A SOURCEBOOK FOR
ENGLISH LYRIC POEMS

A SOURCEBOOK FOR ENGLISH LYRIC POEMS

John Tomarchio

THE CATHOLIC EDUCATION PRESS

WASHINGTON, DC

Copyright ã 2023

The Catholic University of America Press

All rights reserved

The paper used in this publication meets the minimum requirements of American National Standards for Information Science--Permanence of Paper for Printed Library materials, ANSI Z39.48-1984.

[infinity symbol here]

Library of Congress Cataloging-in-Publication Data

[to be supplied]

Title page photo of *Apollo citharoedus* (Musei Capitolini, Rome) by Ricardo André Frantz, 2006, courtesy of Commons.Wikimedia.org: *Apolocitaredo8.jpg*

They, the Muses, once taught Hesiod beautiful song,

while he was shepherding his flocks on holy Mount Helicon;

these goddesses of Olympus, daughters of aegis-bearing Zeus,

first of all spoke this word to me:

Oh, you shepherds of the fields, base and lowly things, little more than bellies,

we know how to tell many falsehoods that seem like truths,

but we also know, when we so desire, how to utter the absolute truth.

Hesiod, *Theogony*

SOURCEBOOKS

FOR LIBERAL ARTS AND SCIENCES

CHRONOLOGY OF THE POETS

CLASSICAL

Thomas Wyatt (1503–42)

Sir Philip Sidney (1554–86)

Edmund Spenser (1552–1599)

William Shakespeare (1564–1616)

Lord Fulke Greville (1554–1628)

John Donne (1573-1631)

George Herbert (1593-1633)

Ben Jonson (1573-1637)

Lady Mary Wroth (1587-1653)

John Milton (1608-74)

Andrew Marvell (1621-78)

Aphra Behn (1640-89)

MODERN

John Keats (1795-1821)

Percy Bysshe Shelley (1792-1822)

William Wordsworth (1770-1850)

Elizabeth Barrett Browning (1806-61)

Samuel Coleridge (1772-1834)

Emily Dickinson (1830-86)

Gerard Manley Hopkins (1844-89)

Herman Melville (1819–91)

Oscar Wilde (1854-1900)

Mary Elizabeth Coleridge (1861-1907)

POST-MODERN

William Butler Yeats (1865-1939)

Edna St. Vincent Millay (1892-1950)

Dylan Thomas (1914-53)

Wallace Stevens (1879-1955)

Hilda Doolittle (1886–1961)

e.e. cummings (1894-1962)

Robert Frost (1874-1963)

T.S. Eliot (1888-1965)

Ezra Pound (1885-1972)

TABLES OF CONTENTS

Preface on Poetry, xi–xviii
Introduction to Lyric, xix–xxix
Sources, xxx–xxxi

Postface on Orpheus, 316–317
Index of Poems by Poet, 318–321

A Grammar of Poetic Verse		
Meter	On Scanning Foot and Line	1–5
Rhyme	Kinds of Rhyme	6–7
Trope	Rhetorical Tropes Sundry	8–31

A Florilegium of English Lyric Verse
Arranged in Five Metrical Modes

The English Sonnet
Fourteen lines of iambic pentameter rhymed alternately.

Thomas Wyatt	*—Whoso list to hunt, I know where is an hind*	35
	—My galley chargèd with forgetfulness	36
	—The longë love that in my thought doth harbour	37
Sir Philip Sidney	*—Loving in truth, and fain in verse my love to show*	38
	—Come, Sleep! O Sleep, the certain knot of peace	39
	—Thou blind man's mark, thou fool's self-chosen snare	40
	—Leave me, O Love, which reachest but to dust	41
Edmund Spenser	**Amoretti LXVII,** *Like as a huntsman*	42
	Amoretti LXXV, *My love is like to ice, and I to fire*	43
William Shakespeare	**Sonnet 12,** *When I do count the clock*	4
	Sonnet 18, *Shall I compare thee to a summer's day?*	5
	Sonnet 1, *From fairest creatures we desire increase*	44
	Sonnet 27, *Weary with toil, I haste me to my bed*	45
	Sonnet 29, *When, in disgrace with fortune and men's eyes*	46
	Sonnet 86, *Was it the proud full sail of his great verse*	47

v

William Shakespeare	**Sonnet 53,** *What is your substance, whereof are you made*	48
	Sonnet 138, *When my love swears she is made of truth*	49
	Sonnet 73, *That time of year thou mayst in me behold*	50
	Sonnet 107, *Not mine own fears, nor the prophetic soul*	51
	Sonnet 94, *They that have power to hurt, and will do none*	52
	Sonnet 121, *'Tis better to be vile than vile esteemed*	53
	Sonnet 97, *How like a winter hath my absence been*	54
	Sonnet 116, *Let me not to the marriage of true minds*	55
	Sonnet 129, *Th' expense of spirit in a waste of shame*	56
	Sonnet 75, *So are you to my thoughts as food to life*	57
Lord Fulke Greville	**Caelica 100,** *In night when colors all to black are cast*	58
	Caelica 29, *The nurse-life wheat within his green husk*	59
John Donne	**Holy Sonnets 5,** *I am a little world*	60
	Holy Sonnets 19, *Oh, to vex me*	61
George Herbert	**Prayer (I),** *Prayer the Church's banquet, angels' age*	62
	Joseph's Coat, *Wounded I sing, tormented I indite*	63
Lady Mary Wroth	**From Pamphilia to Amphilanthus,** Sonnets I–XLVIII	64
John Milton	**Sonnets VII,** *How soon hath Time, the subtle thief*	76
	Sonnet XIX, *When I consider how my light is spent*	77
John Keats	**To Sleep,** *O soft embalmer of the still midnight*	78
Percy Bysshe Shelley	**Ozymandias** *I met a traveller from an antique land*	79
William Wordsworth	*—The world is too much with us*	80
	—Surprised by joy—impatient as the Wind	81
Elizabeth Barrett Browning	**Sonnets from the Portuguese 14,** *If thou must love me*	82
	Sonnets from the Portuguese 43, *How do I love thee?*	83
Gerard Manley Hopkins	*—As kingfishers catch fire*	84
	—Thou art indeed just, Lord, if I contend	85
	—I wake and feel the fell of dark, not day.	86
	—The world is charged with the Grandeur of God	87
Robert Frost	**Design,** *I found a dimpled spider*	88
Edna St. Vincent Millay	*—I, being born a woman and distressed*	89
	—I think I should have loved you presently	90
	—Loving you less than life	91
	—Into the golden vessel of great song	92
	—When I too long have looked upon your face	93
	—Euclid alone has looked on beauty bare	94
	—Still will I harvest beauty where it grows	95

Ballads
A recurring stanza with a distinct scheme of meter and rhyme.

Edmund Spenser	**Prothalamion**, *Calm was the day*	99
John Donne	**The Canonization**, *For God's sake hold your tongue*	106
	Song, *Go and catch a falling star*	108
George Herbert	**Love (III)**, *Love bade me welcome*	109
Lady Mary Wroth	**Song from** *The Countesse of Montgomery's Urania*	110
Aphra Behn	**The Disappointment**, *One Day the Amorous Lisander*	111
John Keats	**La Belle Dame sans Merci**, *Oh, what can ail thee*	118
William Wordsworth	*—I wandered lonely as a cloud*	120
	A Complaint, *There is a change—and I am poor*	121
E. Barrett Browning	**A Musical Instrument**, *What was he doing, the great god*	122
Emily Dickinson	*—There's a certain Slant of light*	124
	—There is a solitude of space	125
	—I died for Beauty	126
	—This world is not conclusion	127
Oscar Wilde	**Requiescat**, *Tread lightly, she is near*	128
	Ballad of Reading Gaol, *He did not wear his scarlet coat*	129
William Butler Yeats	**Song from** *The Player Queen*, *My mother dandled me*	142
	Crazy Jane Talks with the Bishop, *I met the bishop*	143
Robert Frost	**To Earthward**, *Love at the lips was touch*	144
	The Aim Was Song, *Before man came to blow it right*	145

Verses Variable
Regular stress, rhythm, or rhyme measure variable lines.

Thomas Wyatt	*—They flee from me that sometime did me seek*	149
John Donne	**Good Friday, 1613. Riding Westward**, *Let man's soul be*	150
	Nocturnal Upon St. Lucy's Day, *'Tis the year's midnight*	152
	The Sun Rising, *Busy old fool, unruly Sun*	154
	A Valediction: Of Weeping, *Let me pour forth*	155
George Herbert	**The Collar**, *I struck the board, and cried, No more.*	156
	The Altar and **Easter Wings**	158
	Man, *My God, I heard this day*	160

Ben Jonson	On His First Son, *Farewell, thou child of my right hand*	162
	Echo's Song for Narcissus, *Slow, slow, fresh fount*	163
	My Picture Left in Scotland, *I now think Love is*	164
	That Women Are But Men's Shadows, *Follow a shadow*	165
Andrew Marvell	On A Drop of Dew, *See how the orient dew*	166
William Wordsworth	Ode: Intimations of Immortality, *There was a time*	168
Samuel Coleridge	*Kubla Khan, In Xanadu did Kubla Khan*	176
Gerard Manley Hopkins	Preface Introduction to his Sprung Rhythm	178
	Pied Beauty, *Glory be to God for dappled things*	180
	Carrion Comfort, *Not, I'll not, carrion comfort, not feast*	181
	Spring and Fall, *Margaret, are you grieving*	182
	The Windhover, *I caught this morning morning's minion*	183
Mary Elizabeth Coleridge	A Moment, *The clouds had made a crimson crown*	184
	Jealousy, *The myrtle bush grew shady*	185
Herman Melville	Shiloh: A Requiem, *Skimming lightly, wheeling still*	186
Dylan Thomas	*—And death shall have no dominion.*	187
Robert Frost	The Lockless Door, *It went many years*	188
	Tree at my Window, *Tree at my window, window tree*	189

Verse Iterative

A standard line length reiterates indefinitely, with or without rhyme.

Lord Fulke Greville	Caelica 99, *Down in the depth of my iniquity*	193
John Donne	A Valediction Forbidding Mourning, *As virtuous men*	194
George Herbert	Church-monuments, *While that my soul repairs*	196
	Colossians 3:3: *Our life is hid with Christ in God.*	197
Ben Jonson	A Celebration of Charis: His Excuse for Loving	198
	Evening: Barents Sea, *The trawl of unquiet mind*	199
Aphra Behn	Love Armed, *Love in Fantastic Triumph sat*	200
	—A thousand martyrs I have made	201
Andrew Marvell	The Definition of Love, *My love is of a birth as rare*	202
	To His Coy Mistress, *Had we but world enough*	204
	A Dialogue Between the Soul and the Body	206

John Keats	Ode to a Nightingale, *My heart aches*	208
	Ode on a Grecian Urn, *Thou still unravish'd bride*	212
Percy Bysshe Shelley	Mont Blanc, *The everlasting universe of things*	214
Mary Elizabeth Coleridge	*The Other Side of a Mirror*, I sat before my glass	220
William Butler Yeats	Sailing to Byzantium, *That is no country for old men.*	222
	The Second Coming, *Turning and turning*	224
Dylan Thomas	—*Do not go gentle into that good night*	225
Edna St. Vincent Millay	Renascence, *All I could see from where I stood*	226
Robert Frost	For Once, Then, Something, *Others taunt me*	236
	Aquainted with the Night, *I have been one acquainted*	237

Free Verse

Irregular line, rhythm, rhyme, and syntax.

Emily Dickinson	—*Banish Air from Air*	241
	—*After great pain, a formal feeling*	242
	—*One need not be a Chamber*	243
	—*In Winter in my Room*	244
Edna St. Vincent Millay	Spring, *To what purpose, April, do you return again?*	245
Wallace Stevens	The Snow Man, *One must have a mind of winter*	246
	The Emperor of Ice Cream, *Call the roller of big cigars*	247
	Thirteen Ways of Looking at a Blackbird, *Among twenty*	248
H.D. (Hilda Doolittle)	Garden, *You are clear*	250
	At Baia, *I should have thought*	251
	Eurydice, *So you have swept me back*	252
e.e. cummings	—*the bigness of cannon*	257
	—*since feeling is first*	258
	—*in Just-*	259
	—*into the strenuous briefness*	260
	—*when god lets my body be*	261
Ezra Pound	"In A Station at the Metro," *Three years ago in Paris*	262
	Hugh Selwyn Mauberley, *For three years out of key*	266
T.S. Eliot	The Love Song of Alfred J. Prufrock, *Let us go then, you and I*	287
	The Waste Land, *April is the cruelest month*	293

*Apollo crowned with laurel
and Erato, Muse of Lyric Poetry, with lyre.*

PREFACE

Is poetry a liberal art? If when you hear *liberal arts* you think *humanities,* you may think that the question must be rhetorical, for what is itself more humane or more concerned with the humane than poetry? However, the tradition of liberal education is a tradition of sciences as well as arts, and if *humanities* designates the contrary of *sciences*—with connotations of the *soft* versus the *hard,* valuative rather than cognitive—then my question about poetry amounts to a question about knowledge. Does poetry address itself to the human desire to know?

Plato's Socrates cites an ancient dispute between poetry and philosophy when he banishes poetry from the just city he constructs in speech to serve as an image of the just soul. Poets are banished from the just city by him with all due admiration until they can give an account of themselves, to explain what the wonderful things they say mean and to show them to be true, or at least good. In the *Ion* Socrates grants that poets are filled with gods who make them speak divine things, although like actors beautifully reciting lines they do not understand, he says.

Yet in Plato's *Laws* it is granted that Apollo and the Muses begin our education, and muses of poetry featured prominently among the nine muses of antiquity, including individual muses of epic, lyric, tragic, comic, and sacred poetry. Moeover, notwithstanding his indictment of poets, Socrates in the republic he founds "in speech" restricts the early training of youths to gymnastics and music, which includes poetry, for it was sung, and the philosopher reforms poetry in his city for the purpose of educating youths justly. Serious poetry thus retains a place even in the philosopher's just city and soul.

However, the medieval tradition of seven liberal arts and sciences, better known to our own than the ancient, does not place poetry by name, although it hearkens back to an Hellenistic division of liberal arts that does. The Stoics divided a language trivium of grammar, music, and poetry from a philosophical trivum of logic, physics, and ethics, and they subdivided logic into rhetoric, dialectic, and sophistic—which division divides poetry from persuasion and from reasoning. A Latin list of *septem artes liberales* requisite for free citizens is attested by Cicero in his *De inventione*, canonized in the fifth century for the Middle Ages to come by Martianus Capella's *Marriage of Mercury and Philology*. In the medieval schools, a language trivium of Grammar, Logic, and Rhetoric preceded a mathematical quadrivium of Arithmetic, Music, Geometry and Astronomy. However, where is poetry? In humanist Italy, the fifteenth century *Mantegna Tarocchi* engravings group Poetry with Philosophy and Theology, in a theoretical trivium to complete the seven liberal arts in a set of ten. Significantly, this counts Poetry a theoretical science, not a liberal art.

We have yet to hear from Aristotle, who devotes a separate treatise to poetry, his *Poetics*. It is not a treatise on how to write poetry, but rather a contemplation of its kinds, means, and intentions. It is most famous for its attempt to define what tragedy is, namely, an imitation of human action that causes passions of pity and fear in the hearer with the intention of effecting their catharsis. In the course of offering this interpretation of tragedy, he makes an interesting comparision of poetry to philosophy.

Aristotle claims that poetry is more like philosophy than history because history is concerned with the individual as an individual, but poetry in view of a universal. This crediting of poetry with a desire to contemplate universals allys it with contemplation rather than art. On this Aristotolian basis I would like to offer here an apology for poetry—for great poetry, at any rate—to argue a case that it addresses the human desire to understand the natures of things and is as such essentially contemplative.

To begin, let me use Plato's Timaeus to answer Plato's Socrates. Plato's dialogue *Timaeus* is dramatically continuous with his *Republic*, and the foreign visitor Timaeus introduces his cosmogeny to his Athenian hearers with a remark that in the conversation of the previous day led by Socrates the forms themselves were considered. Today, he says, we will consider the forms set into motion by the divine demiurge within the material cosmos of his making. Looking to eternal and immobile numbers and forms for patterns, Timaeus says, the divine craftsman makes bodies heavenly, animal, and mineral, to be moving images of their originals.

Is it not such forms in motion that poetry seeks to contemplate? If Aristotle is right that poetry is like philosophy in its concern with universals, I think it equally important that this concern is with the universal in motion in the individual. Aquinas says in *De ente et essentia* that we call a thing's essence its nature insofar as it is a principle of its motions. What becomes true of a form in motion is more than what is true of it in and by itself. Poetry takes account of existing forms. To grasp the essence as it is in motion in the individual requries a judgment about how it exists in the here and now and how that matters.

Aristotle says in his *Nicomachean Ethics* that besides nature, necessity, and chance, we human beings regard human thought and action as causes. Now it is precisely choice and chance that he singles out in the *Poetics* as tragic poetry's object of contemplation. These two causes are at work in the cosmos variably and conditonally. Natural necessity is the object of the natural sciences. Choice and chance require a different way of knowing, a different sort of causal knowledge—an understanding of conditional necessity and conditioned freedom. Abstraction abstracts from existing and what is true because of existing. Truths of existence require judgments about what is active in the here and now.

If natural sciences study natural necessity and history human action, then what is poetry's proper object of contemplation? In the *Republic* Socrates offers a philosophical sketch of the tyrant's soul, and Tacitus in his *Annals* a historical sketch of the soul of the tyrant Tiberius, but what does the Creon of Sophocles' *Antigone* offer me in contradistinction? What about human agency does Sophocles' Oedipus mean to show?

Not reasons for the factual deeds of singular men, nor ethical cautions, nor only wonder, I think. If Aristotle is right that Sophocles intends to evoke pity and fear, then I do not think it is my sympathy for the individual suffering of his contrived characters. It is rather a philosophical pity and fear, a fear and pity about the existential conditions of human agency, of being responsible for a power to do both good and harm that, limited by ignorance, chance, and necessity, can cause evil it did not intend tragically destructive of the good it did intend. Oedipus is horrified by his own deeds, and we by his story. We should fear for ourselves as for him. Sophocles makes the defectibility and vulnerability of human agency an object of fear and pity for our contemplation, as universal objects of fear and pity for human beings. It is such existential truths that poetry contemplates, truths about our nature at work in us and in the world.

If the poet is not concerned with the necessary as such, he is yet concerned with its effect on the possible and the probable—objects of specifically human concern. If the poet is not concerned with the individual as such, he is still concerned with individuality, and his mode of discourse is as concrete as his mode of consideration. Like the constructed figure of a geometrical demonstration, a poetic construction offers a paradigmatic singular in which and through which to contemplate the universal. The poet incarnates a universal for us in individualized form, to contemplate the significance for us of its being so. The great poet knows how to transfigure the luminous detail, the decisive moment, the language of the sons of man. He gives a vision of a god shedding tears of blood for the death of a man, and he says more than dialectianm historiographer, or theologian could about man, death, and god.

A great poem, large as an epic or small as a lyric, is complete, containing everything its poet intends for the reader to consider: it creates its own context, and selects its own matter, and gives it a form fitted to its own purposes. It creates the object of its own contemplation, like a divine demiurge imaging eternal forms in moving things—or, if poetry is imitation of nature rather than of god, then it is imitation not of its creations but of its creating.

Individual being, individual existence, individuality, though escaping abstraction and quantification, is yet intelligible to individual judgment. In the figurative discourse of poetry, universals are signified by particulars rather than terms. Judgments are individual rather than extensive, existentially determinate rather than logically abstractive. Reason chooses to delve rather than survey.

As personal judgment is the 'unit' of such figurative discourse, so is it of its interpretation. Cognition of it, as well as ability to assess its cogency and verity, requires personal self-cultivation, a reflectivity developed over time *in exercito*. Existential intelligence has proven acquirable, even if not teachable; cognitive, even if not calculable; verifiable, if not ratiocinatively, still reflectively.

Works of human intelligence are themselves intelligent. They are subjective not as arbitrary but as personal, for intellect is the most highly individualized form of being and the most autonomous form of being—its own measure and measurer. It is superior to forms of being liable to quantification and it requires a superior science. There is much about human being that is material and may be measured as any other bodily being. But for a human being to deny that anything not thus measurable is not explicably intelligible is to deny their own human intelligence.

I am arguing this case for poetry of the sort that is studied in liberal education, the sort I have studied as an English major at Columbia College and as a Tutor in the Language Tutorials of the Great Books program of St. John's College. Of course, not all poetry is great poetry, and there is no reason to disparage poetry that not does intend more than personal expression, impression, or affectivity; imaginative fancy or amusement; moral exhortation, laud or celebration. However, that is not the sort that befits an object of study in liberal arts. The sort that does, I submit, is the sort that addresses to its readers a claim about the nature of things they know, a claim of universal human interest and import, a claim that can prove true to the thing, or not, and consequentially.

On this view, the historical facts about the poet and poem become incidental to the intention of a great poem. Homer's epic poem is not about a war, but about war. It does not seek to be true to facts but to the nature of the thing. There is an endeavor to understand something in great poetry that is addressed to a reader likewise seeking understanding. A lyric poem may only question or agonize, but its very framing of its question or passion will disclose their existential stakes for its reader as well. A great poem proposes something to think about, to cross-examine, a representaton of something about which it will matter whether it is true or not—at least to a reader as serious as the poem.

Even if you remain unpersuaded by my account of great poetry as contemplative—as not only valuative but cognitive, defying a dichotomy between subjectivity and objectivity or individuality and universality—the fact remains that students of liberal arts do not study poetry to learn to write poems, and therefore not as an art. The art of creative writing is a separate and special study. My question whether poetry is a liberal art stands, even if my theory of great poetry should not. Study of grammar may be for good writing, and logic for good reasoning, and rhetoric for good speeches, but poetry is not studied for writing good poems. It has a different end, a higher one, I submit, in any case.

In my experience as a lifelong student and teacher of poetry, it is studied for its own sake, for what it contains in itself rather than for anything you can do with it. In this sense, it is quintessentially liberal, even if not a liberal art. Surely it gives pleasure, and as a teacher I will say with Socrates that it can soften hard natures and render souls graceful. But will he say with me that it poetry a good desirable in itself as well? Is not the beautiful that sort of good?

If poetry seeks understanding for its own sake, if it takes pleasure in contemplation for its own sake, then its desire is more like that of theoretical science than liberal art. Its value will be in the self-reflection that renders human life more humane and thus more desirable for a human person to live. That is the stuff of liberal education.

This volume is dedicated to a particular form of poetry, to English lyric poems. One could date the inauguration of this centennial tradition with Sir Philip Sidney's *The Defence of Poesy*, which ushered in the flowering of English lyric poetry in the Elizabethan Renaissance. Sidney's apology looked back to Aristotle's *Poetics*, but it gave it an ethical turn, in contrast to my metaphysical one. Like Aristotle, Sidney says that poetical devices of meter, rhyme, and trope are not of the essence of poetry. He argues that the superiority of poetry to both philosophy and history consists in its ability to inculcate not only reflection but also moral virtue. It concerns itself not only with what must be, has been, or can be, but with what should be. He goes so far as to say poetry outdoes even nature herself in presenting virtue in a more inspiringly ideal form than ever appears in nature. It is this ethical end and efficacy to which Sidney appeals to argue for poetry as mother of all arts, sciences, and education.

Sidney credits the moral efficacy of poetry to its concern with singulars. He credits this for poetry's ability to display virtue more vividly, more ideally, more desirably than can either history's facts or philosophy's abstractions. Such prowess is rhetorical and educational. I credit poetry's attending to the singular with much more than that. My thesis is that poetry takes a metaphysical view of being that is more comprehensive than science's abstractions or history's facts. Poetry looks to immediate experience of individuals for the consequences of universals existing in beings. The student of ethics may well be able to define what courage is in words, even to cite examples, but does he have the courageous man's ability in the moment to recognize the courageous thing to do? Will he even be able in the moment to recognize courage at work in the courageous man in the moment? Something similar may be said about a great poet's judging being's being in the moment.

If the poet is able to recognize the forms of being at work in beings, and the consequences of that for forms and for us, then there is a cognitive virtue there that may be expressible without being teachable, recognizable without being imitable. Perhaps in deference to Socrates we could say such a one need be only a seeker of wisdom rather than wise; or else, if a favorite of a god, perhaps a visionary, but surely more than a mouthpiece. When

Dante credits his Virgil with both wisdom and unsatiated desire of it, it is surely more than poetic hyperbole.

Is not asking the visionary for a dialectical account of what he sees like a deaf man demanding an account of colors, or the eye demanding of the ear an account of music? At best we could show it notes on a page or demonstrate ratios.

On the other hand, there is abuse to answer every right use of power, and the Muses warn Hesiod that they can tell falsehoods as well as the simple truth. If gods and poets lie, how shall we tell the difference? Enter Socrates and the ancient dispute between philosophy and poetry over wisdom.

They, the Muses,
once taught Hesiod beautiful song,
while he was shepherding his flocks on holy Mount Helicon;
these goddesses of Olympus, daughters of aegis-bearing Zeus,
first of all spoke this word to me,
"Oh, you shepherds of the fields, base and lowly things, little more than bellies,
we know how to tell many falsehoods that seem like truths,
but we also know, when we so desire, how to utter the absolute truth."
Thus they spoke, the fluent daughters of great Zeus.
Plucking a branch, to me they gave a staff of laurel, a wondrous thing,
and into me they breathed a divine voice,
so that I might celebrate both the things that are to be and the things that were before;
and they ordered me to honor, in my song,
the race of the blessed gods who exist forever,
but always to sing of them themselves, the Muses,
both first and last.

Hesiod, *Theogony* [1]

---

[1] *Classical Mythology*, M. Morford and R.J. Lenardon (Oxford University Press, 2011).

INTRODUCTION

This sourcebook is not a survey of English lyric poems but rather a florilegium. It singles out great poems worthy of study in the Liberal Arts—in Great Books programs, Core curricula, and in Humanities generally. It singles out these poems not as representative of the author or author's time, but rather as addressed to the reader and reader's time by virtue of its representing the nature of things.

Lyric poetry is not much discussed by our ancient sources. Poetry in the form of song seems taken for granted by them. It was named for the lyre that often accompanied it, images of which decorate this florilegium. But this historical origin of lyric poetry is not its formative essence, not the reason it continues to be what it is for us.

To say it is not narrative, not dramatized, not long or complex, is to define lyric poetry negatively in contradistinction to epic and dramatic. Frankly, this extended use of the term "lyric" to name one of three greatest genera that includes whatever is not in the other two—neither a narration of a complex plot nor a dramatic enactment of one—is perhaps the clearest and safest designation of "lyric" for all practical intents and purposes—including accounting for the selections in this *Sourcebook*. However, as such a definition by default by no means elucidates the essence of lyric, I think it craven not to try to put it into words, even if failure throw us back on a recognition without definition born of experience.

Lyric poems are said to be not only short but personal, and affective. They are said to be melodious in feel, like songs, and to rely on meter and rhyme for their effect. These commonplace descriptions certainly fit some prominent historical forms of lyric poetry, such as sonnets, but I would broaden these terms.

Lyric poems are personal not in the sense that they are about the poet's person. Many may be, but I think it would be hermeneutically naïve to assume lyric poets are speaking historically about themselves as

xix

individuals. A lyric poet may well assume a *persona* for the purposes of the poem, or adapt or contrive occasion or details to purpose. However, it is indeed characteristic that the lyric speaker speaks in the first person, even when the poet is not speaking about themself. In contrast to the impersonal voice of an omniscient narrator, the lyric voice is personified, even if not identified. The extisential determinateness of human subjectivity is thematized: individual perspective, posture, and passiblity. It is an "I" in a transcendental mode, as it were, which any reader can assume. The lyric *ego* offers its reader its personal vantage point on something of universally human significance.

Lyric poems are short because they are self-limited. They are thematic meditations, and their limited size expresses a thematic focus. They attend closely and intensively to something near at hand. It may flood them with radiating asssociations, speculations, questions, but these radiate from its focal point. The poem meditates, muses, emotes about something that affects a human being personally, that is known experientially, affectively, existentially. It addresses its meditation on its own experience to another human being, to the reader as *confrere*. Why? Does it hope for sympathy, or validation? Surely not. After all, the poem lives, the poet does not. Surely it offers something of value *for* its reader, if only its aporia or agony.

Are lyric poems melodious? Often they are, but sometimes only rhythmic. Though many rely on meter or rhyme, free verse is also lyrical and one knows it is a lyric poem even when there is no meter or rhyme. Lyricism is heard by the intellect's sense of music along with the ear's. The lyric poem is not words set to music, but music in words—whether in some conventional poetic meter or in some freer form. But is not all poetry a kind of music? Surely, but the compact size and thematic concentration of the lyric poem offers a synoptic sense of its beginning, middle, and end, so that its music takes on the concision of a song.

Will all the poems of this selection answer to this characterization? I doubt it, and I would not rename or reclassify such a poem as though failing of defintional criteria. It was not my intention to offer a treatise on lyric poetry in this introduction, just to disclose my hermeneutical pinciples of selection. I chose lyrical poems I thought great poems and beautiful, with no attempt at survey or representation or systemization.   I think it a great if easy error to understand Great Books as "canonical". Not even a reading list as extensive as St. John's four-year program could include every Great Book or kind of Great Book—nor should. Not every great book is best for a new learner. The capacities, needs, and interests of students are the principles of selection. I do not teach great books so much as teach students how to read them. I find great books teach themselves if students but learn to read for themselves.

I became enamored of Great Books in the Core Curriculum at Columbia College just because my teachers and classmates happened to prove uninspiring. That the books inspired me none-the-less has made me a great believer in such books' teaching themselves. Inspired by the Columbia Core reading list, I meant to become a Philosophy major. However, the commitment of that academic department to Analytic philosophy took the form of anemic analysis of textual fragments for logical consistency, an exercise as unilluminating to me as uninspiring. The English department, in contrast, did not allow its professional interests in higher crticism to impinge on its undergraduate courses, and it conducted surveys of whole books, as in the Core. Better yet, those professors proved interesting. So, I became a student of English literature, and still am, though I later took my doctorate in Philosophy.

I remain content as a continuing student of Great Books to take them on their own terms and to engage them directly, as interlocutors, rather than as objects to analyze in formal terms indebted to scholarly categories and interests. As a teacher, I would have the book set its own terms and context for an immediate engagement with it by students. In a similar vein, the poems collected here were not selected for reasons either historical or categorical, but for the pedagogical reason that they have worked in the classroom, or at least promise to on the basis of others that have. They are also not presented in historical order, which decision merits yet another apology.

If I take a great lyric poem to be a viable claim about the nature of something I know, then its historical context becomes tangential. Historical coordinates are an extrinsic measure, often allied to epochal divisions that beg criteria of categorization. If each lyric poem can stand on its own as a claim complete, then even the poet's biography becomes tangential. I think it misguided for humanities to imitate the scientific method's exhaustive enumeration and systematic categorization of data based on normative definition. Granted humans are bodies in motion, that is not the aspect of interest in humane studies. Historical standards of research and analysis vouchsafe the humanities a methodological claim to be sciences of a sort (if soft ones), but at the price of reducing their objects of study to archaeological artifacts, testaments to the bygone rather than to the nature of what is still before us and still matters to us. Humanists have become doctors of history rather than of philosophy to imitate scientists.

I do not read Great Books for history, either of periods or of ideas. To arrange the great poems I selected for this sourcebook, I look to the poem itself. Meter is a quantitative measure intrinsic to the poem. Its meter is a constitutive principle not only of a poem as a whole but also of its affect. I would sooner measure a poem by its chosen poetic form than by its poet's biography or cultural era.

The pardigmatic example of this is the classical English sonnet. Fourteen lines of iambic pentameter rhyming in some alternating fashion articulate themselves into three quatrains concluding with a couplet, or else two quatrains and a sextet. This form of the whole gives a sonnet the concision of a syllogistic proof or the syntactic articulation of a periodic sentence. Although the lines are quantitatively fixed in length, the meter acts like a time signature or key in a piece of music, within which proportional boundaries the composer composes his melody. The poet wields the meter like a baton, keeping time, to be sure, but dynamically and affectively. Being conventional, the sonnet form shapes the reader's expectations too, addresses the reader in a familiar form, and delights with the expectation of exposition, development, and culmination, and sometimes surprise.

Such a poetic form is essentially temporal in meaning as in measure. The poet's thought unfolds in time, in a succession significant both logically and rhetorically. To discuss a sonnet as a whole, abstracting its idea from its progressive presentation, quite misses the point. This temporality of poetic form attests to poetry's concern with existing in time, to the kind of being that projects itself into a future it desires out of a past it recollects. What is true of such being is grasped by judgment, not abstraction, and such judgments are likewise temporally situated and existentially singular. A truth materialized in a moment is grasped in the perception of a moment, grasped in an individual insight that explicates itself in a recollective meditation. As with music, one must follow the unfolding, listen to it part by part through time, in order to hear it recollectively as a whole. As with a syllogism, the middle term is the crux of the argument, as is reasoning's progressing through it from its starting point to its conclusion.

Many an English poet has submitted themself to the self-discipline of the sonnet form. The English form was born and flourished in the classical period of English poetry, in Tudor England. But what of that? When Robert Frost chooses to write a sonnet in the twentieth century, shall we associate it more with the poetry of e.e. cummings than of Shakespeare, or for that matter, more with a free verse poem of Frost's than the quincentenary English sonnet tradition his poem invokes for context?

You can choose to supply a historical, cultural, or biographical context to Frost's sonnet according to such poetically extrinsic conditions, but you can also choose to hear the sonnet address you directly in its own chosen form. If it stands on its own in its own poetic form as a thing complete; and if it makes a claim not only about its own author and time but about you and yours; then why not listen to what it has to say to you in its own terms? Why not take for context of intepretation poems of the same form that the poet has selected to orient his reader's expectation and frame his poetic variation or innovation. Such is the contextualization I choose for the poems of this *Sourcebook.*

I have distinguished five metrical modes. The first is the precisely articulated sonnet convention I have already characterized. Second is the far more variable ballad form, as I will call it. I will make use of the term to characterize a form of lyric poem metrically. Like a sonnet, a ballad articulates itself metrically in a salient pattern, but in the form of a repeating stanza rather than a form of the whole. The stanza shapes itself in a distinctive metrical pattern with respect to foot, line, and rhyme, and then the scheme repeats indefinitely. As the stanza may reiterate indefinitely, the poem may iterate *ad libitum* on its theme. One common English ballad stanza is a quatrain of interwoven iambic tetrameter and iabmic trimeter with alternate rhymes, a familiar form of church hymn. A familiar form of folk song is twenty-four lines in three octets with a more complex rhyme scheme.

Poems that make use of ballad form sometimes seem to sing or dance. Often poems adopt the ballad form to tell a tale, but the form can be adopted for any number of less cheerful purposes, as in the solemnity of church hymns. The distinctive line and rhyme schemes of ballads give more individual character to a poem than the conventional sonnet form, more of a metrical figure of its own, even when a quite simple one. Ballads do not so much eschew convention as don one of their own varaition, yet assuring the reader familiar pleasures of theme and variation. If the English sonnet is the Queen's English, then the ballad is a dialect of more local color and popular pedigree.

Next comes what I call variable meters. In this mode the foot dominates over the line because lines vary in length in no conventional or regular way. It is the accentual foot that becomes salient to the ear, or else a regular rhythmic beat, which counts out variable line lengths. One has to stop and scan the whole poem for meter to reveal metric patterns. Like the cartoon of a painting, the metrical form of the whole is structual and foundational rather than syntactical or figural. More personal, variable meter also attests more to the personal rhythms of the poet's thoughts and feelings, can seem more expressive of personal moods and intentions.

Such poems stand out as more personally lyrical, not unlike an aria. The reader may as a result feel all the more an intimate confidante of the poet, if all the more uncertain what to expect next. Yet the poet does speak to the reader in a regular accent or beat, and thus in measured lines, even if erratic measures. Perhaps the effect is more rhythmic than melodic, but it is still sensibly musical. Perhaps more often phrases than lines are lyrical, but lyricism is still expected, or rejected, to effect.

What is the effect when the poet goes to the opposite extreme and adopts a fixed foot and line length in indefinitely reiterative succession? The set metric length may reiterate without variation, or it may punctuate itself intermittently with a standard variation, or punctuate itself according to a rhyme scheme into stanzas. The effect of such metric reiteration is metronomic. Becoming more quantitative than qualitative, the meter becomes less expressive, keeping time more as a metronome does than a baton. Reiterative meter is more an enumerative than a shaping device, like the quantitative uniformity of plainchant. Badly recited, uninflected for sense or syntax, it can be rendered either monotonous or else sing-song. Recited well, the meter lends itself to the rhythyms and cadences of good oratory.

Sometimes rhyme patterns parcel out stanzas of reiterated meter, as a church hymn's recurrent melody frames verses in its successive iteration of a theme. When the poet chooses neither to vary lengths nor to rhyme lines, metronomic reiteration becomes all the more transparent. Such blank verse is the conventional choice for epic poetry, such as Milton's *Paradise Lost*, and it is perhaps for a similar reason that unrhymed reiteration is used by narrative lyric, by which I mean lyric poems that paint a scene, tell a story, or sketch a portrait—a favorite of Romantics. Though the meter is reduced to a *basso continuo*, its effect is still felt as elegance. The poetic discipline of the measured line has an effect like good elocution, and subserves similar purposes.

Now what about the abandonment of meter? Absence of meter in poetry would be heard differently by an ear unused to it. The meter of ancient Greek and Roman poetry is not accentual but quantitative, and I cannot hear it. I know how to approximate it by substituting the accentuation familiar to my ear for the quantities unfamiliar to it, but that is like imagining a body on the basis of its shadow. The Hebrew poetry of the Psalms relies on neither meter or rhyme but rather on iteration of thematic couplets, having the effect of a rhythmic lyricism that can be felt in translation. However, the English ear is tuned from its youth to metrical accentuation and to rhyme, and when it hears English song or poetry eschew it, it hears that too.

Nevertheless, an attuned English ear hears free verse as poetry. Line breaks are still used, even if not line lengths. Rhythm is felt, even if not metrical, and likewise accentuation, even absent an accentual unit. Rhyme or assonance or alliteration is still used, just not schematically. The music of a free verse poem may seem atonal to the ear or aleatoric to the reader, but its phrasing still sounds musical to the mind.

One could argue that with the death of meter in post-modern poetry comes the death of lyricism, but certainly not the death of poetry. However, we said from the start that it is not meter that makes the poem — history or philosophy written in verse is not poetry. Contrariwise, poetry not written in meter still is. Although the meter of a metered poem is an intrinisc measure of it, it is a quanitative one, and quantity does not give essence but rather presupposes it. Absent regularity, a figure is less measurable or intelligible, but not less of a figure for that — it still visibly delimits a space — and perhaps a being. In any case, post-modern free verse does recognizably have poetic shape — the words are sometimes even arranged on the page for a visual effect.

I have arranged my five metrical modes in a progression from a greatest determinacy of form to greatest freedom of form. First of all, the English sonnet alone is a form of the whole: within its fourteen vouchsafed lines the poet uses iambic pentameter to sculpt a figure of elegantly classical proportions. The ballad, instead of a fixed form of the whole, adopts a form of the part, an integral part of its own patterning, a stanza form to be reiterated *ad libitum*.

Variable verse foregoes any fixed form of whole, or part, or line, but retains a metrical unit of stress or of rhythmic beat, with which it counts out and contours its lines variably, as if *ex tempore*. In this respect, it is closer in spirit to the sonnet or the ballad than is iterative verse, which uses a fixed line length more enumeratively than formatively, as a quantitative structure *pro forma*, rather than to contour either the whole or parts. Sometimes one has to count longer lines of iterative poems even to notice there is a meter. Thus rendering meter more transparent, iterative verse moves closer towards doing away with it.

Free verse does away both with any regular line length, any regulative unit of stress, any stanza or rhyme scheme, and with those eschewals free verse becomes poetically idiolectic, each poem *sui generis*, as it were, its own poetic measure—for its language is still recognizably a poetic form of language, even if idiolecti cally so.

My enumeration of five poetic modes do not presume to be exhaustive. I attempted a discerment of forms through inducution rather than a classification by enumeration. In no way do I intend the five modes I arrived at to be definitionally normative, but rather interpretative of practices, and hopefully elucidative of them. I like that my five modes enable me to arrange poems in an interesting way poetically speaking—much more than had historical considerations. Mulling over what the periods of English poetry should be and into which ones individual poets should be put was not mulling over poetry, I found

There is my account, apology, and disclaimer for departing from a conventional arragement of poems according to periods or poets, in favor of one according to the poet's choice of metrical form—or eschewal of any. I should also offer a disclaimer for stopping at the frontier of the public domain in the face of the prohibitive complexities and costs of copyright. Fortunately, on this side of that border is Eliot's *The Waste Land*. I am content for that twentieth century landmark poem to culminate this selection.

Further, although I have emphasized that the study of poetry in the Liberal Arts does not purpose to teach how to write poems but how to contemplate along with them, I recognize that understanding the poetry's means deepens interpretation of its ends. To that end, this *Sourcebook* begins by introducing devices of poetic arts. I dub these study aids a poetic *grammar*, as synopsizing rudiments of poetic literacy.

This propadeutic *grammatica poetica* offers introductions to conventions of meter and of rhyme. There is also some introduction to rhetorical tropes, turns of phrase used by orators and prose writers as much as by poets. They most often have Greek or Latin names hearkening back to antiquity, as the tradition of English letters does. I chose to provide the reader with the name of each trope and its etymology and, absent definition or characterization, delightful English examples. I trust the tropes to speak for themselves, as I do the great poems that follow.

I owe thanks to nameless benefactors. I owe my greatest debt of thanks to anonymous designers and curators of The Poetry Foundation website for its vast and well-ordered storehouse of English lyric poems and *vade mecum* links. I owe thanks to anonymous colleagues at St. John's College Annapolis, who over decades contributed fine poems to the manuals of our Language Tutorials, which formed the kernel of this florilegium. I owe thanks to too many St. John's students to name who over two decades formed this Sourcebook and me.

One I can surely thank by name is Kevin White, a constant friend to all my enterprises. I would like to offer peculiar thanks by name as well to an unwitting friend of this volume, and in his person to the self-abnegation of teachers everywhere. Many a teacher casts many a seed without ever knowing whether it perish on soil rocky or shallow, or if it takes root, whether it be choked by thorns and thistles before it can flower and fruit. Unbeknowst to him, a colleague cast a mustard seed that grew into in this sourcebook. For the sake of the St. John's Graduate Institute's Language Tutorial, a fellow Tutor spliced together a short selection of poems from the two undergraduate poetry manuals for Sophomore and Senior Language tutorials. I found the poetic intelligence of his curation far more illuminating than his sources. His predelictive regard for each poem he selected offered the students singular access to the greatness of poetry, I thought, and his success in doing so seeded this florilegium.

It planted in my mind the idea of a curated florilegium as preferable to representative survey. The academy's canon of methodological objectivity expects historilogical types to be enumerated by comprehensive review of sources, definitional classification of epochs and genres, historical contextualization. The alternative to the methodological dispassion of such scientific survey is a predelictive prudence born of experience—not merely personal experience, but a personal appropriation of communal experience, of the prudence of a living tradition of study—living practices of reading, discussing, and writing poetry. When long cumulative experience provides the sources and horizon, one may confidently select a poem in its own right, to stand on its own as a great poem exemplary of the greatness of poetry: *magnum in parvo*.

Aristotle says that a parent loves their child more than the child the parent because the parent knows better the child's orign and their relation. Seeing themselves grown young and beautiful again, parents labor in love to see their image to full stature anew. But the teacher is, rather, like the figure of friendship Aristotle offers in the mother who gives her child away for its greater good and loves it from afar, putting its happiness over her own. I think that such self-abnegating friendship is what teachers perforce have for their students, and it is a rare delight for a teacher to know the flower and fruit of their labors in their students. I hope that my retired colleague Jonathan Tuck, a lifelong teacher, may take some delight in this florilegium seeded by his predilective understanding of English lyric.

The teacher seeded, and Apollo watered, but God gives the growth, to whom therefore be the thanks in all and above all.

Orpheus
Son of the god Apollo and the muse Calliope

SOURCES

TEXTS, SUBTEXTS, AND CONTEXT

PoetryFoundation.org

Poets.org

Sonnets.org

Best-Poems.net

Wroth.Latrobe.edu.au/all-poems.html

InterestingLiterature.com

EliotsWasteland.tripod.com

John J. Espey, *Ezra Pound's Mauberley: A Study in Composition* (Faber 1955), online:
Google.com/Books/edition/Ezra_Pound_s_Mauberley/UslZwQEACAAJ?hl=en&gbpv=1

Arthur Quinn, *Figures of Speech* (Gibbs–M. Smith, 1982)

Encyclopedia Britannica Online:
Britannica.com/topic/Orpheus-Greek-mythology (Emended)

Wikipedia.org

IMAGES

TITLE PAGE, *Apollo citharoedus* or Apollo with lyre, Musei Capitolini, Rome, Photo by Richardo Andre Frantz, courtesy of Commons.Wikimedia.org:
https://Apolocitaredo8.jpg

GENERAL INTRODUCTION, Apollo crowned with laurel and Muse with tortoise-shell lyre, Attic Kylix ca. 440 BC, attributed to the Carlsruhe Painter, Museum of Fine Arts, Boston, courtesy of Theoi.com: *theoi.com/Gallery/K20.5.html*
—end, Orpheus in red-figured krater, 5th C. BC, Antikensammlung Collection of Classical Antiquities, Staatliche Museen, Berlin, courtesy of LeivithraPark.gr:
https://www.leivithrapark.gr/en/leivithra/myth/

INTRODUCTION TO ENGLISH LYRIC METERS, *Musica*, from *The Seven Liberal Arts,* by Hans Sebald Beham ca.1520, Germany, scanned by Nick Michael, private collection, courtesy of Commons.Wikimedia.org:
https://commons.wikimedia.org/wiki/File:Musica_(Music).jpg

INTRODUCTION TO RHETORICAL TROPES, *Rhetorica*, from *The Seven Liberal Arts,* by Hans Sebald Beham ca. 1520, Germany, private collection, courtesy of Commons.Wikimedia.org:
https://commons.wikimedia.org/wiki/File:Rhetorica.jpg

xxx

SOURCES

ORPHEUS AND EURYDICE VERSOS, Narrative series of eight drawings by Eduard von Engerth (1818-97), titled *Das K. K. Hof-Operntheater In Wien* (The Imperial-Royal Court Opera Theater in Vienna), of which Engerth was the decorator, published by VA Heck Publishing (Vienna), photographs by Friedrich Bruckman Publishing, courtesy of TUGraz DIGITAL Library (University Library of Graz University of Technology):
https://diglib.tugraz.at/download.php?id=5db7da8cdef6d&location=browse

THE ENGLISH SONNET Frontis, *Erato Undressing*, by Angelo Maccagnino (or Angelo di Pietro da Siena), a collaborator of Cosmè Tura (1449-56), in the Pinacoteca Nazionale di Ferrara (*https://gallerie-estensi.beniculturali.it/en/pinacoteca-nazionale/*), courtesy of Commons.Wikimedia.org:
https://upload.wikimedia.org/wikipedia/commons/3/38/Studiolo_di_belfiore%2C_erato_di_angelo_maccagnino_e_collaboratori_di_cosm%C3%A8_tura.jpg

BALLAD Frontis, *Cupids playing with a lyre,* Roman fresco from Herculaneum, at Ercolano, Campania, Italy, courtesy of Commons.Wikimedia.org:
https://commons.wikimedia.org/wiki/File:Herculaneum_-_Lyre_and_Cupids.jpg

VERSES VARIABLE Frontis, *Erato,* The Muse of Love Poetry, painting by Simon Vouet (1590-1649), New Orleans Museum of Art, courtesy of Commons.Wikimedia.org:
https://upload.wikimedia.org/wikipedia/commons/4/47/Erato.jpg

VERSE ITERATIVE Frontis, Muse with Lyre, painting by Henri-Jean Guillaume Martin (1860-1943), courtesy of Commons.Wikimedia.org:
https://commons.wikimedia.org/wiki/File:Martin_-_lady-with-lyre-by-pine-trees-1890.jpg

FREE VERSE Frontis, *La Muse,* Looking in a mirror, Pablo Picasso, 1935, Centre Pompidou, Paris, France, courtesy of Wikiart.org:
https://wikiart.org/en/pablo-picasso/a-muse-1935

Next Page Verso, *The Death of Orpheus,* Painting by Antonio Garcia Vega, recolored for this volume in black-and-white; see Outro below for line to original in dramatic red.

POSTFACE, *Thracian Girl Carrying the Head of Orpheus on His Lyre*, by Gustave Moreau 1865, Musée d'Orsay, courtesy of Commons.Wikimedia.org:
https://commons.wikimedia.org/wiki/File:Head_of_Orpheus.jpg

OUTRO, *The Death of Orpheus*, Painting by Antonio Garcia Vega, courtesy of Commons.Wikimedia.org:
https://commons.wikimedia.org/wiki/File:Muerte_de_OrfeoGarciaVega.jpg

Musica, from *The Seven Liberal Arts*,
by Hans Sebald Beham

ENGLISH LYRIC METERS

Classical English verse is metered: there is a measuring out of sounds in time according to a rule, as in measures of music. Whereas the rhythms of classical Greek and Latin poetry are patterns of syllables longer or shorter to pronounce, classical English verse employs accentual patterns of stressed or unstressed syllables called "long" or "short" by analogy.

Like Greek and Latin, English verse measures itself out in lines of a fixed number of syllables, whether in a standard number per line or a standard variation in stanzas. Each line is also measured out in feet of a fixed pattern of stressed and unstressed syllables. For example, the meter of English sonnets is iambic pentameter: each line has five feet of two syllables, with the accent on the second syllable of each foot (a foot called the iamb). Shakespeare's *When I do tell the clock that tells the time* scans as five iambic feet:

When Ĭ / do tèll / the clòck / that tèlls / the tìme.

Moreover, a classical Shakespearian sonnet arranges its 14 lines of iambic pentameter according to an end-of-line rhyme pattern into 3 quatrains (four-line stanzas) plus a concluding couplet: AB/AB, CD/CD, EF/EF, GG. Another classical sonnet form, the Petrarchan, divides the 14 lines into an octave rhyming ABBA/ABBA and a sestet rhyming CD/CD/CD or CDE/CDE. More variable in stanza than the sonnet are ballad meters—e.g., the "common" meter of hymnody: a quatrain alternates two pairs of iambic tetrameters (four feet) and iambic trimeters (three feet), with rhymes typically on the trimeters.

Ballads are of course conventionally printed in stanzas, but in the case of the sonnet the metrical form of the whole is often heard rather than seen. The first edition of Shakespeare's sonnets, for example, were printed as 14 continuous lines with only the concluding couplet indented. However, Lady Mary Wroth's were written as two quatrains and two sextets with the first line flush and the rest indented, in accord with her Petrarchan rhyme scheme. In this study edition, I insert space between stanzas according to rhyme schemes to occasion reflection on how versification serves meaning.

Metrical rules permit metric variations. For example, the first measure of iambic pentameter may begin with the accent on the first syllable instead of the second—called a trochee. Also, the line typically has a natural syntactical pause in the middle called a caesura, and after this pause the next syllable may be accented instead of the second, as at the beginning of the line. In sum, iambic pentameter permits a trochee in lieu of an iamb in the first foot and after a caesura. Demands of meter will sometimes call for slurring a two-syllable word to one syllable—"oe'r" for "over"—or extenuating one into two—"cru-el" instead of "cruel". This classical meter also permits the line to end with an extra eleventh, unaccented syllable, called a feminine foot.

Sometimes a metrical accent will affect meaning or mood by emphasizing or deemphasizing a word. Thus, scanning a poem for meter is partly a matter of interpretation. For example, one could scan the first foot of this line as iambic or trochaic:

> When 'I / do coùnt / the clòck // that tèlls / the tìme
> Whèn I / do coùnt / the clòck // that tèlls / the tìme

If you interpret the line above to be mimicking the regularity of the ticking clock it speaks about, then an initial *iamb* will give the line a fitting monotony. In contrast, taking the first foot as a *trochee* gives an upbeat to the start of the poem that mimics spontaneous speech, putting an emphasis on the temporal adverb "When" as denoting the moment the poet stops to tell—and reckon—the time. Reading a poem thus entails an interpretation of its meter in light of its meaning, and its meaning in light of its meter.

The grammatical syntax of a line may carry over to the next line—called an enjambment—so that it is only natural to read past the line-stop without pause until the grammatical unit is completed. Likewise, even in lines that are not strictly syntactical enjambments, one may read over metric breaks for reasons of meaning, flow, or feeling. Meter and scansion do not decide reading—that is for each reader/reciter to decide.

A poetic meter might be compared to a musical time-signature—the measure does not rule over melody, dynamics, or tempo, nor does a metronome over performance; rather, both meter and metronome undergird the music-making in silent counterpoint. Likewise, poetic meter measures out or undergirds the poetry, it does not make it. Dialectical tension between rule and variation, meter and meaning, scansion and recitation, gives poetic verse *sprezzatura.*

Following is a delightfully didactic poem by Samuel T. Coleridge that cleverly illustrates poetic meters in use while describing their feel:

Metric Feet
 	
— - / — -
— / — —
 	
— - - /— - -
- — / - —
- - — / - - —
 	
- — - / - — -
— - — / — - —
 	
N.B.
Accented
syllables are
called "long"
and unaccented
ones "short"
by conventions
of Latin and
Greek
quantitative
meters.
	LESSON FOR A BOY
	
	TROCHEE trips from long to short;—
	From long to long in solemn sort
	Slow SPONDEE stalks; strong foot! yet ill able—
	Ever to come up with DACTYL TRISYLLABLE.—
	IAMBICS march from short to long;—
	With a leap and a bound the swift ANAPESTS throng;—
	One syllable long, with one short at each side,
	AMPHIBRACHYS hastes with a stately stride;—
	First and last being long, middle short,
	AMPHIMACER
	Strikes his thundering hoofs like a proud high bred Racer.
	
	If Derwent be innocent, steady and wise,
	And delight in the things of earth, water, and skies;
	Tender warmth at his heart, with these metres to show it,
	With sound sense in his brains, may make Derwent a poet,—
	May crown him with fame, and must win him the love
	Of his father on earth and his Father above.
	      My dear, dear child!
	Could you stand upon Skiddaw,
	      you would not from its whole ridge
	See a man who so loves you as your fond S.T. Coleridge.

Practicum

Scan the following two Shakespeare sonnets.

The meter is iambic pentameter:
five disyllabic feet with accent on the second syllable,
and caesura before or after the middle foot.

Sonnet 12

When I do count the clock that tells the time,
And see the brave day sunk in hideous night;
When I behold the violet past prime,
And sable curls are silvered o'er with white;

When lofty trees I see barren of leaves,
Which erst from heat did canopy the herd,
And summer's green, all girded up in sheaves,
Borne on the bier with white and bristly beard;

Then of thy beauty do I question make,
That thou among the wastes of time must go,
Since sweets and beauties do themselves forsake,
And die as fast as they see others grow,

And nothing 'gainst Time's scythe can make defense,
Save breed, to brave him when he takes thee hence.

William Shakespeare

Sonnet 18

Shall I compare thee to a summer's day?
Thou art more lovely and more temperate:
Rough winds do shake the darling buds of May,
And summer's lease hath all too short a date:

Sometimes too hot the eye of heaven shines,
And often is his gold complexion dimmed;
And every fair from fair sometime declines,
By chance or nature's changing course untrimmed;

But thy eternal summer shall not fade
Nor lose possession of that fair thou ow'st;
Nor shall Death brag thou wand'rest in his shade.
When in eternal lines to time thou grow'st:

So long as men can breathe or eyes can see,
So long lives this, and this gives life to thee.

William Shakespeare

KINDS OF RHYME

Examples gathered from concluding couplets of Shakespeare's Sonnets.

This were to be made new when thou art old, And see thy blood warm when thou feels't it cold.	**Perfect, True, Full,** **or Masculine Rhyme:** *Same vowel sound* *on a single final syllable.*
But if thou live rememb'red not to be, Die single and they image dies with thee.	
But day doth daily draw my sorrows longer, And night doth nightly make grief's length seem stronger.	**Feminine Rhyme** *Disyllabic rhyme of stressed* *plus <u>extra</u> unstressed syllable.*
If my slight Muse do please these curious days, The pain be mine, but thine shall be the praise.	**Rich Rhyme** *Homonyms that sound* *but do not spell the same.*
O, none but unthrifts! Dear my love, you know, You had a father; let you son say so.	
Receiving naught by elements so slow, But heavy tears, badges of either's woe.	**Augmented Rhyme** *One of the rhyming vowels* *is extended by a consonant.*
Lascivious grace, in whom all ill well shows, Kill me with spites; yet we must not be foes.	
Take heed, dear heart, of this large privilege; The hardest knife ill-used doth lose his edge.	**Assonant Rhyme** *Same vowel sounds,* *but differing consonant* *sounds.*
So, till the judgment that yourself arise, You live in this, and dwell in lovers' eyes.	
Presume not on thy heart when mine is slain; Thou gavs't me thine, not to give back again.	**Eye Rhyme** *Precedent of an* *historical pronunciation;* *permitted now by way of* *poetic license.*
But since he died, and poets better prove, Theirs for their style I'll read, his for his love.	

So thou, thyself outgoing in thy noon, Unlooked on diest unless thou get a son.	*Imperfect,* *Slant, Oblique,* *Off / Near /Half* *Rhyme.* *Variant sounds of* *a same vowel.*
And so of you, beauteous and lovely youth, When that shall vade, by verse distills your truth.	
For thee watch I, whilst thou dost wake elsewhere, From me far off, with others all too near.	
And thou is this shall find thy monument When tyrants' crests and tombs of brass are spent.	*Unstressed Rhyme* *Rhymes on unstressed* *syllable.* **Light or Wrenched Rhyme** *Rhymes a stressed with an* *unstressed syllable.*
But thou art all my art and doth advance As high as learning my rude ignorance.	
All days are nights to see till I see thee, And nights bright days when dreams do show thee me.	*Multiple* *Rhyming multiple words*
But here's the joy: my friend and I are one; Sweet flattery! Then she loves but me alone.	**Composite, Mosaic Rhyme** *Rhymes multisyllable word* *with single syllable word.*
Or else of thee this I prognosticate Thy end is truth and beauty's doom and date.	
And, all in war with Time for love of you, As he takes from you, I engraft you new.	**Internal Medial Rhyme** *At both caesura and end of a* *line.* **Caesural Interlaced Rhyme** *Rhymes at both caesuras and* *ends of lines of a couplet.*
Then happy I that love and am beloved Where I may not remove, nor be removed.	
So long as men can breathe, or eyes can see, So long lives this, and this gives life to thee.	**Initial or Internal Rhymes** *Alliteration, repetition, or* *rhymes at beginning of lines,* *or otherwise within a line.*
Blessèd are you whose worthiness gives scope, Being had, to triumph, being lacked, to hope.	

Asyndeton, 10
Polysyndeton, 11
Hendiadys, 12
Zeugma, 13
Aposiopesis, 14
Absolute Ellipsis, 15
Hyperbaton, 16
Anastrophe, 17
Parenthesis, 18
Enallage, Anthimeria, 19
Metonomy, Synecdoche, 20
Catachresis, 21
Polyptoton, 22
Antanaclasis, 23
Isocolon, 24
Anaphora, 25
Epistrophe, 26
Symploce, 27
Epanalepsis, 28
Anadiplosis, Gradatio, 29
Auxesis, 30
Chiasmus, 31

Rhetorica, from *The Seven Liberal Arts,*
by Hans Sebald Beham

RHETORICAL TROPES SUNDRY

Asyndeton

(Fr. α + συνδετοσ unconnected, Fr. συν + δειν to bind together)

And now abides, faith, hope, love, these three;
but the greatest of these is love. ***1 Corinthians***

I came, I saw, I conquered. *Julius Caesar*

O mighty Caesar! Dost thou lie so low?
Are all thy conquests, glories, triumphs, spoils,
Shrunk to this little measure?   *Shakespeare, **Julius Caesar***

I have spoken, you have heard. You know the facts, now give your
decision. *Aristotle, **On Rhetoric***

Eros is bold, enterprising, strong, a mighty hunter, ever weaving some
intrigue or other, keen in the pursuit of wisdom, rich in resources; a
philosopher always, terrible as an enchanter, sorcerer, sophist.
*Plato, **Symposium***

The ring on the finger becomes thin beneath by rubbing,
the fall of dripping water hollows the stone. *Lucretius, **De rerum natura***

O! what a noble mind is here o'er-thrown:
The courtier's, soldier's, scholar's, eye, tongue, sword.
*Shakespeare, **Hamlet***

All hail, great master! Grave sir, hail! I come
To answer thy best pleasure; be't to fly,
To swim, to dive into the fire, to ride
On the curl'd clouds.
*Shakespeare, **The Tempest***

I do not understand. I pause, I examine. *Montaigne, **Essays***

We see these beautiful co-adaptations ... only a little less plainly in the
humblest parasite that clings to the hairs of a quadruped or feathers of a
bird; in the structure of the beetle that dives through the water; in the
plumed seed that is wafted by the gentlest breeze.
*Darwin, **On the Origin of Species***

That government of the people, by the people, for the people,
shall not perish from the earth. *Lincoln, **Gettysburg Address***

Polysyndeton

(πολυσ many + συνδετοσ bound together, Fr. συν + δειν)

And they came to the place which God had told him of; and Abraham built an altar there, and laid the wood in order, and bound Isaac his son, and laid him on the altar upon the wood. And Abraham stretched forth his hand, and took the knife to slay his son. And the Angel of the Lord called unto him out of the heaven, and said, "Abraham, Abraham": and he said, "Here am I". ***Genesis***

And I stood upon the sand of the sea, and saw a beast rise up out of the sea, having seven heads and ten horns, and upon his horns ten crowns, and upon his heads the name of blasphemy. And the beast which I saw was like unto a leopard, and his feet were as the feet of a bear, and his mouth as the mouth of a lion: and the dragon gave him his power, and his seat, and great authority. And I saw one of his heads as it were wounded to death; and his deadly wound was healed: and all the world wondered after the beast. ***Book of Revelation***

Unless hours were cups of sack, and minutes capons, and clocks the tongues of bawds, and dials the signs of leaping houses, and the blessed sun himself a fair hot wench in flame-color'd taffeta, I see no reason why thou shouldst be so superfluous to demand the time of the Week. *Shakespeare,* ***Henry IV***

When men drink, they are rich and successful and win lawsuits and are content and help friends. Quick, bring me a jug of wine. *Aristophanes,* ***The Knights***

Whatever it is that I am, it is a bit of flesh and breath and the ruling part. *Marcus Aurelius,* ***Meditations***

For I have neither wit, nor words, nor worth,
Action, nor utterance, nor the power of speech,
To stir men's blood: I only speak right on.
Shakespeare, ***Julius Caesar*** 3.2

O! that I were as great
As is my grief, or lesser than my name,
Or that I could forget what I have been,
Or not remember what I must be now.
Shakespeare, ***Richard. II*** 3.3

Hendiadys
(? ἑν one + δια through + δυο two ?)

I love the Lord, for he hath heard my voice and my supplication.
Psalm 116

Of arms and a man I sing. *Virgil,* **Aeneid.**

Revenge and satisfaction … hapless hand and blow … *Tacitus,* **Annals**

It is a tale told by an idiot, full of sound and fury, signifying nothing.
Shakespeare, **Macbeth**

The heaviness and the guilt within my bosom
Takes off my manhood. *Shakespeare,* **Cymbeline**

Oh what a rogue and peasant slave am I. *Shakespeare,* **Hamlet**

But you must fear. His greatness weighed, his will is not his own,
For he himself is subject to his birth. He may not, as unvalued persons do,
carve for himself, for on his choice depends the safety and health of this
whole state. And therefore must his choice be circumscribed unto the
voice and yielding of that body whereof he is the head.
Shakespeare, **Hamlet**

But in the gross and scope of my opinion,
This bodes some strange eruption to our state. *Shakespeare,* **Hamlet**

Up! Up! My friend, and clear your looks;
Why all this toil and trouble? *Wordsworth,* **The Tables Turned**

Antiptosis
(? Fr. αντι instead of, πτοσισ a case [i.e., a grammatical case] ?)

Why are thou so far from helping me, from the words of my roaring?
Psalm 22:1

And above all these things put on charity, which is the bond of perfectness.
Colossians 1:17

The King's name is a tower of strength. *Shakespeare,* **Richard III**

Meester, meester! has Betty any right to lather I? *Shakespeare,* **Macbeth**

Zeugma

(Fr ζευγνυναι to join; cf. L. jungere & E. yoke)

But passion lends them power, time means, to meet.
*Shakespeare, **Romeo & Juliet** 2*

How Tarquin wronged me, I Collatine.
*Shakespeare, **Rape of Lucrece***

As you on him Demetrius dote on you!
*Shakespeare, **A Midsummer's Night Dream***

Histories make men wise; poets, witty; the mathematics, subtile; natural philosophy, deep; moral, grave; logic and rhetoric, able to contend. *Francis Bacon, **Essays***

One leaf she lays down, a floor of granite; then a thousand ages, and a bed of slate; a thousand ages, and a measure of coal; a thousand ages, and a layer of marl and mud; vegetable forms appear; her first misshapen animals, zoophyte, trilobium.
*Ralph Waldo Emerson, **The Book of Fate***

One will rarely mistake them if extreme actions are ascribed to vanity, ordinary actions to habit, and mean actions to fear.
*Friedrich Nietzsche, Human, **All Too Human***

A woman takes off her honor along with her garments.
*Herodotus, **Histories***

Let's have a dance ere we are married, that we may lighten our own hearts and our wives' heels.
*Shakespeare, **Much Ado About Nothing***

Neither the sun nor death can be looked upon steadily.
*La Rochefoucauld, **Maximes***

Yet time and her aunt moved slowly — and her patience and her ideas were nearly worn out before the tete-a-tete was over.
*Jane Austen, **Pride and Prejudice***

… in a species of arithmetical desperation, he was alternately cudgeling his brains and his donkey … *Charles Dickens, **Oliver Twist***

Aposiopesis

(Fr. απο + σιωπαν to be quite silent, Fr. σιοπη silence)

And the Lord God said, Behold, the man is become as one of us, to know good and evil; and now, lest he put forth his hand, and take also of the tree of life, and eat, and live forever: therefore the Lord God sent him forth from the garden of Eden, to till the ground from whence he was taken.
Genesis 3:22

Meanwhile Neptune saw the ocean's tumult … and he called out to the winds by name. "What arrogance is this, what pride of your birth, you winds, to interfere here without my nod, raising all this commotion? I'll — No, the waves come first! Heed me: you are going to pay for this!"
Virgil, **Aeneid**

I will have revenges on you both
That all the world shall — I will do such things —
What they are yet, I know not; but they shall be
The terrors of the earth!
Shakespeare, **King Lear**

"You are fond of spectacles," exclaims the stern Tertullian, "expect the greatest of all spectacles, the last and eternal judgment of the universe. How shall I admire, how laugh, how rejoice, how exult, when I behold so many proud monarchs, and fancied gods, groaning in the lowest abyss of darkness; so many magistrates, who persecuted the name of the Lord, liquefying in fiercer fires than they ever kindled against the Christians … so many tragedians, more tuneful in the expression of their own sufferings; so many dancers — " But the humanity of the reader will permit me to draw a veil over the rest of this infernal description, which the zealous African pursues in a long variety of affected and unfeeling witticisms.
Gibbon, **Decline & Fall of the Roman Empire**

She looked perplexed for a moment, and then said, not fiercely, but still loud enough for the furniture to hear: 'Well, I lay if I get hold of you I'll –'
She did not finish, for by this time she was bending down and punching under the bed with the broom, and so she needed breath to punctuate the punches with. *Mark Twain,* **Tom Sawyer**

Thus great with child to speak and helpless in my throes,
Biting my truant pen, beating myself for spite,
"Fool," said my Muse to me, "look in thy heart, and write."
Edmund Spenser

Absolute Ellipsis

(Fr. L. absolutus, Fr. ab + solvere to set free [from])
(Fr. ελλειπσισ ellipsis, Fr. ελλειπειν to leave out, fall short)

Et tu, Brute. **Caesar**

Meats for the belly, and the belly for meats;
but God shall destroy both it and them.
1 Corinthians 6:13

O eyes, no eyes, but fountains fraught with tears;
O life, no life, but lively form of death;
O world, no world, but mass of public wrongs,
Confused and filled with murder and misdeeds.
Thomas Kyd, **The Spanish Tragedy**

Wisely and slow; they stumble that run fast. *Shakespeare,* **Romeo & Juliet**

For what, alas, can these my single arms? What propugnation is in one man's valor? *Shakespeare,* **Troilus and Cressida**

No arts; no letters, no society; and which is worst of all, continual fear and danger of violent death; and the life of man, solitary, poor, nasty, brutish, and short. *Hobbes,* **Leviathan**

Blessed the people whose histories are boring to read.
Montesquieu, **Persian Letters**

The great tragedy of science — the slaying of a beautiful hypothesis by an ugly fact. *T.H. Huxley*

Nearing the end of his tether now. Sober serious man with a bit of the savings-bank I'd say. Wife a good cook and washer. Daughter working the machine in the parlour. Plain Jane, no damn nonsense. *Joyce,* **Ulysses**

After such knowledge, what forgiveness? *Eliot,* **Gerontion**

Rest at pale evening . . .
A tall, slim tree . . .
Night coming tenderly
Black like me.
Langston Hughes, **Dream Variations**

Hyperbaton

(? 'υπερ + βατ– Fr. βαιvo to go, to pass [over] ?)

Whom the Gods would destroy they first make mad.
Longfellow, **The Masque of Pandora**

Of arms and a man I sing.
Virgil, **Aeneid**

Few and singularly blessed are those Jupiter has destined to be cabbage planters. *Rabelais,* **Gargantua and Pantagruel**

Some rise by sin, and some by virtue fall.
Shakespeare, **Measure for Measure**

Yet I'll not shed her blood,
Nor scar that whiter skin of hers than snow.
Shakespeare, **Othello**

From such crooked wood as man is made of,
nothing right can be fashioned.
Kant, **Idea for a Universal History**

The queen was preparing furious ruins for the Roman capitol.
Horace, **Odes**

Ah! When will this long weary day have end,
And lend me leave to come unto my love?
Edmund Spenser, **Epithalamion**

Cursing, swearing, reviling, and the like do not signify as speech
but as the actions of a tongue accustomed.
Hobbes, **Leviathan**

Alas, what ignorant sin have I committed?
Shakespeare, **Othello**

The eye of man hath not heard, the ear of man hath not seen, man's hand is not able to taste, his tongue to conceive, nor his heart to report, what my dream was…
Shakespeare, **A Midsummer Night's Dream**

Anastrophe
(Fr. αναστροθη a turning back, Fr. ανα + στρεθειν to turn [back])

How many ages hence
Shall this our lofty scene be acted o'er
In states unborn and accents yet unknown!
Shakespeare, **Julius Caesar**

Are you good men and true? *Shakespeare,* **Much Ado About Nothing**

Figures pedantical … *Shakespeare,* **Love's Labor's Lost**

Military glory pure and simple withers in time into mere recognition by specialists and military historians. *Jacob Burckhardt*

The old bear … not even a mortal but an anachronism indomitable and invincible out of an old dead time. *William Faulkner,* **Go Down Moses**

Time present and time past
Are both perhaps present in time future,
And time future contained in time past. *Eliot,* **Four Quartets**

For if he a madman lived, at least he a wise one died.
Cervantes, **Don Quixote**

You may my glories and my state depose,
But not my griefs; still am I king of those. *Shakespeare,* **Richard II**

Hysteron-proteron
('υστερον the latter + προτερον first)

Let us die and rush into the heart of battle. *Virgil,* **Aeneid**

Naught, naught, all naught. I can behold no longer
Thanatoid, the Egyptian admiral,
With all their sixty, fly and turn the rudder.
Shakespeare, **Anthony & Cleopatra**

We granted his prayer and gave him John,
and we made his wife fertile for him. **Quran**

Parenthesis
(Fr. παρεντιθεναι to insert,
Fr. παρα– + εν– + τιθεναι place with-in)

And it came to pass after all thy wickedness (woe, woe unto thee! saith the Lord God,) That thou hast also built unto thee an eminent place, and hast made thee a high place in every street. ***Ezekiel***

Wherefore if ye be dead with Christ from the rudiments of the world, why, as though living in the world, are ye subject to ordinances, (Touch not; taste not; handle not; Which all are to perish with the using;) after the commandments and doctrines of men? ***Colossians***

Next Mettus asunder tore the swift chariots,
(Better, false Alban, to have kept your pledge!)
And Tullus dragged the traitor's mangled limbs.
Virgil, ***Aeneid***

 I love thilike lasse, (alas why does I love?)
And am forlorne, (alas why am I lorne?)
Edmund Spenser, ***The Shepheardes Calendar***

Why she, even she—
O heaven! A beast, that wants discourse of reason,
Would have mourn'd longer—married with my uncle,
My father's brother.
Shakespeare, ***Hamlet***

Poetry and Religion (and it is really worth knowing) are "a product of the smaller intestines."
Thomas Carlyle, ***Signs of the Times***

Nothing is easier than to admit in words the truth of the universal struggle for life, or more difficult—at least I have found it so—than constantly to bear this conclusion in mind.
Darwin, ***The Origin of Species***

—Even losing you (the joking voice, a gesture
I love) I shan't have lied. It's evident
the art of losing's not too hard to master
though it may look like (Write it!) like disaster.
Elizabeth Bishop, ***One Art***

Enallage
(? Fr. εναλλαγηναι to be changed, diverted from one thing to another?)

The wages of sin is death. **Romans**

The posture of your blows are yet unknown.
Shakespeare, ***Julius Caesar***

To show an unfelt sorrow is an office
Which the false man does easy.
Shakespeare, ***Macbeth***

The idols are broke in the temple of Baal.
Lord Byron, ***The Destruction of Sennacherib***

Curiouser and curiouser …
Lewis Carroll, ***Alice in Wonderland***

Anthimeria
(? Fr. αντι + –θι in the place of, μερισ a part [i.e., of speech?] ?)

The painful warrior famoused for fight.
Shakespeare, ***Sonnet*** 25

Such stuff as madmen / Tongue, and brain not …
Shakespeare, ***Cymbeline***

Thank me no thankings, nor proud me no prouds.
Shakespeare, ***Romeo & Juliet***

Every why hath a wherefore.
Shakespeare, ***A Comedy of Errors***

Is there not wars? Is there not employment?
Shakespeare, ***Henry V***

I go in search of a great perhaps. *Rabelais*

The hot of him is purest in the heart. *Wallace Stevens*

he sang his didn't he danced his did. *e.e. cummings*

Metonymy
(Fr. μετωνυμια change of name/noun, Fr. μετα + ονομα)

And the Lord said unto her, Two nations are in thy womb. *Genesis*

Rome has spoken, the case is closed. *Augustine*

I must comfort the weaker vessel, as doublet and hose ought to show itself courageous to petticoat. *Shakespeare,* **As You Like It**

Bell, book, and candle shall not drive me back. *Shakespeare,* **King John**

Amazement seized / The rebel thrones. *Milton,* **Paradise Lost**

As learned Commentators view / In Homer more than Homer knew. *Jonathan Swift,* **On Poetry**

The pen is mightier than the sword. *Edward Bulwer-Lytton*

Synecdoche
(Fr. συνεκδοχη sense, interpretation, Fr. συν– + εκδοχη a receiving)

For dust thou art, and unto dust shalt thou return. **Genesis**

I have sinned in this, that I have betrayed innocent blood. **Matthew**

Was this the face that launched a thousand ships,
And burnt the topless towers of Ilium?
Christopher Marlowe, **Doctor Faustus**

I saw them in the war / Like to a pair of lions smear'd with prey.
Shakespeare, **Two Noble Kinsmen**

There was never yet fair woman but she made mouths in a glass.
Shakespeare, **King Lear**

A hungry stomach has no ears. *Jean de La Fontaine*

I should have been a pair of ragged claws
Scuttling across the floor of silent seas.
Eliot, **The Love Song of J. Alfred Prufrock**

Catachresis

(Fr. καταχρησισ misuse, Fr. κατα + χρησθαι to use [up], [mis]use)

For the Lord knoweth the way of the righteous: but the way of the ungodly shall perish. ***Psalms***

Ye have made our savour to be abhorred in the eyes of Pharaoh. ***Exodus***

Why do ye not understand my speech? even because ye cannot hear my word. ***Gospel of John***

I do not ask much: I beg cold comfort. *Shakespeare,* ***King John***

A man that studies revenge keeps his own wounds green.
Francis Bacon, ***Of Revenge***

Her who still weeps with spongy eyes. *Donne,* ***The Indifferent***

Blind mouths. *John Milton,* ***Lycidas***

This dark brightness that falls from the stars. *Pierre Corneille,* ***Le Cid***

Cold War. *Bernard Baruch*

The pink itself of courtesy. *Miguel Cervantes,* ***Don Quixote***

His complexion is perfect gallows. *Shakespeare,* ***The Tempest***

A man may see how this world goes with no eyes. Look with thine ears: see how yond justice rails upon yon simple thief.
Shakespeare, ***King Lear***

The Oriel Common room stank of logic. *John Henry Newman*

I shall not live in vain
If I can ease one Life the Aching
Or cool one Pain.
Emily Dickinson

the voice of your eyes is deeper than all roses. *e.e. cummings*

Polyptoton

(Fr. πολυ– many/multi + πτωμα a fall/grammatical case, Fr. πιπτειν)

Cursed be Canaan; a servant of servants shall he be unto his brethren.
Genesis

When he ascended up on high, he led captivity captive, and gave gifts to men.
Ephesians

Light be the earth upon you, lightly rest. *Euripides,* **Alcestis**

Nothing is enough to the man for whom enough is too little. *Epicurus*

He cures most in whom most have faith. *Galen of Pergamon*

We both exist and know we exist, and rejoice in this existing and this knowledge. *Augustine,* **City of God**

He was not born to shame: upon his brow shame is asham'd to sit.
Shakespeare, **Romeo & Juliet**

But when I tell him he hates flatterers, he says he does, being then most flattered. *Shakespeare,* **Julius Caesar**

Few men speak humbly of humility, chastely of chastity, skeptically of skepticism. *Pascal,* **Pensées**

The religion most prevalent in our northern colonies is a refinement of the principle of resistance: it is the dissidence of dissent, and the Protestantism of the Protestant religion. *Edmund Burke*

Let the people think they Govern and they will be Govern'd. This cannot fail if Those they Trust, are Trusted. *William Penn,* **Some Fruits of Solitude**

Man would sooner have void for his purpose than be void of purpose.
Nietzsche, **The Genealogy of Morals**

With eager feeding food doth choke the feeder … *Shakespeare,* **Richard II**

Love is not love
that alters when it alteration finds
or bends with the remover to remove. *Shakespeare,* **Sonnets**

Antanaclasis

(Fr. αντι opposite, corresponding + κλησισ a calling on?)

Follow me; and let the dead bury their dead. **Matthew**

And when he had given thanks, he brake it, and said, Take, eat; this is my body, which is broken for you. *1 Corinthians*

They are not all Israel, which are of Israel. *Romans*

Mortal man, think mortal thoughts! *Attributed to Euripides*

On however high a throne he sits, a man still sits on his bottom.
Montaigne, **Essays**

It seems to me most strange that men should fear;
Seeing that death, a necessary end,
Will come when it will come.
Shakespeare, *Julius Caesar*

To England will I steal, and there I'll steal. *Shakespeare,* **Henry V 5.1**

True eloquence heeds not eloquence, true morality heeds not morality.
Pascal, **Pensées**

We must all hang together, or assuredly we shall all hang separately.
Benjamin Franklin

Experience is only the half of experience. *Goethe,* **Verses in Prose**

That night, that year of now done darkness I wretch lay wrestling with (my God) my God. *Gerard Manley Hopkins,* **Carrion Comfort**

And tell the pleasant prince this mock of his
Hath turned his balls to gun-stones, and his soul
Shall stand sore chargèd for the wasteful vengeance
That shall fly with them; for many a thousand widows
Shall this his mock mock out of their dear husbands,
Mock mothers from their sons, mock castles down,
And some are yet ungotten and unborn
That shall have cause to curse the Dauphin's scorn…
Shakespeare, **Henry V**

Isocolon

(? Fr. ισοσ equal + ολκοσ furrow, track & 'ελκω to draw or drag ?)

But in all things approving ourselves as the ministers of God, in much patience, in afflictions, in necessities, in distresses. In stripes, in imprisonments, in tumults, in afflictions, in labors, in watchings, in fastings; by pureness, by knowledge, by long-suffering, by kindness, by the Holy Ghost, by love unfeigned, by the word of truth, by the power of God, by the armor of righteousness on the right hand and on the left. By honor and dishonor, by evil report and good report: as deceivers, and yet true; as unknown, and yet well known; as dying, and, behold, we live; as chastened, and not killed; as sorrowful, yet always rejoicing; as poor, yet making many rich; as having nothing, and yet possessing all things.
2 Corinthians

In peace, sons bury their fathers; in war, fathers bury their sons.
Herodotus, **The Persian Wars**

Human Life! Its duration is but a moment, its substance in perpetual flux, its senses dim, its physical frame perishable, its consciousness a whirl, its destiny dim its reputation uncertain — in fact, the material part is a rolling stream, the spiritual part dreams and vapor, life a war and journeying in a far-away country, fame forgetfulness. What can see us through?
Marcus Aurelius, **Meditations**

If you prick us, do we not bleed? if you tickle us, do we not laugh? if you poison us, do we not die? and if you wrong us, shall we not revenge? *Shakespeare,* **The Merchant of Venice** 3.1

Always the dullness of the fool is the whetstone of the wits.
Shakespeare, **As You Like It** 1.2.59

The various modes of worship, which prevailed in the Roman world, were all considered by the people, as equally true; by the philosopher, as equally false; and by the magistrate, as equally useful.
Edward Gibbon, **History of the Decline and Fall of the Roman Empire**

We are as students of nature pantheists, as poets polytheists, as moral beings monotheists. *Goethe,* **Maxims and Reflections**

The world will ever bow to those who hold principle above policy, truth above diplomacy, and right about consistency.
Thomas Babington Macaulay

Anaphora

(Fr. ανα + φερειν to carry [back], refer)

That day is a day of wrath, a day of trouble and distress, a day of wasteness and desolation, a day of darkness and gloominess, a day of clouds and thick darkness. *Zephaniah*

Blessed are the poor in spirit: for theirs is the kingdom of heaven. Blessed are they that mourn: for they shall be comforted. Blessed are the meek: for they shall inherit the earth. *Matthew*

Through me the way unto the woeful city,
Through me the way to eternal woe,
Through me the way among people lost.
Dante, Inferno

This royal throne of kings, this scepter'd isle,
This earth of majesty, this seat of Mars …
This blessed plot, this earth, this realm, this England.
Shakespeare, Richard II

Mad world! Mad kings! Mad composition! *Shakespeare, King John*

Everything is good when it leaves the hands of the Creator;
everything degenerates when it is in the hands of man. *Rousseau, Emile*

She was not quite what you would call refined. She was not quite what you would call unrefined. She was the kind of person that keeps a parrot.
Mark Twain, Following the Equator

We shall not flag or fail. We shall go on to the end. We shall fight in France, we shall fight on the seas and oceans, we shall fight with growing confidence and growing strength in the air, we shall defend our island, whatever the cost may be, we shall fight on the beaches, we shall fight on the landing grounds, we shall fight in the fields and in the streets, we shall fight in the hills; we shall never surrender.
Churchill, Address to the House of Commons

Go back to Mississippi, go back to Alabama, go back to South Carolina, go back to Georgia, go back to Louisiana, go back to the slums and ghettos of our northern cities, knowing that somehow this situation can and will be changed. *Martin Luther King Jr., Address at the Lincoln Memorial*

Epistrophe
(Fr. επι + στροφη a turning [about])

O Israel, trust thou in the Lord: he is their help and their shield. O house of Aaron, trust in the Lord: he is their help and their shield. Ye that fear the Lord, trust in the Lord: he is their help and their shield.
Psalms

When I was a child, I spake as a child, I understood as a child, I thought as a child: but when I became a man, I put away childish things.
1 Corinthians

The grove of Angita mourned you,
The glassy watered Fuccinus mourned you,
All the lucid lakes lamented you.
Virgil, **Aeneid**

For truth is one, and right is ever one. *Spenser,* **Faerie Queene**

Unhappy spirits that fell with Lucifer,
Conspired against our God with Lucifer,
And are forever damned with Lucifer.
Christopher Marlow, **Doctor Faustus**

Julia: they do not love that do not show their love.
Lucetta: O! they love least that let men know their love.
Shakespeare, **Two Gentlemen of Verona**

Why I should fear I know not,
Since guiltiness I know not; but yet I feel fear.
Shakespeare, **Othello**

Selfishness is not living as one wishes to live. It is asking others to live as one wishes to live. *Oscar Wilde,* **The Soul of Man and Prison Writings**

Men have never been good, they are not good, they never will be good.
Karl Barth

There is no Negro problem. There is no Southern problem. There is no Northern problem. There is only an American problem.
Lyndon Johnson, Address to Congress

Symploce

(? Fr. συμπλοκη an intertwining ?)

Cursed be he that removeth his neighbor's landmark: and all the people shall say, Amen. Cursed be he that maketh the blind to wander out of the way: and all the people shall say, Amen .... Cursed be he that lieth with any manner of beast: and all the people shall say, Amen.
Deuteronomy

Are they Hebrews? So am I. Are they Israelites? So am I. Are they of the seed of Abraham? So am I.
2 Corinthians

Who are the ones that have so often broken treaties? The Carthaginians. Who are the ones that have waged war with such atrocious cruelty? The Carthaginians. Who are the ones that have laid Italy to waste? The Carthaginians. Who are the ones that pray for pardon? The Carthaginians. *Cicero, in* **Institutio Oratoria**

If thou has any sound, or use of voice,
Speak to me.
If there be any good thing to be done,
That may to thee do ease and grace to me,
Speak to me.
Shakespeare, **Hamlet**

I'll tell you who Time ambles withal, who Time trots withal, who Time gallops withal, and who he stands still withal.
Shakespeare, **As You Like It**

Son:	How will my mother for a father's death
	Take on with me, and ne'er be satisfied!
Father:	How will my wife for slaughter of my son
	She seas of tears, and ne'er be satisfied!
King:	How will the country for these woeful chances
	Misthink the Kind, and not be satisfied.

Shakespeare, **Henry VI**, Part 3

The madman is not the man who has lost his reason. The madman is the man who has lost everything except his reason.
G.K. Chesterton, **Orthodoxy**

Epanalepsis

(? Fr. επι + αναληπσισ a taking up[on], taking [on] again ?)

Rejoice in the Lord always: and again I say, Rejoice. **Philippians**

In the world, ye shall have tribulation, but be of good cheer -- I have overcome the world. **John**

Nothing can be made out of nothing. *Lucretius,* **De rerum natura**

Judges need to be many, for a few will always do the will of a few. *Machiavelli,* **Discourses on Livy**

Blood hath brought blood, and blows have answer'd blows; Strength match'd with strength, and power confronted power. *Shakespeare,* **King Jame**s

Men of few words are the best men. *Shakespeare,* **Henry V**

Kings it makes gods, and meaner creatures kings. *Shakespeare,* **Richard III**

Once more unto the breach, dear friends, once more. *Shakespeare,* **Henry V**

It takes time to ruin a world, but all it takes is time. *Fontenelle*

Common sense is not very common. *Voltaire*

Harm, violation, exploitation, destruction, cannot be wrong in themselves, for life essentially presupposes harm, violation, exploitation, and destruction. *Nietzsche,* **On the Genealogy of Morals**

Hugo was a madman who believed he was Hugo. *Jean Cocteau,* **Opium**

Say over again, and yet once over again, That thou dost love me. *Elizabeth Barret Browning,* **Sonnets from the Portuguese**

He smiled the most exquisite smile, veiled by memory, tinged by dreams. *Virginia Woolf,* **To the Lighthouse**

Possessed by what we now no more possessed. *Robert Frost,* **The Gift Outright**

Anadiplosis

(Fr. αναδιπλωσισ repetition, Fr. ανα + διπλουν to double)

I will lift up mine eyes unto the hills, from whence cometh my help.
My help cometh from the Lord which made heaven and earth. ***Psalms***

Therefore shall his calamity come suddenly; suddenly shall he be broken
without remedy. ***Proverbs***

Does the silk worm expend her yellow labours for thee? For thee does she
undo herself? *Cyril Tourneur,* ***The Revenger's Tragedy***

Death, as the Psalmist saith, is certain to all; all shall die.
Shakespeare, ***Henry IV,*** Part 2

Who has not the spirit of his age, of his age has all the unhappiness. *Voltaire*

Talent is an adornment; an adornment is also a concealment.
Nietzsche, ***Beyond Good and Evil***

Everything that can be said, can be said clearly. *Wittgenstein,* ***Tractactus***

Gradatio

We glory in tribulations also: Knowing that tribulation worketh patience;
And patience, experience; And experience, hope: And hope maketh not
ashamed. ***Romans***

The boy is the most powerful of all the Hellenes; for the Hellenes are
commanded by the Athenians, the Athenians by myself, myself by the
boy's mother, and the mother by her boy. *Plutarch,* ***Themistocles***

[F]or your brother and my sister no sooner met but they looked; no sooner
looked but they loved; no sooner loved but they sighed; no sooner sighed
but they asked one another the reason; no sooner knew the reason but they
sought the remedy; and in these degrees have they made a pair of stairs to
marriage which they will climb incontinent, or else be incontinent before
marriage *Shakespeare, As You Like It*

Men often hate each other because they fear each other; they fear each other
because they don't know each other; they don't know each other because
they can not communicate; they can not communicate because they are
separated. ***Martin Luther King Jr.***

Auxesis

(Fr. αυξησισ increase, Fr. αυξειν to increase)

Blessed is the man that walketh not in the counsel of the ungodly, nor standeth in the way of sinners, nor sitteth in the seat of the scornful. **Psalms**

Let this mind be in you, which was also in Christ Jesus:
Who, being in the form of God, though it not robbery to be equal with God: But made himself of no reputation, and took upon him the form of a servant, and was made in the likeness of men: And being found in fashion as a man, he humbled himself, and became obedient unto death, even the death of the cross. **Philippians**

It is a sin to bind a Roman citizen, a crime to scourge him, little short of the most unnatural murder to put him to death; what then shall I call this crucifixion? *Cicero, in* **Institutio Oratoria**

Pleasure might cause her to read, reading might make her know,
Knowledge might pitie winne, and pitie grace obtain.
Sidney, **Astrophil and Stella**

Since brass, nor stone, nor earth, nor boundless sea,
But sad mortality o'er-sways their power …
How with this rage shall beauty hold a plea,
Whose action is no stronger than a flower?
Shakespeare, **Sonnets**

Nurse, O my love is slain, I saw him go
O'er the white Alps alone; I saw him I,
Assailed, fight, taken, stabbed, bleed, fall, and die.
John Donne, **Elegies**

What shall point out them,
When they shall bow, and kneel, and fall down flat
To kisse those heaps, which now they have in trust?
George Herbert, **Church Monuments**

Some have at first for Wits, then Poets past,
Turn'd Critics next, and prov'd plain fools at last.
Alexander Pope, **An Essay on Criticism**

Chiasmus

(From the Greek letter χ)

Woe unto them that call evil good, and good evil; that put darkness for light, and light for darkness; that put bitter for sweet, and sweet for bitter. *Isaiah*

The Sabbath was made for man, and not man for the Sabbath. *Mark*

Circumstances rule men; men do not rule circumstances.
Herodotus, **The Histories**

Every man seeks peace by waging war, but no man seeks war by making peace. *Augustine,* **City of God**

It is not titles that reflect honor on men, but men on their titles.
Machiavelli, **The Prince**

Those who have compared our life to a dream were right …
we sleeping wake and waking sleep.
Montaigne, **Essays**

If a man will begin with certainties, he shall end in doubts;
but if he will be content to begin with doubts he shall end in certainties.
Francis Bacon, **The Advancement of Learning**

Fair is foul, and foul is fair. *Shakespeare,* **Macbeth**

That he is mad, 'tis true; 'tis true 'tis pity;
And pity 'tis 'tis true. *Shakespeare,* **Hamlet**

I wasted time, and now doth time waste me.
Shakespeare, **Richard II**

For 'tis a question left us yet to prove,
Whether love lead fortune, or else fortune love.
Shakespeare, **Hamlet**

More safe I sing with mortal voice, unchang'd
To hoarse or mute, though fall'n on evil days,
On evil days though fall'n and evil tongues.
Milton, **Paradise Lost VII**

Thomas Wyatt, 35

Sir Philip Sidney, 38

Edmund Spenser, 42

William Shakespeare, 44

Lord Fulke Greville, 58

John Donne, 60

George Herbert, 62

Lady Mary Wroth, 64

John Milton, 76

Percy Bysshe Shelley, 79

John Keats, 78

William Wordsworth, 80

Elizabeth Barrett Browning, 82

Gerard Manley Hopkins, 84

Robert Frost, 88

Edna St. Vincent Millay, 89

Erato Undressing
Muse of erotic lyric with roses.

THE ENGLISH SONNET

Fourteen lines of iambic pentameter rhymed alternately.

The Marriage of Eurydice and Orpheus

The Death of Eurydice

Whoso list to hunt, I know where is an hind,

But as for me, hélas, I may no more.

The vain travail hath wearied me so sore,

4   I am of them that farthest cometh behind.

Yet may I by no means my wearied mind

Draw from the deer, but as she fleeth afore

8   Fainting I follow. I leave off therefore,

Sithens in a net I seek to hold the wind.

Who list her hunt, I put him out of doubt,

12   As well as I may spend his time in vain.

And graven with diamonds in letters plain

There is written, her fair neck round about:

16   Noli me tangere, for Caesar's I am,

And wild for to hold, though I seem tame.

Sir Thomas Wyatt

36 | Sonnets

My galley chargèd with forgetfulness

Thorough sharp seas in winter nights doth pass

'Tween rock and rock; and eke mine enemy, alas,

4   That is my lord, steereth with cruelness;

And every oar a thought in readiness,

As though that death were light in such a case.

8   An endless wind doth tear the sail apace

Of forcèd sighs and trusty fearfulness.

A rain of tears, a cloud of dark disdain,

12   Hath done the wearèd cords great hinderance;

Wreathed with error and eke with ignorance.

The stars be hid that led me to this pain;

Drownèd is reason that should me consort,

16   And I remain despairing of the port.

Sir Thomas Wyatt

The longë love that in my thought doth harbour

And in mine heart doth keep his residence,

Into my face presseth with bold pretense

4   And therein campeth, spreading his banner.

She that me learneth to love and suffer

And will that my trust and lust's negligence

Be reined by reason, shame, and reverence,

8   With his hardiness taketh displeasure.

Wherewithal unto the heart's forest he fleeth,

Leaving his enterprise with pain and cry,

12   And there him hideth and not appeareth.

What may I do when my master feareth

But in the field with him to live and die?

For good is the life ending faithfully.

Sir Thomas Wyatt

38 | *Sonnets*

Loving in truth, and fain in verse my love to show,

That she, dear she, might take some pleasure of my pain,—

Pleasure might cause her read, reading might make her know,

4   Knowledge might pity win, and pity grace obtain,—

I sought fit words to paint the blackest face of woe;

Studying inventions fine her wits to entertain,

8   Oft turning others' leaves, to see if thence would flow

Some fresh and fruitful showers upon my sunburn'd brain.

But words came halting forth, wanting invention's stay;

12   Invention, Nature's child, fled step-dame Study's blows;

And others' feet still seem'd but strangers in my way.

Thus great with child to speak and helpless in my throes,

16   Biting my truant pen, beating myself for spite,

"Fool," said my Muse to me, "look in thy heart, and write."

Sir Philip Sidney

Come, Sleep! O Sleep, the certain knot of peace,

The baiting-place of wit, the balm of woe,

The poor man's wealth, the prisoner's release,

4   Th' indifferent judge between the high and low;

With shield of proof shield me from out the press

Of those fierce darts Despair at me doth throw!

8   O make in me those civil wars to cease!—

I will good tribute pay if thou do so.

Take thou of me smooth pillows, sweetest bed,

12   A chamber deaf of noise and blind of light,

A rosy garland, and a weary head;

And if these things, as being thine in right,

16   Move not thy heavy grace, thou shalt in me,

Livelier than elsewhere, Stella's image see.

Sir Philip Sidney

40 | *Sonnets*

Thou blind man's mark, thou fool's self-chosen snare,

Fond fancy's scum, and dregs of scattered thought;

Band of all evils, cradle of causeless care;

4   Thou web of will, whose end is never wrought;

Desire, desire! I have too dearly bought,

With price of mangled mind, thy worthless ware;

Too long, too long, asleep thou hast me brought,

8   Who shouldst my mind to higher things prepare.

But yet in vain thou hast my ruin sought;

In vain thou madest me to vain things aspire;

12   In vain thou kindlest all thy smoky fire;

For virtue hath this better lesson taught,—

Within myself to seek my only hire,

Desiring nought but how to kill desire.

Sir Philip Sidney

Leave me, O Love, which reachest but to dust;

And thou, my mind, aspire to higher things;

Grow rich in that which never taketh rust;

4   Whatever fades but fading pleasure brings.

Draw in thy beams and humble all thy might

To that sweet yoke where lasting freedoms be;

8   Which breaks the clouds and opens forth the light,

That both doth shine and give us sight to see.

O take fast hold; let that light be thy guide

12   In this small course which birth draws out to death,

And think how evil becometh him to slide,

Who seeketh heav'n, and comes of heav'nly breath.

16   Then farewell, world; thy uttermost I see:

Eternal Love, maintain thy life in me.

Sir Philip Sidney

Amoretti LXVII

Like as a huntsman after weary chase,

Seeing the game from him escap'd away,

Sits down to rest him in some shady place,

4   With panting hounds beguiled of their prey:

So after long pursuit and vain assay,

When I all weary had the chase forsook,

The gentle deer return'd the self-same way,

8   Thinking to quench her thirst at the next brook.

There she beholding me with milder look,

Sought not to fly, but fearless still did bide:

Till I in hand her yet half trembling took,

12   And with her own goodwill her firmly tied.

Strange thing, me seem'd, to see a beast so wild,

So goodly won, with her own will beguil'd.

Edmund Spenser

Amoretti LXXV

My love is like to ice, and I to fire:

How comes it then that this her cold so great

Is not dissolved through my so hot desire,

4   But harder grows the more I her entreat?

Or how comes it that my exceeding heat

Is not allayed by her heart-frozen cold,

But that I burn much more in boiling sweat,

8   And feel my flames augmented manifold?

What more miraculous thing may be told,

That fire, which all things melts, should harden ice,

And ice, which is congeal'd with senseless cold,

12   Should kindle fire by wonderful device?

Such is the power of love in gentle mind,

That it can alter all the course of kind.

Edmund Spenser

Sonnet 1

From fairest creatures we desire increase,

That thereby beauty's rose might never die,

But as the riper should by time decease,

His tender heir might bear his memory;

But thou, contracted to thine own bright eyes,

Feed'st thy light's flame with self-substantial fuel,

Making a famine where abundance lies,

Thyself thy foe, to thy sweet self too cruel.

Thou that art now the world's fresh ornament

And only herald to the gaudy spring

Within thine own bud buriest thy content,

And, tender churl, mak'st waste in niggarding.

Pity the world, or else this glutton be,

To eat the world's due, by the grave and thee.

William Shakespeare

Sonnet 27

Weary with toil, I haste me to my bed,

The dear repose for limbs with travel tired;

But then begins a journey in my head,

4   To work my mind, when body's work's expired:

For then my thoughts (from far where I abide)

Intend a zealous pilgrimage to thee,

And keep my drooping eyelids open wide,

8   Looking on darkness which the blind do see:

Save that my soul's imaginary sight

Presents thy shadow to my sightless view,

Which, like a jewel hung in ghastly night,

12   Makes black night beauteous and her old face new.

Lo, thus, by day my limbs, by night my mind,

For thee, and for myself, no quiet find.

William Shakespeare

46 | *Sonnets*

Sonnet 29

When, in disgrace with fortune and men's eyes,

I all alone beweep my outcast state,

And trouble deaf heaven with my bootless cries,

4   And look upon myself and curse my fate,

Wishing me like to one more rich in hope,

Featured like him, like him with friends possessed,

Desiring this man's art and that man's scope,

8   With what I most enjoy contented least;

Yet in these thoughts myself almost despising,

Haply I think on thee, and then my state,

(Like to the lark at break of day arising

12   From sullen earth) sings hymns at heaven's gate;

For thy sweet love remembered such wealth brings

That then I scorn to change my state with kings.

William Shakespeare

Sonnet 86

Was it the proud full sail of his great verse,

Bound for the prize of all too precious you,

That did my ripe thoughts in my brain inhearse,

4   Making their tomb the womb wherein they grew?

Was it his spirit, by spirits taught to write

Above a mortal pitch, that struck me dead?

No, neither he, nor his compeers by night

8   Giving him aid, my verse astonished.

He, nor that affable familiar ghost

Which nightly gulls him with intelligence,

As victors of my silence cannot boast;

12   I was not sick of any fear from thence:

But when your countenance filled up his line,

Then lacked I matter; that enfeebled mine.

William Shakespeare

48 | *Sonnets*

Sonnet 53

What is your substance, whereof are you made,

That millions of strange shadows on you tend?

Since every one hath, every one, one shade,

4 And you, but one, can every shadow lend.

Describe Adonis, and the counterfeit

Is poorly imitated after you;

On Helen's cheek all art of beauty set,

8 And you in Grecian tires are painted new.

Speak of the spring and foison of the year:

The one doth shadow of your beauty show,

The other as your bounty doth appear;

12 And you in every blessed shape we know.

In all external grace you have some part,

But you like none, none you, for constant heart.

William Shakespeare

Sonnet 138

When my love swears that she is made of truth,

I do believe her, though I know she lies,

That she might think me some untutored youth,

4   Unlearnèd in the world's false subtleties.

Thus vainly thinking that she thinks me young,

Although she knows my days are past the best,

8   Simply I credit her false-speaking tongue:

On both sides thus is simple truth suppressed.

But wherefore says she not she is unjust?

12   And wherefore say not I that I am old?

Oh, love's best habit is in seeming trust,

And age in love loves not to have years told.

16   Therefore I lie with her and she with me,

And in our faults by lies we flattered be.

William Shakespeare

Sonnet 73

That time of year thou mayst in me behold

When yellow leaves, or none, or few, do hang

Upon those boughs which shake against the cold,

4   Bare ruin'd choirs, where late the sweet birds sang.

In me thou see'st the twilight of such day

As after sunset fadeth in the west,

8   Which by and by black night doth take away,

Death's second self, that seals up all in rest.

In me thou see'st the glowing of such fire

12   That on the ashes of his youth doth lie,

As the death-bed whereon it must expire,

Consum'd with that which it was nourish'd by.

16   This thou perceiv'st, which makes thy love more strong,

To love that well which thou must leave ere long.

William Shakespeare

Sonnet 107

Not mine own fears, nor the prophetic soul

Of the wide world dreaming on things to come,

Can yet the lease of my true love control,

4   Supposed as forfeit to a cónfined doom.

The mortal moon hath her eclipse endured

And the sad augurs mock their own preságe;

Incertainties now crown themselves assured,

8   And peace proclaims olives of endless age.

Now with the drops of this most balmy time

My love looks fresh, and death to me subscribes,

Since spite of him I'll live in this poor rhyme,

12   While he insults o'er dull and speechless tribes.

And thou in this shalt find thy monument,

When tyrants' crests and tombs of brass are spent.

William Shakespeare

52 | *Sonnets*

Sonnet 94

They that have pow'r to hurt, and will do none,

That do not do the thing they most do show,

Who moving others are themselves as stone,

4   Unmovèd, cold, and to temptation slow—

They rightly do inherit heaven's graces,

And husband nature's riches from expense;

They are the lords and owners of their faces,

8   Others but stewards of their excellence.

The summer's flow'r is to the summer sweet,

Though to itself it only live and die;

But if that flow'r with base infection meet,

12   The basest weed outbraves his dignity.

For sweetest things turn sourest by their deeds;

Lilies that fester smell far worse than weeds.

William Shakespeare

Sonnet 121

’Tis better to be vile than vile esteemed

When not to be receives reproach of being,

And the just pleasure lost, which is so deemed

4   Not by our feeling but by others’ seeing.

For why should others’ false adulterate eyes

Give salutation to my sportive blood?

Or on my frailties why are frailer spies,

8   Which in their wills count bad that I think good?

No, I am that I am; and they that level

At my abuses reckon up their own:

I may be straight though they themselves be bevel;

12   By their rank thoughts my deeds must not be shown,

Unless this general evil they maintain:

All men are bad and in their badness reign

William Shakespeare

Sonnet 97

How like a winter hath my absence been
From thee, the pleasure of the fleeting year!
What freezings have I felt, what dark days seen,
What old December's bareness everywhere!

And yet this time removed was summer's time,
The teeming autumn, big with rich increase,
Bearing the wanton burden of the prime,
Like widowed wombs after their lords' decease:

Yet this abundant issue seemed to me
But hope of orphans and unfathered fruit;
For summer and his pleasures wait on thee,
And thou away, the very birds are mute;

Or if they sing, 'tis with so dull a cheer
That leaves look pale, dreading the winter's near.

William Shakespeare

Sonnet 116

Let me not to the marriage of true minds

Admit impediments. Love is not love

Which alters when it alteration finds,

4   Or bends with the remover to remove.

O no! it is an ever-fixed mark

That looks on tempests and is never shaken;

It is the star to every wand'ring bark,

8   Whose worth's unknown, although his height be taken.

Love's not Time's fool, though rosy lips and cheeks

Within his bending sickle's compass come;

Love alters not with his brief hours and weeks,

12   But bears it out even to the edge of doom.

If this be error and upon me prov'd,

I never writ, nor no man ever lov'd.

William Shakespeare

56 | *Sonnets*

Sonnet 129

Th' expense of spirit in a waste of shame

Is lust in action; and till action, lust

Is perjured, murd'rous, bloody, full of blame,

4   Savage, extreme, rude, cruel, not to trust,

Enjoyed no sooner but despisèd straight,

Past reason hunted; and, no sooner had

8   Past reason hated as a swallowed bait

On purpose laid to make the taker mad;

Mad in pursuit and in possession so,

12   Had, having, and in quest to have, extreme;

A bliss in proof and proved, a very woe;

Before, a joy proposed; behind, a dream.

16   All this the world well knows; yet none knows well

To shun the heaven that leads men to this hell.

William Shakespeare

Sonnet 75

So are you to my thoughts as food to life,

Or as sweet seasoned showers are to the ground;

And for the peace of you I hold such strife

4 As 'twixt a miser and his wealth is found;

Now proud as an enjoyer, and anon

Doubting the filching age will steal his treasure;

Now counting best to be with you alone,

8 Then better'd that the world may see my pleasure;

Sometime all full with feasting on your sight,

And by and by clean starved for a look;

Possessing or pursuing no delight

12 Save what is had or must from you be took.

Thus do I pine and surfeit day by day,

Or gluttoning on all, or all away.

William Shakespeare

Caelica 100

In night when colors all to black are cast,

Distinction lost, or gone down with the light;

The eye a watch to inward senses placed,

Not seeing, yet still having powers of sight,

Gives vain alarums to the inward sense,

Where fear stirred up with witty tyranny,

Confounds all powers, and thorough self-offense,

Doth forge and raise impossibility:

Such as in thick depriving darknesses,

Proper reflections of the error be,

And images of self-confusednesses,

Which hurt imaginations only see;

And from this nothing seen, tells news of devils,

Which but expressions be of inward evils.

Lord Brooke Fulke Greville

Caelica 29

The nurse-life wheat within his green husk growing,

Flatters our hope, and tickles our desire,

Nature's true riches in sweet beauties showing,

4 Which sets all hearts, with labor's love, on fire.

No less fair is the wheat when golden ear

Shows unto hope the joys of near enjoying;

Fair and sweet is the bud, more sweet and fair

8 the rose, which proves that time is not destroying.

Caelica, your youth, the morning of delight,

Enamel'd o'er with beauties white and red,

All sense and thoughts did to belief invite,

12 That love and glory there are brought to bed;

And your ripe year's love-noon; he goes no higher,

Turns all the spirits of man into desire.

Lord Brooke Fulke Greville

Holy Sonnets, 5

I am a little world made cunningly

Of elements, and an angelic sprite,

But black sin hath betrayed to endless night

4   My world's both parts, and oh, both parts must die.

You, which beyond that heav'n that was most high

Have found new spheres, and of new lands can write,

Pour new seas in mine eyes, so that I might

8   Drown my world with my weeping earnestly,

Or wash it, if it must be drowned no more:

But oh it must be burnt; alas, the fire

Of lust and envy have burnt it heretofore,

12   And made it fouler; let their flames retire,

And burn me, O Lord, with a fiery zeal

Of thee and thy house, which doth in eating heal.

John Donne

Holy Sonnets, 19

Oh, to vex me, contraries meet in one:

Inconstancy unnaturally hath begot

A constant habit; that when I would not,

4   I change in vows, and in devotion.

As humorous is my contrition

As my profane love, and as soon forgot:

As riddlingly distempered, cold and hot,

8   As praying, as mute; as infinite, as none.

I durst not view heav'n yesterday; and today

In prayers and flattering speeches I court God:

Tomorrow I quake with true fear of his rod.

12   So my devout fits come and go away

Like a fantastic ague: save that here

Those are my best days, when I shake with fear.

John Donne

Prayer (I)

Prayer the Church's banquet, angels' age,
God's breath in man returning to his birth,
The soul in paraphrase, heart in pilgrimage,
The Christian plummet sounding heav'n and earth;

Engine against th'Almighty, sinner's tower,
Reversèd thunder, Christ-side-piercing spear,
The six-days' world transposing in an hour,
A kind of tune, which all things hear and fear;

Softness, and peace, and joy, and love, and bliss,
Exalted Manna, gladness of the best,
Heaven in ordinary, man well dressed,
The milky way, the bird of Paradise,

Church-bells beyond the stars heard, the soul's blood,
The land of spices, something understood.

George Herbert

Joseph's Coat

Wounded I sing, tormented I indite,

Thrown down I fall into a bed, and rest:

Sorrow hath chang'd its note: such is his will

4   Who changeth all things, as him pleaseth best.

For well he knows, if but one grief and smart

Among my many had his full career,

Sure it would carry with it ev'n my heart,

8   And both would run until they found a bier

To fetch the body; both being due to grief.

But he hath spoil'd the race; and giv'n to anguish

One of Joy's coats, 'ticing it with relief

12   To linger in me, and together languish.

I live to shew his power, who once did bring

My joys to weep, and now my griefs to sing.

George Herbert

64 | *Pamphilia to Amphilanthus*

I

When night's black mantle could most darkness
prove,
And sleep, death's image, did my senses hire
From knowledge of myself, then thoughts did move
Swifter than those most swiftness need require:
In sleep, a chariot drawn by winged desire
I saw, where sat bright Venus, Queen of love,
And at her feet her son, still adding fire
To burning hearts, which she did hold above.

But one heart flaming more than all the rest
The Goddess held, and put it to my breast.
'Dear son, now shoot,' said she, 'thus must we win.'
He her obeyed, and martyred my poor heart.
I waking hoped as dreams it would depart;
Yet since, O me, a lover I have been.

II

Dear eyes, how well, indeed, you do adorn
That blessed sphere which gazing eyes hold dear,
The loved place of Cupid's triumphs near,
The court of glory, where his force was not borne,
How may they term you April's sweetest morn
When pleasing looks from those bright lights appear
A sunshine day, from clouds and mists still clear
Kind nursing fires for wishes yet unborn.

Two stars of Heaven sent down to grace the earth,
Placed in that throne which gives all joys their birth,
Shining and burning, pleasing, yet their charms
Which wounding, yet in hurts are deemed delights,
So pleasant is their force, so great their mights
As, happy, they can triumph in their harms.

III

Yet is there hope. Then love but play thy part;
Remember well thyself and think on me,
Shine in those eyes which conquered have my
heart,
And see if mine be slack to answer thee.
Lodge in that breast and, pity move to be
For flames which in mine burn in truest smart,
Exiling thoughts that touch inconstancy,
Or those which waste not in the constant art.

Watch but my sleep, if I take any rest
For thought of you, my spirit so distressed
As, pale and famished, I for mercy cry.
Will not your servant leave? Think but on this:
Who wears love's crown must not do so amiss,
But seek their god who on thy force rely.

IV

Venus unto the Gods a suit did move,
That since she was of love the goddess styled,
She only might the power have of love,
And not as now a partner with her child,
The cause to this which stirred the Goddess mild
Was that of late her servant false did prove
Hurt as she said afresh by Cupid wild,
And to a Nymph his passions did remove;

Or else that they would eyes unto him give
That he might see, how he his shafts did drive,
This they denied: For if he blind did ill,
What would he seeing? But thus much they did
To shoot without her leave they him forbid
He this observed, and since obeys her will.

Lady Mary Wroth | 65

V

Can pleasing sight, misfortune ever bring?
Can firm desire ever, torments try?
Can winning eyes prove to the hart a sting?
Or can sweet lips in treason hidden lie?
The Sun most pleasing blinds the strongest eye
If too much look'd on, breaking the sight's string;
Desires crossed must unto mischiefs hie,
And as despair, a luckless chance may fling.

Eyes, having won, rejecting proves a sting
Killing the bud before the tree doth spring,
Sweet lips not loving doth as poison prove.
Desire, sight, eyes, lips, seek, see, prove, and find
You love may win, but curses if unkind,
Then show you harm's dislike, and joy in Love.

VI

O strive not still to heap disdain on me
Nor pleasure take your cruelty to show
On hapless me, on whom all sorrows flow,
And biding make: as given, and lost by thee,
Alas; even grief is grown to pity me;
Scorn cries out 'gainst itself such ill to show,
And would give place for joy's delights to flow;
Yet wretched I, all tortures bear from thee,

Long have I suffered, and esteemed it dear
Since you so willed, yet grew my pains more near.
Wish you my end? Say so, you shall it have;
For all the depth of my heart-killed despair
Is that for you I feel not death for care;
But now I'll seek it, since you will not save.

VII

Love leave to urge, thou know'st thou hast the hand;
T'is cowardice to strive where none resist:
Pray thee leave of, I yield unto thy band;
Do not thus, still, in thine own power persist,
Behold I yield: let forces be dismissed;
I am your subject conquered, bound do stand,
Never your foe, but did your claim assist
Seeking your due of those who did withstand;

But now, it seems, you would I should you love;
I do confess, 'twas you, made me first choose;
And your faire shows made me a lover prove
when I my freedom did, for pain refuse
Yet this Sir God, your boyship I despise;
Your charms I obey, but love not want of eyes.

VIII

Led by the power of grief, to wailings brought
By false conceit of change fallen on my part,
I seek for some small ease by lines, which bought,
Increaseth pain; grief is not cured by art:
Ah! how unkindness moves within the heart
Which still is true, and free from changing thought
What unknown woe it breeds; what endless smart
With ceaseless tears which causelessly are brought.

It makes me now to shun all shining light,
And seek for blackest clouds me light to give,
Which to all others, only darkness drive,
They on me shine, for sun disdains my sight
Yet though I dark do live I triumph may
Unkindness, nor this wrong shall love allay.

66 | *Pamphilia to Amphilanthus*

IX

Be you all pleased? Your pleasures grieve not me;

Do you delight? I envy not your joy;

Have you content? Contentment with you be:

Hope you for bliss? Hope still, and still enjoy:

Let sad misfortune hapless me destroy,

Leave crosses to rule me, and still rule free,

While all delights their contraries employ

To keep good back, and I but torments see,

Joys are bereaved, and harms do only tarry;

Despair takes place, disdain hath got the hand;

Yet firm love holds my senses in such band

As since despised, I, with sorrow marry;

Then if with grief I now must coupled be

Sorrow I'll wed: despair thus governs me.

X

The weary traveller who tired sought

In places distant far, yet found no end

Of pain, or labour, nor his state to mend,

At last with joy is to his home back brought,

Finds not more ease, though he with joy be

fraught,

When past is fear, content like souls ascend,

Than I, on whom new pleasures do descend,

Which now as high as first-born bliss is wrought;

He tired with his pains, I, with my mind;

He all content receives by ease of limbs;

I, greatest happiness that I do find

Belief for faith, while hope in pleasure swims;

Truth says 'twas wrong conceit bred my despite

Which once acknowledged, brings my heart's

delight.

XI

You endless torments that my rest oppress

How long will you delight in my sad pain?

Will never love your favour more express?

Shall I still live, and ever feel disdain?

Alas now stay, and let my grief obtain

Some end; feed not my heart with sharp distress:

Let me once see my cruel fortunes gain

At least release, and long felt woes redress;

Let not the blame of cruelty disgrace

The honoured title of your Godhead, Love:

Give not just cause for me to say a place

Is found for rage alone on me to move;

O quickly end, and do not long debate

My needful aid least help do come too late.

XII

Cloyed with the torments of a tedious night

I wish for day; which come, I hope for joy:

When cross I find new tortures to destroy

My woe-killed heart, first hurt by mischief's might,

Then cry for night, and once more day takes

flight

And brightness gone; what rest should here enjoy

Usurped is; hate will her force employ;

Night cannot grief entomb though black as spite

My thoughts are sad; her face as sad doth seem:

My pains are long; her hours tedious are:

My grief is great, and endless is my care:

Her face, her force, and all of woes esteem:

Then welcome Night, and farewell flattering day

Which all hopes breed, and yet our joys delay.

Lady Mary Wroth | 67

XIII

Dear, famish not what you yourself gave food,
Destroy not what your glory is to save;
Kill not that soul to which you spirit gave;
In pity, not disdain your triumph stood;
An easy thing it is to shed the blood
Of one, who at your will, yields to the grave;
But more you may true worth by mercy crave
When you preserve, not spoil, but nourish good;

Your sight is all the food I doe desire;
Then sacrifice me not in hidden fire,
Or stop that breath which did your praises move:
Think butt how easy 'tis a sight to give;
Nay even desert; since by it I doe live,
I but Chameleon-like would live, and love.

XIV

Am I thus conquered? Have I lost the powers
That to withstand, which joys to ruin me?
Must I bee still while it my strength devours.
And captive, leads me prisoner, bound, unfree?
Love first shall leave men's fancies to them free,
Desire shall quench love's flames, spring hate
sweet showers,
Cupid shall lose his darts, have sight, and see
His shame, and Venus hinder happy hours;

Why should wee not love's purblind charms
resist?
Must we be servile, doing what he list?
No; seek some host to harbour thee: I fly
Thy babyish tricks, and freedom do profess;
But O my hurt makes my lost heart confess
I love, and must: so farewell liberty.

XV

Love like a juggler, comes to play his prize,
And all minds draw his wonders to admire,
To see how cunningly he, wanting eyes,
Can yet deceive the best sight of desire:
The wanton child, how he can fain his fire
So prettily, as none sees his disguise;
How finely do his tricks, while we fools hire
The mask and service of his tyrannies,

For in the end, such juggling doth he make
As he our hearts, in stead of eyes doth take
For men can only by their sleights abuse
The sight with nimble, and delightful skill;
But if he play, his gain is our lost will:
Yet childlike, we cannot his sports refuse.

XVI

My pain, still smothered in my grieved breast,
Seeks for some ease, yet cannot passage find
To be discharged of this unwelcome guest;
When most I strive, more fast his burdens bind,
Like to a ship, on Goodwins cast by wind
The more she strives, more deep in sand is
pressed
Till she bee lost; so am I, in this kind
Sunk, and devoured, and swallowed by unrest,

Lost, shipwrecked, spoiled, debarred of smallest
hope,
Nothing of pleasure left; save thoughts have scope,
Which wander may: Go then, my thoughts, and cry
'Hope's perished; Love tempest-beaten; joy lost
Killing despair hath all these blessing crossed.'
Yet faith still cries, 'Love will not falsify.'

68 | *Pamphilia to Amphilanthus*

XVII

Poor Love in chains, and fetters, like a thief
I met led forth, as chaste Diana's gain,
Vowing the untaught Lad should no relief
From her receive, who gloried in fond pain.
She called him thief; with vows he did maintain
He never stole; butt some slight touch of grief
Had given to those who did his power disdain,
In which revenge, his honour, was the chief:

She said he murdered, and therefore must die;
He, that he caused but love: did harms deny,
But, while she thus discoursing with him stood
The Nymphs untied him, and his chains took off
Thinking him safe; butt he, loose, made a scoff
Smiling, and scorning them, flew to the wood.

XVIII

Which should I better like of, day, or night,
Since all the day I live in bitter woe
Enjoying light more clear my wrongs to know,
And yet most sad, feeling in it all spite;
In night, when darkness doth forbid all light
Yet see I grief apparent to the show
Followed by jealousy whose fond tricks flow,
And on unconstant waves of doubt alight,

I can behold rage cowardly to feed
Upon foul error, which these humours breed,
Shame, doubt, and fear, yet boldly will think ill,
All these in both I feel, then which is best:
Dark to joy by day, light in night oppressed.
Leave both, and end, these but each other spill.

XIX

Come darkest night, becoming sorrow best;
Light, leave thy light; fit for a lightsome soul;
Darkness doth truly suit with me oppressed,
Whom absence power doth from mirth control:
The very trees with hanging heads condole
Sweet summer's parting, and of leaves distressed
In dying colors make a grief-full role;
So much (alas) to sorrow are they pressed

Thus of dead leaves her farewell carpet's made;
Their fall, their branches, all their mournings prove;
With leafless, naked bodies, whose hues fade
From hopeful green, to wither in their love,
If trees, and leaves for absence, mourners be,
No marvel that I grieve, who like want see.

XX

The Sun which glads the earth at his bright sight
When in the morn he shows his golden face,
And takes the place from tedious drowsy night
Making the world still happy by his grace;
Shows happiness remains not in one place,
Nor may the heavens, alone to us give light,
But hide that cheerful face, though no long space,
Yet long enough for trial of their might;

But never sunset could be so obscure
No desert ever have a shade so sad,
Nor could black darkness ever prove se bad
As pains which absence makes me now endure;
The missing of the sun awhile makes night,
But absence of my joy sees never Light.

Lady Mary Wroth | 69

XXI

When I last saw thee, I did not thee see,
It was thy Image, which in my thoughts lay
So lively figured, as no time's delay
Could suffer me in heart to parted be;
And sleep so favourable is to me,
As not to let thy loved remembrance stray,
Lest that I waking might have cause to say
There was one minute found to forget thee;

Then since my faith is such, so kind my sleep
That gladly thee presents into my thought:
And still true lover-like thy face doth keep
So as some pleasure shadow-like is wrought,
Pity my loving, nay of conscience give
Reward to me in whom thy self doth live.

XXII

Cupid would needs make me a lover be
When I did little think of loving thought
Or ever to be tied; till he told me
That none can live, but to his bands are brought;
I, ignorant, did grant, and so was bought,
And sold again to lover's slavery;
The duty to the god of love once taught
Such band is, as we will not seek to free,

Yet when I well did understand his might
How he enflamed, and forced one to affect
I loved, and smarted, counting it delight
So still to waste, which reason did reject,
When love came blindfold, and did challenge me.
Indeed I loved but, wanton boy, not he.

XXIII

When every one to pleasing pastime hies
Some hunt, some hawk, some play, while some
delight
In sweet discourse, and music shows joy's might
Yet I my thoughts do far above these prize
The joy which I take, is that free from eyes
I sit, and wonder at this day-like night
So to dispose themselves, as void of right;
And leave true pleasure for poor vanities

When others hunt, my thoughts I have in chase;
If hawk, my mind at wished end doth fly,
Discourse, I, with my spirit talk, and cry
While others, music is their greatest grace.
O God, say I, can these fond pleasures move?
Or music be but in dear thoughts of love?

XXIV

Once did I hear an aged father say
Unto his son who with attention hears
What age and wise experience ever clears
From doubts of fear, or reason to betray,
'My Son,' said he, 'behold thy father, grey:
I once had as thou hast, fresh tender years,
And like thee sported, destitute of fears,
But my young faults made me too soon decay;

Love once I did, and like thee feared my love,
Led by the hateful thread of jealousy,
Striving to keep, I lost my liberty,
And gained my grief which still my sorrows move.
In time shun this; to love is no offence
But doubt in youth, in age breeds penitence.'

70 | *Pamphilia to Amphilanthus*

XXV

Poor eyes be blind, the light behold no more
Since that is gone which is your dear delight,
Ravished from you by greater power, and might,
Making your loss a gain to others' store,
O'erflow, and drown, till sight to you restore
That blessed star, and as in hateful spite
Send forth your tears in floods, to kill all sight,
And looks, that lost, wherein you joyed before.

Bury those beams, which in some kindled fires,
And conquered have their love-burnt hearts'
desires
Losing, and yet no gain by you esteemed,
Till that bright star do once again appear
Brighter than Mars when he doth shine most clear
See not: then by his might be you redeemed.

XXVI

Most blessed Night, the happy time for love,
The shade for Lovers and their love's delight,
The reign of Venus' servants, free from spite,
The hopeful season, for joy's sports to move;
Now hast thou made thy glory higher prove
Than did the God, whose pleasant reed did smite
All Argus' eyes into a deathlike night
Till they were safe, that love could none reprove,

But thou hast closed those eyes from prying sight
That nourish jealousy more than joy's right
While vain suspicion fosters their mistrust,
Making sweet sleep to master all suspect
Which else their private fears would not neglect
But would embrace both blinded, and unjust.

XXVII

Fie treacherous Hope, why do you still rebel?
Is it not yet enough you flattered me?
But cunningly you seek to use a spell
How to betray, must these your trophies be?
I looked from you far sweeter fruit to see
But blasted were your blossoms when they fell,
And those delights expected late from thee
Withered, and dead, and what seemed bliss proves
Hell.

No town was won by a more plotted slight
Than I by you, who may my fortune write
In embers of that fire which ruined me,
Thus Hope, your falsehood calls you to be tried
You're loath, I see, the trial to abide;
Prove true at last, and I will set thee free.

XXVIII

Grief, killing grief, have not my torments been
Already great, and strong enough, but still
Thou dost increase, nay glory in my ill,
And woes new past, afresh new woes begin!
Am I the only purchase you can win?
Was I ordained to give despair her fill
Or fittest I should mount misfortune's hill
Who in the plain of joy cannot live in?

If it be so, grief come as welcome guest
Since I must suffer, for another's rest:
Yet this good grief, let me entreat of thee,
Use still thy force, but not from those I love
Let me all pains, and lasting torments prove
So I miss these, lay all thy weights on me.

Lady Mary Wroth | 71

XXIX

Fly hence, O joy, no longer here abide,
Too great thy pleasures are for my despair
To look on, losses now must prove my fare
Who not long since, on better food relied;
But fool, how oft had I heaven's changing spied
Before of my own fate I could take care,
Yet now past time, too late I can beware
Now nothing's left but sorrow's faster tide;

While I enjoyed that sun whose sight did lend
Me joy, I thought that day could have no end
But oh! a night came clothed in absence dark,
Absence more sad, more bitter then is gall
Or death, when on true lovers it doth fall
Whose fires of love, disdaineth rest's poor spark.

XXX

You blessed shades, which give me silent rest,
Witness but this when death hath closed mine eyes,
And separated me from earthly ties,
Being from hence to higher place addressed;
How oft in you I have lain here oppressed
And have my miseries in woeful cries
Delivered forth, mounting up to the skies
Yet helpless back returned to wound my breast,

Which wounds did but strive how to breed
more harm
To me, who can be cured by no one charm
But that of love, which yet may me relieve.
If not, let death my former pains redeem,
And you my trusty friends, my faith esteem
And witness I well could love, who so could grieve.

XXXI

After long trouble in a tedious way
Of love's unrest, laid down to ease my pain,
Hoping for rest, new torments I did gain
Possessing me as if I ought t'obey:
When Fortune came, though blinded, yet did stay,
And in her blessed arms did me enchain;
I, cold with grief, thought no warmth to obtain
Or to dissolve that ice of joy's decay;

Till, 'Rise,' said she, 'Venus to thee doth send
By me, the servant of true lovers, joy:
Banish all clouds of doubt, all fears destroy,
And now on Fortune, and on Love, depend.'
I her obeyed, and rising felt that love
Indeed was best, when I did least it move.

XXXII

How fast thou fliest, O Time, on love's swift wings
To hopes of joy, that flatters our desire
Which to a lover, still, contentment brings!
Yet, when we should enjoy, thou dost retire.
Thou stayest thy pace, false time, from our
desire,
When to our ill thou hast'st with Eagle's wings,
Slow, only to make us see thy retire
Was for despair, and harm, which sorrow brings;

O! slack thy pace, and milder pass to love
Be like the bee, whose wings she doth but use
To bring home profit, masters good to prove
Laden, and weary, yet again pursues,
So lade thyself with honey of sought joy
And do not me the hive of love destroy.

72 | *Pamphilia to Amphilanthus*

XXXIII

How many eyes hast thou, poor Love, to guard
Thee from thy most desired wish, and end?
Is it because some say thou' art blind, that barred
From sight, thou should'st no happiness attend?
Who blame thee so, small justice can pretend,
Since 'twixt thee, and the sun no question hard
Can be, his sight but outward, thou canst bend
The heart, and guide it freely; thus unbarred

Art thou, while we both blind and bold thus dare
Accuse thee of the harms, ourselves should find
Who led with folly, and by rashness blind,
Thy sacred power do with a child's compare
Yet Love this boldness pardon: for admire
Thee sure we must, or be born without fire.

XXXIV

Take heed mine eyes, how you your looks do cast
Lest they betray my heart's most secret thought;
Be true unto your selves for nothing's bought
More dear than doubt which brings a lover's fast.
Catch you all watching eyes, ere they be past,
Or take yours fixed where your best love hath sought
The pride of your desires; let them be taught
Their faults with shame, they could no truer last.

Then look, and look with joy for conquest won
Of those that searched your hurt in double kind;
So you kept safe, let them themselves look blind
Watch, gaze, and mark till they to madness run,
While you, my eyes enjoy full sight of love
Contented that such happinesses move.

XXXV

My heart is lost, what can I now expect,
An evening fair after a drowsy day?
Alas fond fancy, this is not the way
To cure a mourning hurt, or salve neglect,
They who should help, do me, and help reject,
Embracing loose desires, and wanton play,
While Venus' base delights do bear the sway,
And impudency reigns without respect;

O Cupid, let thy mother know her shame
'Tis time for her to leave this youthful flame
Which doth dishonour her, is age's blame,
And takes away the greatness of thy name;
Thou God of love, she only Queen of lust,
Yet strives by weakening thee, to be unjust.

XXXVI

Juno, still jealous of her husband Jove,
Descended from above, on earth to try
Whether she there could find his chosen love
Which made him from the Heaven so often fly,
Close by the place, where I for shade did lie
She chafing came; but when she saw me move
'Have you not seen this way,' said she 'to hie
One in whom virtue never ground did prove,

He in whom love doth breed to stir more hate,
Courting a wanton Nymph for his delight.
His name is Jupiter, my Lord by fate,
Who for her, leaves me, heaven, his throne, and light.
'I saw not him,' said I, 'although here are
Many in whose hearts love hath made like war.'

Lady Mary Wroth | 73

XXXVII

Night, welcome art thou to my mind distressed,
Dark, heavy, sad, yet not more sad than I;
Never could'st thou find fitter company
For thine own humour then I thus oppressed.
If thou be dark, my wrongs still unredressed
Saw never light, nor smallest bliss can spy;
If heavy, joy from me too fast doth hie
And care outgoes my hope of quiet rest,

Then now in friendship join with hapless me,
Who am as sad, and dark as thou canst bee
Hating all pleasure, or delight in life;
Silence, and grief, with thee I best do love
And from you three, I know I cannot move.
Then let us live companions without strife.

XXXVIII

What pleasure can a banished creature have
In all the pastimes that invented are
By wit or learning, absence making war
Against all peace that may a biding crave;
Can we delight but in a welcome grave
Where we may bury pains, and so be far
From loathed company who always jar
Upon the string of mirth that pastime gave;

The knowing part of joy is deemed the heart,
If that be gone what joy can joy impart
When senseless is the feeler of our mirth?
No, I am banished, and no good shall find
But all my fortunes must with mischief bind,
Who but for misery did gain a birth.

XXXIX

If I were given to mirth 'twould be more cross
Thus to bee robbed of my chiefest joy;
But silently I bear my greatest loss:
Who's used to sorrow, grief will not destroy;
Nor can I as these pleasant wits enjoy
My own framed words, which I account the dross
Of purer thoughts, or reckon them as moss
While they (wit-sick) themselves to breathe employ,

Alas, think I, your plenty shows your want,
For where most feeling is, words are more scant,
Yet pardon me, live, and your pleasure take,
Grudge not if I, neglected, envy show
'Tis not to you that I dislike do owe,
But crossed myself, wish some like me to make.

XL

It is not love which you poor fools do deem
That doth appear by fond and outward shows
Of kissing, toying, or by swearing's gloze.
O no, these far are off from love's esteem;
Alas, these are not them that can redeem
Love lost, or winning, keep those chosen blows
Though oft with face and looks love overthrows
Yet so slight conquest doth not him beseem,

'Tis not a show of sighs, or tears can prove
Who loves indeed: which blasts of feigned love
Increase, or die as favours from them slide;
But in the soul true love in safety lies
Guarded by faith which to desert still hies,
And yet true looks do many blessing hide.

74 | *Pamphilia to Amphilanthus*

XLI

Late in the forest I did Cupid see
Cold, wet, and crying, he had lost his way,
And being blind was farther like to stray:
Which sight a kind compassion bred in me,
I kindly took and dried him, while that he,
Poor child, complained he starved was with stay,
And pined for want of his accustomed prey,
For none in that wild place his host would be,

I glad was of his finding, thinking sure
This service should my freedom still procure
And in my arms I took him then unharmed
Carrying him unto a myrtle bower
But in the way he made me feel, his power,
Burning my heart who had him kindly warmed.

XLII

If ever love had force in human breast,
If ever he could move in pensive heart,
Or if that he such power could but impart
To breed those flames whose heat brings joy's
unrest,
Then look on me; I am to these addressed:
I am the soul that feels the greatest smart;
I am that heartless trunk of heart's depart;
And I that one by love and grief oppressed;

None ever felt the truth of love's great miss
Of eyes, till I deprived was of bliss;
For had he seen, he must have pity showed,
I should not have been made the stage of woe
Where sad disasters have their open show;
O no, more pity he had sure bestowed.

XLIII

O dearest eyes the lights, and guides of love,
The joys of Cupid who, himself born blind,
To your bright shining doth his triumphs bind
For in your seeing doth his glory move;
How happy are those places where you prove
Your heavenly beams, which makes the Sun to find
Envy, and grudging he so long hath shined
That your clear light should match his beams above

But now, alas, your sight is here forbid
And darkness must these poor lost rooms possess
So be all blessed lights from henceforth hid
That this black deed in darkness have excess,
For why should heaven afford least light to those
Who for my misery this darkness chose.

XLIV

How fast thou hastest (O Spring) with swiftest speed
To catch thy waters which before are run,
And of the greater rivers welcome won,
Ere these thy new-born streams these places feed,
Yet do you well lest staying here might breed
Dangerous floods your sweetest banks t' o'er-run,
And yet much better my distress to shun
Which makes my tears but your course to
succeed,

But best you do when with so hasty flight,
You fly my ills which now my self outgo,
Whose broken heart can testify such woe,
Which so o'ercharged my life blood wasteth quite
Sweet spring then keep your way, be never spent
And my ill days, or griefs asunder rent.

Lady Mary Wroth | 75

XLV

Good now be still, and do not me torment
With multitudes of questions; be at rest,
And only let me quarrel with my breast
Which still lets in new storms my soul to rent.
Fie, will you still my mischiefs more augment?
You say I answer cross, I that confessed
Long since, yet must I ever be oppressed
With your tongue-torture which will ne'er be
spent?

Well then I see no way but this will fright
That Devil speech; alas I am possessed,
And mad folks senseless are of wisdom's right,
The hellish spirit absence doth arrest
All my poor senses to his cruel might;
Spare me then till I am myself, and blest.

XLVI

Love, thou hast all, for now thou hast me made
So thine, as if for thee I were ordained;
Then take thy conquest, nor let me be pained
More in thy sun, when I do seek thy shade,
No place for help have I left to invade,
That showed a face where least ease might be
gained;
Yet found I pain increase, and but obtained
That this no way was to have love allayed,

When hot, and thirsty to a well I came
Trusting by that to quench part of my flame,
But there I was by Love afresh embraced;
Drink I could not, but in it I did see
Myself a living glass as well as she,
For Love to see himself in, truly placed.

XLVII

O stay mine eyes, shed not these fruitless tears
Since hope is past to win you back again
That treasure which, being lost, breeds all your
pain;
Cease from this poor betraying of your fears,
Think this too childish is, for where grief rears
So high a power for such a wretched gain,
Sighs, nor laments, should thus be spent in vain:
True sorrow, never outward wailing bears;

Be ruled by me, keep all the rest in store,
Till no room is that may contain one more,
Then in that sea of tears, drown hapless me,
And I'll provide such store of sighs as part
Shall be enough to break the strongest heart.
This done, we shall from torments freed be.

XLVIII

How like a fire doth love increase in me,
The longer that it lasts, the stronger still,
The greater, purer, brighter, and doth fill
No eye with wonder more; then hopes still be
Bred in my breast, where fires of love are free
To use that part to their best pleasing will,
And now impossible it is to kill
The heat so great where Love his strength doth see.

Mine eyes can scarce sustain the flames, my heart
Doth trust in them my longings to impart,
And languishingly strive to show my love;
My breath not able is to breathe least part
Of that increasing fuel of my smart;
Yet love I will till I but ashes prove.

Sonnet VII

How soon hath Time, the subtle thief of youth,

Stol'n on his wing my three-and-twentieth year!

My hasting days fly on with full career,

But my late spring no bud or blossom shew'th.

Perhaps my semblance might deceive the truth

That I to manhood am arriv'd so near;

And inward ripeness doth much less appear,

That some more timely-happy spirits endu'th.

Yet be it less or more, or soon or slow,

It shall be still in strictest measure ev'n

To that same lot, however mean or high,

Toward which Time leads me, and the will of Heav'n:

All is, if I have grace to use it so

As ever in my great Task-Master's eye.

John Milton

Milton | 77

Sonnet XIX

When I consider how my light is spent,
Ere half my days in this dark world and wide,
And that one talent which is death to hide
Lodged with me useless, though my soul more bent
To serve therewith my Maker, and present
My true account, lest He returning chide;
"Doth God exact day-labor, light denied?"
I fondly ask. But Patience, to prevent

That murmur, soon replies, "God doth not need
Either man's work or His own gifts. Who best
Bear His mild yoke, they serve Him best. His state
Is kingly: thousands at His bidding speed,
And post o'er land and ocean without rest;
They also serve who only stand and wait.

John Milton

To Sleep

O soft embalmer of the still midnight,
Shutting, with careful fingers and benign,
Our gloom-pleas'd eyes, embower'd from the light,
Enshaded in forgetfulness divine:
O soothest Sleep! if so it please thee, close
In midst of this thine hymn my willing eyes,
Or wait the "Amen," ere thy poppy throws
Around my bed its lulling charities.

Then save me, or the passed day will shine
Upon my pillow, breeding many woes,—
Save me from curious Conscience, that still lords
Its strength for darkness, burrowing like a mole;
Turn the key deftly in the oiled wards,
And seal the hushed Casket of my Soul.

John Keats

Ozymandias

I met a traveller from an antique land
Who said: 'Two vast and trunkless legs of stone
Stand in the desert. Near them, on the sand,
Half sunk, a shattered visage lies, whose frown,
And wrinkled lip, and sneer of cold command,
Tell that its sculptor well those passions read
Which yet survive, stamped on these lifeless things,
The hand that mocked them and the heart that fed:

And on the pedestal these words appear:
"My name is Ozymandias, king of kings:
Look on my works, ye Mighty, and despair!"
Nothing beside remains. Round the decay
Of that colossal wreck, boundless and bare
The lone and level sands stretch far away.

Percy Bysshe Shelley

80 | *Sonnets*

The world is too much with us; late and soon,

Getting and spending, we lay waste our powers;

Little we see in Nature that is ours;

We have given our hearts away, a sordid boon!

This Sea that bares her bosom to the moon;

The winds that will be howling at all hours,

And are up-gathered now like sleeping flowers,

For this, for everything, we are out of tune;

It moves us not.—Great God! I'd rather be

A pagan suckled in a creed outworn;

So might I, standing on this pleasant lea,

Have glimpses that would make me less forlorn;

Have sight of Proteus rising from the sea;

Or hear old Triton blow his wreathèd horn.

William Wordsworth

Surprised by joy—impatient as the Wind
I turned to share the transport—Oh! with whom
But Thee, long buried in the silent Tomb,
That spot which no vicissitude can find?
Love, faithful love, recalled thee to my mind—
But how could I forget thee?—Through what power,
Even for the least division of an hour,
Have I been so beguiled as to be blind

To my most grievous loss!—That thought's return
Was the worst pang that sorrow ever bore,
Save one, one only, when I stood forlorn,
Knowing my heart's best treasure was no more;
That neither present time, nor years unborn
Could to my sight that heavenly face restore.

William Wordsworth

82 | *Sonnets*

Sonnets from the Portuguese, 14

If thou must love me, let it be for nought
Except for love's sake only. Do not say,
"I love her for her smile—her look—her way
Of speaking gently,—for a trick of thought
That falls in well with mine, and certes brought
A sense of pleasant ease on such a day"—
For these things in themselves, Belovèd, may
Be changed, or change for thee—and love, so wrought,

May be unwrought so. Neither love me for
Thine own dear pity's wiping my cheeks dry:
A creature might forget to weep, who bore
Thy comfort long, and lose thy love thereby!
But love me for love's sake, that evermore
Thou mayst love on, through love's eternity.

Elizabeth Barrett Browning

Sonnets from the Portuguese, 43

How do I love thee? Let me count the ways.
I love thee to the depth and breadth and height
My soul can reach, when feeling out of sight
For the ends of being and ideal grace.
I love thee to the level of every day's
Most quiet need, by sun and candle-light.
I love thee freely, as men strive for right.
I love thee purely, as they turn from praise.

I love thee with the passion put to use
In my old griefs, and with my childhood's faith.
I love thee with a love I seemed to lose
With my lost saints. I love thee with the breath,
Smiles, tears, of all my life; and, if God choose,
I shall but love thee better after death.

Elizabeth Barrett Browning

84 | *Sonnets*

As kingfishers catch fire, dragonflies draw flame;

As tumbled over rim in roundy wells

Stones ring; like each tucked string tells, each hung bell's

Bow swung finds tongue to fling out broad its name;

Each mortal thing does one thing and the same:

Deals out that being indoors each one dwells;

Selves—goes itself; myself it speaks and spells,

Crying Whát I dó is me: for that I came.

I say móre: the just man justices;

Keeps grace: thát keeps all his goings graces;

Acts in God's eye what in God's eye he is—

Chríst—for Christ plays in ten thousand places,

Lovely in limbs, and lovely in eyes not his

To the Father through the features of men's faces.

Gerard Manley Hopkins

*Justus quidem tu es, Domine, si disputem tecum; verumtamen
justa loquar ad te: Quare via impiorum prosperatur? &c.*[2]

Thou art indeed just, Lord, if I contend

With thee; but, sir, so what I plead is just.

Why do sinners' ways prosper? and why must

Disappointment all I endeavour end?

Wert thou my enemy, O thou my friend,

How wouldst thou worse, I wonder, than thou dost

Defeat, thwart me? Oh, the sots and thralls of lust

Do in spare hours more thrive than I that spend,

Sir, life upon thy cause. See, banks and brakes

Now, leavèd how thick! lacèd they are again

With fretty chervil, look, and fresh wind shakes

Them; birds build – but not I build; no, but strain,

Time's eunuch, and not breed one work that wakes.

Mine, O thou lord of life, send my roots rain.

Gerard Manley Hopkins

---

[2] Thou indeed, O Lord, art just, if I plead with thee, but yet I will speak what is just to thee: Why doth the way of the wicked prosper? Jeremiah 12:1 (Douay-Rheims)

86 | *Sonnets*

I wake and feel the fell of dark, not day.
What hours, O what black hours we have spent
This night! what sights you, heart, saw; ways you went!
And more must, in yet longer light's delay.
With witness I speak this. But where I say
Hours I mean years, mean life. And my lament
Is cries countless, cries like dead letters sent
To dearest him that lives alas! away.

I am gall, I am heartburn. God's most deep decree
Bitter would have me taste: my taste was me;
Bones built in me, flesh filled, blood brimmed the curse.
Selfyeast of spirit a dull dough sours. I see
The lost are like this, and their scourge to be
As I am mine, their sweating selves; but worse.

Gerard Manley Hopkins

God's Grandeur

The world is charged with the grandeur of God.

It will flame out, like shining from shook foil;

It gathers to a greatness, like the ooze of oil

Crushed. Why do men then now not reck his rod?

Generations have trod, have trod, have trod;

And all is seared with trade; bleared, smeared with toil;

And wears man's smudge and shares man's smell: the soil

Is bare now, nor can foot feel, being shod.

And for all this, nature is never spent;

There lives the dearest freshness deep down things;

And though the last lights off the black West went

Oh, morning, at the brown brink eastward, springs—

Because the Holy Ghost over the bent

World broods with warm breast and with ah! bright wings.

Gerard Manley Hopkins

Design

I found a dimpled spider, fat and white,
On a white heal-all, holding up a moth
Like a white piece of rigid satin cloth--
Assorted characters of death and blight
Mixed ready to begin the morning right,
Like the ingredients of a witches' broth--
A snow-drop spider, a flower like a froth,
And dead wings carried like a paper kite.

What had that flower to do with being white,
The wayside blue and innocent heal-all?
What brought the kindred spider to that height,
Then steered the white moth thither in the night?
What but design of darkness to appall?--
If design govern in a thing so small.

Robert Frost

I, being born a woman and distressed

By all the needs and notions of my kind,

Am urged by your propinquity to find

Your person fair, and feel a certain zest

To bear your body's weight upon my breast:

So subtly is the fume of life designed,

To clarify the pulse and cloud the mind,

And leave me once again undone, possessed.

Think not for this, however, the poor treason

Of my stout blood against my staggering brain,

I shall remember you with love, or season

My scorn with pity, —let me make it plain:

I find this frenzy insufficient reason

For conversation when we meet again.

Edna St. Vincent Millay

90 | *Sonnets*

I think I should have loved you presently,
And given in earnest words I flung in jest;
And lifted honest eyes for you to see,
And caught your hand against my cheek and breast;
And all my pretty follies flung aside
That won you to me, and beneath your gaze,
Naked of reticence and shorn of pride,
Spread like a chart my little wicked ways.

I, that had been to you, had you remained,
But one more waking from a recurrent dream,
Cherish no less the certain stakes I gained,
And walk your memory's halls, austere, supreme,
A ghost in marble of a girl you knew
Who would have loved you in a day or two.

Edna St. Vincent Millay

Loving you less than life, a little less

Than bitter-sweet upon a broken wall

Or bush-wood smoke in autumn, I confess

I cannot swear I love you not at all.

For there is that about you in this light--

A yellow darkness, sinister of rain--

Which sturdily recalls my stubborn sight

To dwell on you, and dwell on you again.

And I am made aware of many a week

I shall consume, remembering in what way

Your brown hair grows about your brow and cheek,

And what divine absurdities you say:

Till all the world, and I, and surely you,

Will know I love you, whether or not I do.

Edna St. Vincent Millay

92 | *Sonnets*

Into the golden vessel of great song
Let us pour all our passion; breast to breast
Let other lovers lie, in love and rest;
Not we,--articulate, so, but with the tongue
Of all the world: the churning blood, the long
Shuddering quiet, the desperate hot palms pressed
Sharply together upon the escaping guest,
The common soul, unguarded, and grown strong.

Longing alone is singer to the lute;
Let still on nettles in the open sigh
The minstrel, that in slumber is as mute
As any man, and love be far and high,
That else forsakes the topmost branch, a fruit
Found on the ground by every passer-by.

Edna St. Vincent Millay

When I too long have looked upon your face,

Wherein for me a brightness unobscured

Save by the mists of brightness has its place,

4   And terrible beauty not to be endured,

I turn away reluctant from your light,

And stand irresolute, a mind undone,

A silly, dazzled thing deprived of a sight

8   From having looked too long upon the sun.

Then is my daily life a narrow room

In which a little while, uncertainly,

Surrounded by impenetrable gloom,

12   Among familiar things grown strange to me

Making my way, I pause, and feel, and hark,

Till I become accustomed to the dark.

Edna St. Vincent Millay

94 | *Sonnets*

Euclid alone has looked on Beauty bare.
Let all who prate of Beauty hold their peace,
And lay them prone upon the earth and cease
4   To ponder on themselves, the while they stare
At nothing, intricately drawn nowhere
In shapes of shifting lineage; let geese
Gabble and hiss, but heroes seek release
8   From dusty bondage into luminous air.

O blinding hour, O holy, terrible day,
When first the shaft into his vision shone
Of light anatomized! Euclid alone
12 Has looked on Beauty bare. Fortunate they
Who, though once only and then but far away,
Have heard her massive sandal set on stone.

Edna St. Vincent Millay

Still will I harvest beauty where it grows:
In colored fungus and the spotted fog
Surprised on foods forgotten; in ditch and bog
4   Filmed brilliant with irregular rainbows
Of rust and oil, where half a city throws
Its empty tins; and in some spongy log
Whence headlong leaps the oozy emerald frog.
8   And a black pupil in the green scum shows.

Her the inhabiter of divers places
Surmising at all doors, I push them all.
Oh, you that fearful of a creaking hinge
12   Turn back forevermore with craven faces,
I tell you Beauty bears an ultrafringe
Unguessed of you upon her gossamer shawl!

Edna St. Vincent Millay

Edmund Spenser, 99

John Donne, 106

George Herbert, 109

Lady Mary Wroth, 110

Aphra Behn, 111

John Keats, 118

William Wordsworth, 120

Elizabeth Barrett Browning, 122

Emily Dickinson, 124

Oscar Wilde, 128

William Butler Yeats, 142

Robert Frost, 144

Lyre and Cupids
Roman Fresco at Herculaneum

BALLAD

Recurring Stanza Scheme

Orpheus at the Tomb of Eurydice

Orpheus Rides Across the Styx

Prothalamion

CALM was the day, and through the trembling air
Sweet breathing Zephyrus did softly play,
A gentle spirit, that lightly did delay
Hot Titan's beams, which then did glister fair;
When I whose sullen care,
Through discontent of my long fruitless stay
In prince's court, and expectation vain
Of idle hopes, which still do fly away
Like empty shadows, did afflict my brain,
Walked forth to ease my pain
Along the shore of silver streaming Thames,
Whose rutty bank, the which his river hems,
Was painted all with variable flowers,
And all the meads adorned with dainty gems,
Fit to deck maidens' bowers,
And crown their paramours,
Against the bridal day, which is not long:
Sweet Thames, run softly, till I end my song.

There, in a meadow, by the river's side,
A flock of nymphs I chanced to espy,
All lovely daughters of the flood thereby,
With goodly greenish locks, all loose untied,
As each had been a bride;
And each one had a little wicker basket,
Made of fine twigs, entrailed curiously,
In which they gathered flowers to fill their flasket,
And with fine fingers cropt full featously
The tender stalks on high.

100 | Ballads

Of every sort, which in that meadow grew,

They gathered some; the violet pallid blue,

The little daisy, that at evening closes,

32   The virgin lily, and the primrose true,

With store of vermeil roses,

To deck their bridegrooms' posies

Against the bridal day, which was not long:

36   Sweet Thames, run softly, till I end my song.

With that, I saw two swans of goodly hue

Come softly swimming down along the Lee;

Two fairer birds I yet did never see.

40   The snow which doth the top of Pindus strew,

Did never whiter shew,

Nor Jove himself, when he a swan would be

For love of Leda, whiter did appear:

44   Yet Leda was they say as white as he,

Yet not so white as these, nor nothing near.

So purely white they were,

That even the gentle stream, the which them bare,

48   Seemed foul to them, and bade his billows spare

To wet their silken feathers, lest they might

Soil their fair plumes with water not so fair,

And mar their beauties bright,

52   That shone as heaven's light,

Against their bridal day, which was not long:

Sweet Thames, run softly, till I end my song.

	Eftsoons the nymphs, which now had flowers their fill,
56	
	Ran all in haste, to see that silver brood,
	As they came floating on the crystal flood.
	Whom when they saw, they stood amazed still,
60	Their wondering eyes to fill.
	Them seemed they never saw a sight so fair,
	Of fowls so lovely, that they sure did deem
	Them heavenly born, or to be that same pair
64	Which through the sky draw Venus' silver team;
	For sure they did not seem
	To be begot of any earthly seed,
	But rather angels, or of angels' breed:
68	Yet were they bred of Somers-heat they say,
	In sweetest season, when each flower and weed
	The earth did fresh array,
	So fresh they seemed as day,
72	Even as their bridal day, which was not long:
	Sweet Thames, run softly, till I end my song.

56 Eftsoons the nymphs, which now had flowers their fill,
Ran all in haste, to see that silver brood,
As they came floating on the crystal flood.
Whom when they saw, they stood amazed still,
60 Their wondering eyes to fill.
Them seemed they never saw a sight so fair,
Of fowls so lovely, that they sure did deem
Them heavenly born, or to be that same pair
64 Which through the sky draw Venus' silver team;
For sure they did not seem
To be begot of any earthly seed,
But rather angels, or of angels' breed:
68 Yet were they bred of Somers-heat they say,
In sweetest season, when each flower and weed
The earth did fresh array,
So fresh they seemed as day,
72 Even as their bridal day, which was not long:
Sweet Thames, run softly, till I end my song.

Then forth they all out of their baskets drew
Great store of flowers, the honour of the field,
76 That to the sense did fragrant odours yield,
All which upon those goodly birds they threw,
And all the waves did strew,
That like old Peneus' waters they did seem,
80 When down along by pleasant Tempe's shore,
Scattered with flowers, through Thessaly they stream,
That they appear through lilies' plenteous store,
Like a bride's chamber floor.

102 | Ballads

84   Two of those nymphs meanwhile, two garlands bound,
      Of freshest flowers which in that mead they found,
      The which presenting all in trim array,
      Their snowy foreheads therewithal they crowned,
88   Whilst one did sing this lay,
      Prepared against that day,
      Against their bridal day, which was not long:
      Sweet Thames, run softly, till I end my song.

92   'Ye gentle birds, the world's fair ornament,
      And heaven's glory, whom this happy hour
      Doth lead unto your lovers' blissful bower,
      Joy may you have and gentle heart's content
96   Of your love's complement:
      And let fair Venus, that is queen of love,
      With her heart-quelling son upon you smile,
      Whose smile, they say, hath virtue to remove
100   All love's dislike, and friendship's faulty guile
      For ever to assoil.
      Let endless peace your steadfast hearts accord,
      And blessed plenty wait upon your board,
104   And let your bed with pleasures chaste abound,
      That fruitful issue may to you afford,
      Which may your foes confound,
      And make your joys redound
108   Upon your bridal day, which is not long:
      Sweet Thames, run softly, till I end my song.'

So ended she; and all the rest around

To her redoubled that her undersong,

112   Which said their bridal day should not be long.

And gentle echo from the neighbour ground

Their accents did resound.

So forth those joyous birds did pass along,

116   Adown the Lee, that to them murmured low,

As he would speak, but that he lacked a tongue,

Yet did by signs his glad affection show,

Making his stream run slow.

120   And all the fowl which in his flood did dwell

Gan flock about these twain, that did excel

The rest so far as Cynthia doth shend

The lesser stars. So they, enranged well,

124   Did on those two attend,

And their best service lend,

Against their wedding day, which was not long:

Sweet Thames, run softly, till I end my song.

128   At length they all to merry London came,

To merry London, my most kindly nurse,

That to me gave this life's first native source;

Though from another place I take my name,

132   An house of ancient fame.

There when they came, whereas those bricky towers,

The which on Thames' broad aged back do ride,

Where now the studious lawyers have their bowers

136   There whilom wont the Templar Knights to bide,

Till they decayed through pride:

104 | Ballads

Next whereunto there stands a stately place,

Where oft I gained gifts and goodly grace

140   Of that great lord, which therein wont to dwell,

Whose want too well now feels my friendless case.

But ah, here fits not well

Old woes but joys to tell

144   Against the bridal day, which is not long:

Sweet Thames, run softly, till I end my song.

Yet therein now doth lodge a noble peer,

Great England's glory, and the world's wide wonder,

148   Whose dreadful name late through all Spain did thunder,

And Hercules' two pillars standing near

Did make to quake and fear:

Fair branch of honour, flower of chivalry,

152   That fillest England with thy triumph's fame,

Joy have thou of thy noble victory,

And endless happiness of thine own name

That promiseth the same:

156   That through thy prowess and victorious arms,

Thy country may be freed from foreign harms;

And great Elisa's glorious name may ring

Through all the world, filled with thy wide alarms,

160   Which some brave Muse may sing

To ages following,

Upon the bridal day, which is not long:

Sweet Thames, run softly, till I end my song.

164   From those high towers this noble lord issuing,
Like radiant Hesper when his golden hair
In th'Ocean billows he hath bathed fair,
Descended to the river's open viewing,
168   With a great train ensuing.
Above the rest were goodly to be seen
Two gentle knights of lovely face and feature
Beseeming well the bower of any queen,
172   With gifts of wit and ornaments of nature,
Fit for so goodly stature;
That like the twins of Jove they seemed in sight,
Which deck the baldric of the heavens bright.
176   They two forth pacing to the river's side,
Received those two fair birds, their love's delight;
Which, at th' appointed tide,
Each one did make his bride
180   Against their bridal day, which is not long:
Sweet Thames, run softly, till I end my song.

Edmund Spenser

The Canonization

For God's sake hold your tongue, and let me love,
Or chide my palsy, or my gout,
3   My five gray hairs, or ruined fortune flout,
With wealth your state, your mind with arts improve,
Take you a course, get you a place,
6   Observe his honor, or his grace,
Or the king's real, or his stampèd face
Contemplate; what you will, approve,
9   So you will let me love.

Alas, alas, who's injured by my love?
What merchant's ships have my sighs drowned?
12   Who says my tears have overflowed his ground?
When did my colds a forward spring remove?
When did the heats which my veins fill
15   Add one more to the plaguy bill?
Soldiers find wars, and lawyers find out still
Litigious men, which quarrels move,
18   Though she and I do love.

Call us what you will, we are made such by love;
Call her one, me another fly,
21   We're tapers too, and at our own cost die,
And we in us find the eagle and the dove.

Donne | 107

The phœnix riddle hath more wit

24   By us; we two being one, are it.

So, to one neutral thing both sexes fit.

We die and rise the same, and prove

27   Mysterious by this love.

We can die by it, if not live by love,

And if unfit for tombs and hearse

30   Our legend be, it will be fit for verse;

And if no piece of chronicle we prove,

We'll build in sonnets pretty rooms;

33   As well a well-wrought urn becomes

The greatest ashes, as half-acre tombs,

And by these hymns, all shall approve

36   Us canonized for Love.

And thus invoke us: "You, whom reverend love

Made one another's hermitage;

39   You, to whom love was peace, that now is rage;

Who did the whole world's soul contract, and drove

Into the glasses of your eyes

42   (So made such mirrors, and such spies,

That they did all to you epitomize)

Countries, towns, courts: beg from above

45   A pattern of your love!"

John Donne

Song

Go and catch a falling star,

Get with child a mandrake root,

3 Tell me where all past years are,

Or who cleft the devil's foot,

Teach me to hear mermaids singing,

6 Or to keep off envy's stinging,

And find

What wind

9 Serves to'advance an honest mind.

If thou beest born to strange sights,

Things invisible to see,

12 Ride ten thousand days and nights,

Till age snow white hairs on thee;

Thou, when thou return'st will tell me

15 All strange wonders that befell thee

And swear

Nowhere

18 Lives a woman true and fair.

If thou find'st one, let me know;

Such a pilgrimage were sweet:

21 Yet do not, I would not go,

Though at next door we might meet;

though she were true, when you met her,

24 And last, till you write your letter,

Yet she

Will be

27 False, ere I come, to two, or three.

John Donne

Love (III)

Love bade me welcome. Yet my soul drew back
Guilty of dust and sin.
But quick-eyed Love, observing me grow slack
From my first entrance in,
Drew nearer to me, sweetly questioning,
If I lacked any thing.

A guest, I answered, worthy to be here:
Love said, You shall be he.
I the unkind, ungrateful? Ah my dear,
I cannot look on thee.
Love took my hand, and smiling did reply,
Who made the eyes but I?

Truth Lord, but I have marred them: let my shame
Go where it doth deserve.
And know you not, says Love, who bore the blame?
My dear, then I will serve.
You must sit down, says Love, and taste my meat:
So I did sit and eat.

George Herbert

Song from *The Countesse of Montgomery's Urania*

Love peruse me, seeke, and finde
How each corner of my minde
Is a twine
4   Woven to shine.

Not a Webb ill made, foule fram'd,
Bastard not by Father nam'd,
Such in me
8   Cannot bee.

Deare behold me, you shall see
Faith the Hive, and love the Bee,
Which doe bring
12   Gaine and sting.

Pray desect me, sinewes, vaines,
Hold, and loves life in those gaines;
Lying bare
16   To despaire,

When you thus anotamise
All my body, my heart prise;
Being true
20   Just to you.

Close the Truncke, embalme the Chest,
Where your power still shall rest,
Joy entombe,
24   Loves just doome.

Lady Mary Wroth

The Disappointment

One day the Amorous Lisander,
By an impatient Passion sway'd,
Surpris'd fair Cloris, that lov'd Maid,
Who cou'd defend her self no longer;

5   All things did with his Love conspire,
The gilded Planet of the Day,
In his gay Chariot, drawn by Fire,
Was now descending to the Sea,

And left no Light to guide the World,
10   But what from Cloris brighter Eyes was hurl'd.

In alone Thicket, made for Love,
Silent as yielding Maids Consent,
She with a charming Languishment
Permits his force, yet gently strove?

15   Her Hands his Bosom softly meet,
But not to put him back design'd,
Rather to draw him on inclin'd,
Whilst he lay trembling at her feet;

Resistance 'tis to late to shew,
20   She wants the pow'r to say—Ah! what do you do?

112 | Ballads

Her bright Eyes sweat, and yet Severe,
Where Love and Shame confus'dly strive,
Fresh Vigor to Lisander give:
And whisp'ring softly in his Ear,

25 She Cry'd—Cease—cease—your vain desire,
Or I'll call out—What wou'd you do?
My dearer Honour, ev'n to you,
I cannot—must not give—retire,

Or take that Life whose chiefest part
30 I gave you with the Conquest of my Heart.

But he as much unus'd to fear,
As he was capable of Love,
The blessed Minutes to improve,
Kisses her Lips, her Neck, her Hair!

35 Each touch her new Desires alarms!
His burning trembling Hand he pres't
Upon her melting Snowy Breast,
While she lay panting in his Arms !

All her unguarded Beauties lie
40 The Spoils and Trophies of the Enemy.

And now, without Respect or Fear,
He seeks the Objects of his Vows;
His Love no Modesty allows:
By swift degrees advancing where

His daring Hand that Alter seiz'd,
Where Gods of Love do Sacrifice;
That awful Throne, that Paradise,
Where Rage is tam'd, and Anger pleas'd;

That Living Fountain, from whose Trills
The melted Soul in liquid Drops distils.

Her balmy Lips encount'ring his,
Their Bodies as their Souls are joyn'd,
Where both in Transports were confin'd,
Extend themselves upon the Moss.

Cloris half dead and breathless lay,
Her Eyes appear'd like humid Light,
Such as divides the Day and Night;
Or falling Stars, whose Fires decay;

And now no signs of Life she shows,
But what in short-breath-sighs returns and goes.

He saw how at her length she lay,
He saw her rising Bosom bare,
Her loose thin Robes, through which appear
A Shape design'd for Love and Play;

65 Abandon'd by her Pride and Shame,
She do's her softest Sweets dispense,
Off'ring her Virgin-Innocence
A Victim to Loves Sacred Flame;

Whilst th' or'e ravish'd Shepherd lies,
70 Unable to perform the Sacrifice.

Ready to taste a Thousand Joys,
Thee too transported hapless Swain,
Found the vast Pleasure turn'd to Pain:
Pleasure, which too much Love destroys!

75 The willing Garments by he laid,
And Heav'n all open to his view;
Mad to possess, himself he threw
On the defenseless lovely Maid.

But oh! what envious Gods conspire
80 To snatch his Pow'r, yet leave him the Desire!

Natures support, without whose Aid
She can no humane Being give,
It self now wants the Art to live,
Faintness it slacken'd Nerves invade:

85 In vain th' enraged Youth assay'd
To call his fleeting Vigour back,
No Motion 'twill from Motion take,
Excess of Love his Love betray'd;

In vain he Toils, in vain Commands,
90 Th' Insensible fell weeping in his Hands.

In this so Am'rous cruel strife,
Where Love and Fate were too severe,
The poor Lisander in Despair,
Renounc'd his Reason with his Life.

95 Now all the Brisk and Active Fire
That should the Nobler Part inflame,
Unactive Frigid, Dull became,
And left no Spark for new Desire;

Not all her Naked Charms cou'd move,
100 Or calm that Rage that had debauch'd his Love.

116 | Ballads

Cloris returning from the Trance
Which Love and soft Desire had bred,
Her tim'rous Hand she gently laid,
Or guided by Design or Chance,

105 Upon that Fabulous Priapus,
That Potent God (as Poets feign.)
But never did young Shepherdess
(Gath'ring of Fern upon the Plain)

More nimbly draw her Fingers back,
110 Finding beneath the Verdant Leaves a Snake.

Then Cloris her fair Hand withdrew,
Finding that God of her Desires
Disarm'd of all his pow'rful Fires,
And cold as Flow'rs bath'd in the Morning-dew.

115 Who can the Nymphs Confusion guess ?
The Blood forsook the kinder place,
And strew'd with Blushes all her Face,
Which both Disdain and Shame express;

And from Lisander's Arms she fled,
120 Leaving him fainting on the gloomy Bed.

Like Lightning through the Grove she hies,
Or Daphne from the Delphic God;
No Print upon the Grassie Road
125   She leaves, t' instruct pursuing Eyes.

The Wind that wanton'd in her Hair,
And with her ruffled Garments plaid,
Discover'd in the flying Maid
All that the Gods e're made of Fair.

130   So Venus, when her Love was Slain,
With fear and haste flew o're the fatal Plain.

The Nymphs resentments, none but I
Can well imagine, and Condole;
But none can guess Lisander's Soul,
135   But those who sway'd his Destiny:

His silent Griefs, swell up to Storms,
And not one God, his Fury spares,
He Curst his Birth, his Fate, his Stars,
But more the Shepherdesses Charms;

140   Whose soft bewitching influence,
Had Damn'd him to the Hell of Impotence.

Aphra Behn

La Belle Dame sans Merci: A Ballad

O what can ail thee, knight-at-arms,
Alone and palely loitering?
The sedge has withered from the lake,
And no birds sing.

O what can ail thee, knight-at-arms,
So haggard and so woe-begone?
The squirrel's granary is full,
And the harvest's done.

I see a lily on thy brow,
With anguish moist and fever-dew,
And on thy cheeks a fading rose
Fast withereth too.

I met a lady in the meads,
Full beautiful—a faery's child,
Her hair was long, her foot was light,
And her eyes were wild.

I made a garland for her head,
And bracelets too, and fragrant zone;
She looked at me as she did love,
And made sweet moan

I set her on my pacing steed,
And nothing else saw all day long,
For sidelong would she bend, and sing
A faery's song.

Keats | _119_

She found me roots of relish sweet,
And honey wild, and manna-dew,
28 And sure in language strange she said—
'I love thee true'.

She took me to her Elfin grot,
And there she wept and sighed full sore,
32 And there I shut her wild wild eyes
With kisses four.

And there she lullèd me asleep,
And there I dreamed—Ah! woe betide!—
36 The latest dream I ever dreamt
On the cold hill side.

I saw pale kings and princes too,
Pale warriors, death-pale were they all;
40 They cried—'La Belle Dame sans Merci
Thee hath in thrall!'

I saw their starved lips in the gloam,
With horrid warning gapèd wide,
44 And I awoke and found me here,
On the cold hill's side.

And this is why I sojourn here,
Alone and palely loitering,
48 Though the sedge is withered from the lake,
And no birds sing.

John Keats

I wandered lonely as a cloud
That floats on high o'er vales and hills,
3 When all at once I saw a crowd,
A host, of golden daffodils;
Beside the lake, beneath the trees,
6 Fluttering and dancing in the breeze.

Continuous as the stars that shine
And twinkle on the milky way,
9 They stretched in never-ending line
Along the margin of a bay:
Ten thousand saw I at a glance,
12 Tossing their heads in sprightly dance.

The waves beside them danced; but they
Out-did the sparkling waves in glee:
15 A poet could not but be gay,
In such a jocund company:
I gazed—and gazed—but little thought
18 What wealth the show to me had brought:

For oft, when on my couch I lie
In vacant or in pensive mood,
21 They flash upon that inward eye
Which is the bliss of solitude;
And then my heart with pleasure fills,
24 And dances with the daffodils.

William Wordsworth

A Complaint

There is a change—and I am poor;
Your love hath been, nor long ago,
A fountain at my fond heart's door,
Whose only business was to flow;
And flow it did; not taking heed
Of its own bounty, or my need.

What happy moments did I count!
Blest was I then all bliss above!
Now, for that consecrated fount
Of murmuring, sparkling, living love,
What have I? shall I dare to tell?
A comfortless and hidden well.

A well of love—it may be deep—
I trust it is,—and never dry:
What matter? if the waters sleep
In silence and obscurity.
—Such change, and at the very door
Of my fond heart, hath made me poor.

William Wordsworth

A Musical Instrument

WHAT was he doing, the great god Pan,
Down in the reeds by the river?
Spreading ruin and scattering ban,
Splashing and paddling with hoofs of a goat,
And breaking the golden lilies afloat
With the dragon-fly on the river.

He tore out a reed, the great god Pan,
From the deep cool bed of the river:
The limpid water turbidly ran,
And the broken lilies a-dying lay,
And the dragon-fly had fled away,
Ere he brought it out of the river.

High on the shore sate the great god Pan,
While turbidly flowed the river;
And hacked and hewed as a great god can,
With his hard bleak steel at the patient reed,
Till there was not a sign of a leaf indeed
To prove it fresh from the river.

He cut it short, did the great god Pan,
(How tall it stood in the river!)
Then drew the pith, like the heart of a man,
Steadily from the outside ring,
And notched the poor dry empty thing
In holes, as he sate by the river.

'This is the way,' laughed the great god Pan,

27   (Laughed while he sate by the river,)
'The only way, since gods began
To make sweet music, they could succeed.'

30 Then, dropping his mouth to a hole in the reed,
He blew in power by the river.

Sweet, sweet, sweet, O Pan!

33   Piercing sweet by the river!
Blinding sweet, O great god Pan!
The sun on the hill forgot to die,

36 And the lilies revived, and the dragon-fly
Came back to dream on the river.

Yet half a beast is the great god Pan,

39   To laugh as he sits by the river,
Making a poet out of a man:
The true gods sigh for the cost and pain,—

42 For the reed which grows nevermore again
As a reed with the reeds in the river.

Elizabeth Barrett Browning

124 | Ballads

There's a certain Slant of light,
Winter Afternoons -
That oppresses, like the Heft
Of Cathedral Tunes -

Heavenly Hurt, it gives us -
We can find no scar,
But internal difference -
Where the Meanings, are -

None may teach it - Any -
'Tis the seal Despair -
An imperial affliction
Sent us of the Air -

When it comes, the Landscape listens -
Shadows - hold their breath -
When it goes, 'tis like the Distance
On the look of Death -

Emily Dickinson

There is a solitude of space

A solitude of sea

A solitude of death, but these

4   Society shall be

Compared with that profounder site

That polar privacy

A soul admitted to itself—

8   Finite infinity.

Emily Dickinson

126 | Ballads

I died for beauty, but was scarce
Adjusted in the tomb,
When one who died for truth was lain
4   In an adjoining room.

He questioned softly why I failed?
"For beauty," I replied.
"And I for truth—the two are one;
8   We brethren are," he said.

And so, as kinsmen met a-night,
We talked between the rooms,
Until the moss had reached our lips,
12   And covered up our names.

Emily Dickinson

This World is not Conclusion.
A Species stands beyond—
Invisible, as Music—
4   But positive, as Sound -

It beckons, and it baffles—
Philosophy, don't know—
And through a Riddle, at the last—
8   Sagacity, must go—

To guess it, puzzles scholars—
To gain it, Men have borne
Contempt of Generations
12 And Crucifixion, shown -

Faith slips—and laughs, and rallies—
Blushes, if any see—
Plucks at a twig of Evidence—
16 And asks a Vane, the way—

Much Gesture, from the Pulpit—
Strong Hallelujahs roll—
Narcotics cannot still the Tooth
20 That nibbles at the soul -

Emily Dickinson

Requiescat

Tread lightly, she is near
Under the snow,
Speak gently, she can hear
The daisies grow.

All her bright golden hair
Tarnished with rust,
She that was young and fair
Fallen to dust.

Lily-like, white as snow,
She hardly knew
She was a woman, so
Sweetly she grew.

Coffin-board, heavy stone,
Lie on her breast,
I vex my heart alone
She is at rest.

Peace, Peace, she cannot hear
Lyre or sonnet,
All my life's buried here,
Heap earth upon it.

Oscar Wilde

The Ballad of Reading Gaol

I

He did not wear his scarlet coat,
For blood and wine are red,
And blood and wine were on his hands
When they found him with the dead,
The poor dead woman whom he loved,
And murdered in her bed.

He walked amongst the Trial Men
In a suit of shabby grey;
A cricket cap was on his head,
And his step seemed light and gay;
But I never saw a man who looked
So wistfully at the day.

I never saw a man who looked
With such a wistful eye
Upon that little tent of blue
Which prisoners call the sky,
And at every drifting cloud that went
With sails of silver by.

I walked, with other souls in pain,
Within another ring,
And was wondering if the man had done
A great or little thing,
When a voice behind me whispered low,
"That fellow's got to swing."

Dear Christ! the very prison walls
Suddenly seemed to reel,
And the sky above my head became
Like a casque of scorching steel;
And, though I was a soul in pain,
My pain I could not feel.

I only knew what hunted thought
Quickened his step, and why
He looked upon the garish day
With such a wistful eye;
The man had killed the thing he loved
And so he had to die.

Yet each man kills the thing he loves
By each let this be heard,
Some do it with a bitter look,
Some with a flattering word,
The coward does it with a kiss,
The brave man with a sword!

Some kill their love when they are young,
And some when they are old;
Some strangle with the hands of Lust,
Some with the hands of Gold:
The kindest use a knife, because
The dead so soon grow cold.

130 | Ballads

Some love too little, some too long,
Some sell, and others buy;
Some do the deed with many tears,
And some without a sigh:
For each man kills the thing he loves,
Yet each man does not die.

He does not die a death of shame
On a day of dark disgrace,
Nor have a noose about his neck,
Nor a cloth upon his face,
Nor drop feet foremost through the floor
Into an empty place

He does not sit with silent men
Who watch him night and day;
Who watch him when he tries to weep,
And when he tries to pray;
Who watch him lest himself should rob
The prison of its prey.

He does not wake at dawn to see
Dread figures throng his room,
The shivering Chaplain robed in white,
The Sheriff stern with gloom,
And the Governor all in shiny black,
With the yellow face of Doom

He does not rise in piteous haste
To put on convict-clothes,
While some coarse-mouthed Doctor
gloats, and notes
Each new and nerve-twitched pose,
Fingering a watch whose little ticks
Are like horrible hammer-blows.

He does not know that sickening thirst
That sands one's throat, before
The hangman with his gardener's gloves
Slips through the padded door,
And binds one with three leathern thongs,
That the throat may thirst no more.

He does not bend his head to hear
The Burial Office read,
Nor, while the terror of his soul
Tells him he is not dead,
Cross his own coffin, as he moves
Into the hideous shed.

He does not stare upon the air
Through a little roof of glass;
He does not pray with lips of clay
For his agony to pass;
Nor feel upon his shuddering cheek
The kiss of Caiaphas.

II

Six weeks our guardsman walked the yard,
In a suit of shabby grey:
His cricket cap was on his head,
And his step seemed light and gay,
But I never saw a man who looked
So wistfully at the day.

I never saw a man who looked
With such a wistful eye
Upon that little tent of blue
Which prisoners call the sky,
And at every wandering cloud that trailed
Its raveled fleeces by.

He did not wring his hands, as do
Those witless men who dare
To try to rear the changeling Hope
In the cave of black Despair:
He only looked upon the sun,
And drank the morning air.

He did not wring his hands nor weep,
Nor did he peek or pine,
But he drank the air as though it held
Some healthful anodyne;
With open mouth he drank the sun
As though it had been wine!

And I and all the souls in pain,
Who tramped the other ring,
Forgot if we ourselves had done

A great or little thing,
And watched with gaze of dull amaze
The man who had to swing.

And strange it was to see him pass
With a step so light and gay,
And strange it was to see him look
So wistfully at the day,
And strange it was to think that he
Had such a debt to pay.

For oak and elm have pleasant leaves
That in the spring-time shoot:
But grim to see is the gallows-tree,
With its adder-bitten root,
And, green or dry, a man must die
Before it bears its fruit!

The loftiest place is that seat of grace
For which all worldlings try:
But who would stand in hempen band
Upon a scaffold high,
And through a murderer's collar take

His last look at the sky?
It is sweet to dance to violins
When Love and Life are fair:
To dance to flutes, to dance to lutes
Is delicate and rare:
But it is not sweet with nimble feet
To dance upon the air!

132 | *Ballads*

So with curious eyes and sick surmise
We watched him day by day,
And wondered if each one of us
Would end the self-same way,
For none can tell to what red Hell
His sightless soul may stray.

At last the dead man walked no more
Amongst the Trial Men,
And I knew that he was standing up
In the black dock's dreadful pen,
And that never would I see his face
In God's sweet world again.

Like two doomed ships that pass in storm
We had crossed each other's way:
But we made no sign, we said no word,
We had no word to say;
For we did not meet in the holy night,
But in the shameful day.

A prison wall was round us both,
Two outcast men were we:
The world had thrust us from its heart,
And God from out His care:
And the iron gin that waits for Sin
Had caught us in its snare.

III

In Debtors' Yard the stones are hard,
And the dripping wall is high,
So it was there he took the air
Beneath the leaden sky,
And by each side a Warder walked,
For fear the man might die.

Or else he sat with those who watched
His anguish night and day;
Who watched him when he rose to weep,
And when he crouched to pray;
Who watched him lest himself should rob
Their scaffold of its prey.

The Governor was strong upon
The Regulations Act:
The Doctor said that Death was but
A scientific fact:
And twice a day the Chaplain called
And left a little tract.

And twice a day he smoked his pipe,
And drank his quart of beer:
His soul was resolute, and held
No hiding-place for fear;
He often said that he was glad
The hangman's hands were near.

Oscar Wilde | 133

But why he said so strange a thing
No Warder dared to ask:
For he to whom a watcher's doom
Is given as his task,
Must set a lock upon his lips,
And make his face a mask.

Or else he might be moved, and try
To comfort or console:
And what should Human Pity do
Pent up in Murderers' Hole?
What word of grace in such a place
Could help a brother's soul?

With slouch and swing around the ring
We trod the Fool's Parade!
We did not care: we knew we were
The Devil's Own Brigade:
And shaven head and feet of lead
Make a merry masquerade.

We tore the tarry rope to shreds
With blunt and bleeding nails;
We rubbed the doors, and scrubbed the floors,
And cleaned the shining rails:
And, rank by rank, we soaped the plank,
And clattered with the pails

We sewed the sacks, we broke the stones,
We turned the dusty drill:
We banged the tins, and bawled the hymns,

And sweated on the mill:
But in the heart of every man
Terror was lying still.

So still it lay that every day
Crawled like a weed-clogged wave:
And we forgot the bitter lot
That waits for fool and knave.
Till once, as we tramped in from work,
We passed an open grave.

With yawning mouth the yellow hole
Gaped for a living thing;
The very mud cried out for blood
To the thirsty asphalte ring:
And we knew that ere one dawn grew fair
Some prisoner had to swing.

Right in we went, with soul intent
On Death and Dread and Doom:
The hangman, with his little bag,
Went shuffling through the gloom
And each man trembled as he crept
Into his numbered tomb.

That night the empty corridors
Were full of forms of Fear,
And up and down the iron town
Stole feet we could not hear,
And through the bars that hide the stars
White faces seemed to peer.

134 | Ballads

He lay as one who lies and dreams
In a pleasant meadow-land,
The watcher watched him as he slept,
And could not understand
How one could sleep so sweet a sleep
With a hangman close at hand?

But there is no sleep when men must weep
Who never yet have wept:
So we—the fool, the fraud, the knave—
That endless vigil kept,
And through each brain on hands of pain
Another's terror crept.

Alas! it is a fearful thing
To feel another's guilt!
For, right within, the sword of Sin
Pierced to its poisoned hilt,
And as molten lead were the tears we shed
For the blood we had not spilt.

The Warders with their shoes of felt
Crept by each padlocked door,
And peeped and saw, with eyes of awe,
Grey figures on the floor,
And wondered why men knelt to pray
Who never prayed before.

All through the night we knelt and prayed,
Mad mourners of a corpse!
The troubled plumes of midnight were

The plumes upon a hearse:
And bitter wine upon a sponge
Was the savior of Remorse.

The cock crew, the red cock crew,
But never came the day:
And crooked shape of Terror crouched,
In the corners where we lay:
And each evil sprite that walks by night
Before us seemed to play.

They glided past, they glided fast,
Like travelers through a mist:
They mocked the moon in a rigadoon
Of delicate turn and twist,
And with formal pace and loathsome grace
The phantoms kept their tryst.

With mop and mow, we saw them go,
Slim shadows hand in hand:
About, about, in ghostly rout
They trod a saraband:
And the damned grotesques made
arabesques,
Like the wind upon the sand!

With the pirouettes of marionettes,
They tripped on pointed tread:
But with flutes of Fear they filled the ear,
As their grisly masque they led,
And loud they sang, and loud they sang,
For they sang to wake the dead.

Oscar Wilde | 135

"Oho!" they cried, "The world is wide,
But fettered limbs go lame!
And once, or twice, to throw the dice
Is a gentlemanly game,
But he does not win who plays with Sin
In the secret House of Shame."

No things of air these antics were
That frolicked with such glee:
To men whose lives were held in gyves,
And whose feet might not go free,
Ah! wounds of Christ! they were living
things,
Most terrible to see.

Around, around, they waltzed and wound;
Some wheeled in smirking pairs:
With the mincing step of demirep
Some sidled up the stairs:
And with subtle sneer, and fawning leer,
Each helped us at our prayers.

The morning wind began to moan,
But still the night went on:
Through its giant loom the web of gloom
Crept till each thread was spun:
And, as we prayed, we grew afraid
Of the Justice of the Sun.

The moaning wind went wandering round
The weeping prison-wall:
Till like a wheel of turning-steel

We felt the minutes crawl:
O moaning wind! what had we done
To have such a seneschal?

At last I saw the shadowed bars
Like a lattice wrought in lead,
Move right across the whitewashed wall
That faced my three-plank bed,
And I knew that somewhere in the world
God's dreadful dawn was red.

At six o'clock we cleaned our cells,
At seven all was still,
But the sough and swing of a mighty wing
The prison seemed to fill,
For the Lord of Death with icy breath
Had entered in to kill.

He did not pass in purple pomp,
Nor ride a moon-white steed.
Three yards of cord and a sliding board
Are all the gallows' need:
So with rope of shame the Herald came
To do the secret deed.

We were as men who through a fen
Of filthy darkness grope:
We did not dare to breathe a prayer,
Or give our anguish scope:
Something was dead in each of us,
And what was dead was Hope.

136 | Ballads

For Man's grim Justice goes its way,
  And will not swerve aside:
It slays the weak, it slays the strong,
  It has a deadly stride:
With iron heel it slays the strong,
  The monstrous parricide!

We waited for the stroke of eight:
  Each tongue was thick with thirst:
For the stroke of eight is the stroke of Fate
  That makes a man accursed,
And Fate will use a running noose
  For the best man and the worst.

We had no other thing to do,
  Save to wait for the sign to come:
So, like things of stone in a valley lone,
  Quiet we sat and dumb:
But each man's heart beat thick and quick
  Like a madman on a drum!

With sudden shock the prison-clock
  Smote on the shivering air,
And from all the gaol rose up a wail
  Of impotent despair,
Like the sound that frightened marshes
      hear
  From a leper in his lair.

And as one sees most fearful things
  In the crystal of a dream,
We saw the greasy hempen rope
  Hooked to the blackened beam,
And heard the prayer the hangman's snare
  Strangled into a scream.

And all the woe that moved him so
  That he gave that bitter cry,
And the wild regrets, and the bloody
      sweats,
  None knew so well as I:
For he who lives more lives than one
  More deaths than one must die.

IV

There is no chapel on the day
  On which they hang a man:
The Chaplain's heart is far too sick,
  Or his face is far too wan,
Or there is that written in his eyes
  Which none should look upon.

So they kept us close till nigh on noon,
  And then they rang the bell,
And the Warders with their jingling keys
  Opened each listening cell,
And down the iron stair we tramped,
  Each from his separate Hell.

Oscar Wilde | 137

Out into God's sweet air we went,
But not in wonted way,
For this man's face was white with fear,
And that man's face was grey,
And I never saw sad men who looked
So wistfully at the day.

I never saw sad men who looked
With such a wistful eye
Upon that little tent of blue
We prisoners called the sky,
And at every careless cloud that passed
In happy freedom by.

But there were those amongst us all
Who walked with downcast head,
And knew that, had each got his due,
They should have died instead:
He had but killed a thing that lived
Whilst they had killed the dead.

For he who sins a second time
Wakes a dead soul to pain,
And draws it from its spotted shroud,
And makes it bleed again,
And makes it bleed great gouts of blood
And makes it bleed in vain!

Like ape or clown, in monstrous garb
With crooked arrows starred,
Silently we went round and round

The slippery asphalte yard;
Silently we went round and round,
And no man spoke a word.

Silently we went round and round,
And through each hollow mind
The memory of dreadful things
Rushed like a dreadful wind,
And Horror stalked before each man,
And terror crept behind.

The Warders strutted up and down,
And kept their herd of brutes,
Their uniforms were spick and span,
And they wore their Sunday suits,
But we knew the work they had been at
By the quicklime on their boots.

For where a grave had opened wide,
There was no grave at all:
Only a stretch of mud and sand
By the hideous prison-wall,
And a little heap of burning lime,
That the man should have his pall.

For he has a pall, this wretched man,
Such as few men can claim:
Deep down below a prison-yard,
Naked for greater shame,
He lies, with fetters on each foot,
Wrapt in a sheet of flame!

138 | Ballads

And all the while the burning lime
Eats flesh and bone away,
It eats the brittle bone by night,
And the soft flesh by the day,
It eats the flesh and bones by turns,
But it eats the heart alway.

For three long years they will not sow
Or root or seedling there:
For three long years the unblessed spot
Will sterile be and bare,
And look upon the wondering sky
With unreproachful stare.

They think a murderer's heart would taint
Each simple seed they sow.
It is not true! God's kindly earth
Is kindlier than men know,
And the red rose would but blow more
red,
The white rose whiter blow.

Out of his mouth a red, red rose!
Out of his heart a white!
For who can say by what strange way,
Christ brings his will to light,
Since the barren staff the pilgrim bore
Bloomed in the great Pope's sight?

But neither milk-white rose nor red
May bloom in prison air;
The shard, the pebble, and the flint,

Are what they give us there:
For flowers have been known to heal
A common man's despair.

So never will wine-red rose or white,
Petal by petal, fall
On that stretch of mud and sand that lies
By the hideous prison-wall,
To tell the men who tramp the yard
That God's Son died for all.

Yet though the hideous prison-wall
Still hems him round and round,
And a spirit man not walk by night
That is with fetters bound,
And a spirit may not weep that lies
In such unholy ground,

He is at peace—this wretched man—
At peace, or will be soon:
There is no thing to make him mad,
Nor does Terror walk at noon,
For the lampless Earth in which he lies
Has neither Sun nor Moon.

They hanged him as a beast is hanged:
They did not even toll
A requiem that might have brought
Rest to his startled soul,
But hurriedly they took him out,
And hid him in a hole.

They stripped him of his canvas clothes,
And gave him to the flies;
They mocked the swollen purple throat
And the stark and staring eyes:
And with laughter loud they heaped the
shroud
In which their convict lies.

The Chaplain would not kneel to pray
By his dishonored grave:
Nor mark it with that blessed Cross

That Christ for sinners gave,
Because the man was one of those
Whom Christ came down to save.

Yet all is well; he has but passed
To Life's appointed bourne:
And alien tears will fill for him
Pity's long-broken urn,
For his mourners will be outcast men,
And outcasts always mourn.

V

I know not whether Laws be right,
Or whether Laws be wrong;
All that we know who lie in gaol
Is that the wall is strong;
And that each day is like a year,
A year whose days are long.

But this I know, that every Law
That men have made for Man,
Since first Man took his brother's life,
And the sad world began,
But straws the wheat and saves the chaff
With a most evil fan.

This too I know—and wise it were
If each could know the same—
That every prison that men build

Is built with bricks of shame,
And bound with bars lest Christ should see
How men their brothers maim.

With bars they blur the gracious moon,
And blind the goodly sun:
And they do well to hide their Hell,
For in it things are done
That Son of God nor son of Man
Ever should look upon!

The vilest deeds like poison weeds
Bloom well in prison-air:
It is only what is good in Man
That wastes and withers there:
Pale Anguish keeps the heavy gate,
And the Warder is Despair.

140 | Ballads

For they starve the little frightened child
Till it weeps both night and day:
And they scourge the weak, and flog the
fool,
And gibe the old and grey,
And some grow mad, and all grow bad,
And none a word may say.

Each narrow cell in which we dwell
Is foul and dark latrine,
And the fetid breath of living Death
Chokes up each grated screen,
And all, but Lust, is turned to dust
In Humanity's machine.

The brackish water that we drink
Creeps with a loathsome slime,
And the bitter bread they weigh in scales
Is full of chalk and lime,
And Sleep will not lie down, but walks
Wild-eyed and cries to Time.

But though lean Hunger and green Thirst
Like asp with adder fight,
We have little care of prison fare,
For what chills and kills outright
Is that every stone one lifts by day
Becomes one's heart by night.

With midnight always in one's heart,
And twilight in one's cell,
We turn the crank, or tear the rope,

Each in his separate Hell,
And the silence is more awful far
Than the sound of a brazen bell.

And never a human voice comes near
To speak a gentle word:
And the eye that watches through the door
Is pitiless and hard:
And by all forgot, we rot and rot,
With soul and body marred.

And thus we rust Life's iron chain
Degraded and alone:
And some men curse, and some men
weep,
And some men make no moan:
But God's eternal Laws are kind
And break the heart of stone.

And every human heart that breaks,
In prison-cell or yard,
Is as that broken box that gave
Its treasure to the Lord,
And filled the unclean leper's house
With the scent of costliest nard.

Ah! happy day they whose hearts can break
And peace of pardon win!
How else may man make straight his plan
And cleanse his soul from Sin?
How else but through a broken heart
May Lord Christ enter in?

And he of the swollen purple throat.
And the stark and staring eyes,
Waits for the holy hands that took
The Thief to Paradise;
And a broken and a contrite heart
The Lord will not despise.

The man in red who reads the Law
Gave him three weeks of life,
Three little weeks in which to heal

His soul of his soul's strife,
And cleanse from every blot of blood
The hand that held the knife.

And with tears of blood he cleansed the
hand,
The hand that held the steel:
For only blood can wipe out blood,
And only tears can heal:
And the crimson stain that was of Cain
Became Christ's snow-white seal.

VI

In Reading gaol by Reading town
There is a pit of shame,
And in it lies a wretched man
Eaten by teeth of flame,
In burning winding-sheet he lies,
And his grave has got no name.

And there, till Christ call forth the dead,
In silence let him lie:
No need to waste the foolish tear,

Or heave the windy sigh:
The man had killed the thing he loved,
And so he had to die.

And all men kill the thing they love,
By all let this be heard,
Some do it with a bitter look,
Some with a flattering word,
The coward does it with a kiss,
The brave man with a sword!

Oscar Wilde

142 | Ballads

Song from *The Player Queen*

My mother dandled me and sang,
'How young it is, how young!'
And made a golden cradle
That on a willow swung.

'He went away,' my mother sang,
'When I was brought to bed,'
And all the while her needle pulled
The gold and silver thread.

She pulled the thread and bit the thread
And made a golden gown,
And wept because she had dreamt that I
Was born to wear a crown.

'When she was got,' my mother sang,
'I heard a sea-mew cry,
And saw a flake of the yellow foam
That dropped upon my thigh.'

How therefore could she help but braid
The gold into my hair,
And dream that I should carry
The golden top of care.

William Butler Yeats

Crazy Jane Talks with the Bishop

I met the Bishop on the road
And much said he and I.
"Those breasts are flat and fallen now
Those veins must soon be dry;
Live in a heavenly mansion,
Not in some foul sty."

"Fair and foul are near of kin,
And fair needs foul," I cried.
"My friends are gone, but that's a truth
Nor grave nor bed denied,
Learned in bodily lowliness
And in the heart's pride.

"A woman can be proud and stiff
When on love intent;
But Love has pitched his mansion in
The place of excrement;
For nothing can be sole or whole
That has not been rent."

William Butler Yeats

To Earthward

Love at the lips was touch
As sweet as I could bear;
And once that seemed too much;
I lived on air

That crossed me from sweet things,
The flow of—was it musk
From hidden grapevine springs
Downhill at dusk?

I had the swirl and ache
From sprays of honeysuckle
That when they're gathered shake
Dew on the knuckle.

I craved strong sweets, but those
Seemed strong when I was young;
The petal of the rose
It was that stung.

Now no joy but lacks salt,
That is not dashed with pain
And weariness and fault;
I crave the stain.

Of tears, the aftermark
Of almost too much love,
The sweet of bitter bark
And burning clove.

When stiff and sore and scarred
I take away my hand
From leaning on it hard
In grass and sand,

The hurt is not enough:
I long for weight and strength
To feel the earth as rough
To all my length.

Robert Frost

The Aim Was Song

Before man came to blow it right
The wind once blew itself untaught,
And did its loudest day and night
In any rough place where it caught.

Man came to tell it what was wrong:
It hadn't found the place to blow;
It blew too hard—the aim was song.
And listen—how it ought to go!

He took a little in his mouth,
And held it long enough for north
To be converted into south,
And then by measure blew it forth.

By measure. It was word and note,
The wind the wind had meant to be—
A little through the lips and throat.
The aim was song—the wind could see.

Robert Frost

Thomas Wyatt, 149

John Donne, 150

George Herbert, 156

Ben Jonson, 162

Andrew Marvell, 166

William Wordsworth, 168

Samuel Coleridge, 176

Gerard Manley Hopkins, 178

Mary Elizabeth Coleridge, 184

Herman Melville, 186

Dylan Thomas, 187

Robert Frost, 188

Erato, Muse of Love Poetry, with Mirror
by Simon Vouet

VERSES VARIABLE

Regular Stress Measures Out Irregular Lines

Orpheus at the Entrance to Hades

Orpheus Begs Pluto for Eurydice

They flee from me that sometime did me seek

With naked foot, stalking in my chamber.[3]

4 I have seen them gentle, tame, and meek,

That now are wild and do not remember

That sometime they put themself in danger

To take bread at my hand; and now they range,

8 Busily seeking with a continual change.

Thanked be fortune it hath been otherwise

Twenty times better; but once in special,

In thin array after a pleasant guise,

12 When her loose gown from her shoulders did fall,

And she me caught in her arms long and small;

Therewithal sweetly did me kiss

And softly said, "Dear heart, how like you this?"

16 It was no dream: I lay broad waking.

But all is turned thorough my gentleness

Into a strange fashion of forsaking;

And I have leave to go of her goodness,

20 And she also, to use newfangleness.

But since that I so kindly am served

I would fain know what she hath deserved.

Sir Thomas Wyatt

---

[3] This line does not scan: *chamber* does not accent as an iamb. Several lines to follow will not scan for this same reason—e.g., its rhyming fourth line—or else for lack of a tenth syllable. *Suggestion:* if we allow for a silent syllable at the caesura, like a rest in music, as a dramatic pause; and allow for a final feminine foot as needed; then do the lines not only scan, but even sing? As follows: With ná/ked foót, /—stálk/ing ín/ my chámber.... That nów/ are wíld /—ánd/ do nót/ remémber

Good Friday, 1613.
Riding Westward

Let man's soul be a sphere, and then, in this,
The intelligence that moves, devotion is,
And as the other spheres, by being grown
Subject to foreign motions, lose their own,
And being by others hurried every day, 5
Scarce in a year their natural form obey:
Pleasure or business, so, our souls admit
For their first mover, and are whirled by it.
Hence is't, that I am carried towards the West
This day, when my soul's form bends toward the East.
There I should see a sun, by rising set,
And by that setting endless day beget;
But that Christ on this cross did rise and fall,
Sin had eternally benighted all.
Yet dare I'almost be glad, I do not see
That spectacle of too much weight for me.
Who sees God's face, that is self life, must die;
What a death were it then to see God die?
It made his own lieutenant Nature shrink,
It made his footstool crack, and the sun wink.

Could I behold those hands which span the poles,

And turn all spheres at once, pierced with those holes?

25 Could I behold that endless height which is

Zenith to us, and to'our antipodes,

Humbled below us? Or that blood which is

The seat of all our souls, if not of his,

Make dirt of dust, or that flesh which was worn

30 By God, for his apparel, ragg'd, and torn?

If on these things I durst not look, durst I

Upon his miserable mother cast mine eye,

Who was God's partner here, and furnished thus

Half of that sacrifice which ransomed us?

35 Though these things, as I ride, be from mine eye,

They'are present yet unto my memory,

For that looks towards them; and thou look'st towards me,

O Savior, as thou hang'st upon the tree;

I turn my back to thee, but to receive

40 Corrections, till thy mercies bid thee leave.

O think me worth thine anger, punish me,

Burn off my rusts, and my deformity,

Restore thine image, so much, by thy grace,

That thou may'st know me, and I'll turn my face.

John Donne

A Nocturnal Upon St. Lucy's Day

'Tis the year's midnight, and it is the day's,

Lucy's, who scarce seven hours herself unmasks;

3   The sun is spent, and now his flasks

Send forth light squibs, no constant rays;

The world's whole sap is sunk;

6 The general balm th' hydroptic earth hath drunk,

Whither, as to the bed's feet, life is shrunk,

Dead and interr'd; yet all these seem to laugh,

9   Compar'd with me, who am their epitaph.

Study me then, you who shall lovers be

At the next world, that is, at the next spring;

12   For I am every dead thing,

In whom Love wrought new alchemy.

For his art did express

15   A quintessence even from nothingness,

From dull privations, and lean emptiness;

He ruin'd me, and I am re-begot

18 Of absence, darkness, death: things which are not.

All others, from all things, draw all that's good,

Life, soul, form, spirit, whence they being have;

21   I, by Love's limbec, am the grave

Of all that's nothing. Oft a flood

Have we two wept, and so

24 Drown'd the whole world, us two; oft did we grow

Donne | 153

To be two chaoses, when we did show

27   Care to aught else; and often absences

Withdrew our souls, and made us carcasses.

30   But I am by her death (which word wrongs her)

Of the first nothing the elixir grown;

Were I a man, that I were one

33   I needs must know; I should prefer,

If I were any beast,

Some ends, some means; yea plants, yea stones detest,

36   And love; all, all some properties invest;

If I an ordinary nothing were,

As shadow, a light and body must be here.

39

But I am none; nor will my sun renew.

You lovers, for whose sake the lesser sun

42   At this time to the Goat is run

To fetch new lust, and give it you,

Enjoy your summer all;

45   Since she enjoys her long night's festival,

Let me prepare towards her, and let me call

This hour her vigil, and her eve, since this

48   Both the year's, and the day's deep midnight is.

John Donne

154 | Variable

Busy old fool, unruly Sun,

Why dost thou thus,

Through windows and through curtains call on us?

Must to thy motions lovers' seasons run?

Saucy pedantic wretch, go chide

Late schoolboys, and sour prentices,

Go tell Court-huntsmen that the King will ride,

Call country ants to harvest offices;

Love, all alike, no season knows, nor clime,

Nor hours, days, months, which are the rags of time.

Thy beams so reverend and strong

Why shouldst thou think?

I could eclipse and cloud them with a wink,

But that I would not lose her sight so long;

If her eyes have not blinded thine,

Look, and tomorrow late, tell me

Whether both th'Indias of spice and mine

Be where thou leftst them, or lie here with me.

Ask for those kings whom thou saw'st yesterday,

And thou shalt hear, All here in one bed lay.

She'is all States, and all Princes, I,

Nothing else is.

Princes do but play us; compared to this,

All honor's mimic, all wealth alchemy.

Thou, sun, art half as happy as we,

In that the world's contracted thus;

Thine age asks ease, and since thy duties be

To warm the world, that's done in warming us.

Shine here to us, and thou art every where;

This bed thy center is, these walls, thy sphere.

John Donne

A Valediction: Of Weeping

Let me pour forth

My tears before thy face, whilst I stay here,

For thy face coins them, and thy stamp they bear,

And by this mintage they are something worth,

For thus they be

Pregnant of thee;

Fruits of much grief they are, emblems of more:

When a tear falls, that thou falls which it bore;

So thou and I are nothing then, when on a diverse shore.

On a round ball

A workman that hath copies by, can lay

An Europe, Afrique, and an Asia,

And quickly make that which was nothing, all;

So doth each tear,

Which thee doth wear,

A globe, yea world, by that impression grow,

Till thy tears mixed with mine do overflow

This world, by waters sent from thee, my heav'n dissolvèd so.

O more than moon,

Draw not up seas to drown me in thy sphere;

Weep me not dead in thine arms, but forbear

To teach the sea what it may do too soon;

Let not the wind

Example find,

To do me more harm than it purposeth;

Since thou and I sigh one another's breath,

Whoe'er sighs most, is cruelest, and hastes the other's death.

John Donne

The Collar

I struck the board, and cried, "No more;
I will abroad!
What? shall I ever sigh and pine?
My lines and life are free, free as the road,
Loose as the wind, as large as store.
Shall I be still in suit?
Have I no harvest but a thorn
To let me blood, and not restore
What I have lost with cordial fruit?
Sure there was wine
Before my sighs did dry it; there was corn
Before my tears did drown it.
Is the year only lost to me?
Have I no bays to crown it,
No flowers, no garlands gay? All blasted?
All wasted?
Not so, my heart; but there is fruit,
And thou hast hands.

Recover all thy sigh-blown age

On double pleasures: leave thy cold dispute

21   Of what is fit and not. Forsake thy cage,

Thy rope of sands,

Which petty thoughts have made, and made to thee

24   Good cable, to enforce and draw,

And be thy law,

While thou didst wink and wouldst not see.

27   Away! take heed;

I will abroad.

Call in thy death's-head there; tie up thy fears;

30   He that forbears

To suit and serve his need

Deserves his load."

33   But as I raved and grew more fierce and wild

At every word,

Methought I heard one calling, Child!

36   And I replied My Lord.

George Herbert

The Altar

A broken ALTAR, Lord, thy servant rears,
Made of a heart and cemented with tears:
Whose parts are as thy hand did frame;
No workman's tool hath touch'd the same.
A HEART alone
Is such a stone,
As nothing but
Thy pow'r doth cut.

Wherefore each part
Of my hard heart
Meets in this frame,
To praise thy name:
That if I chance to hold my peace,
These stones to praise thee may not cease.
Oh, let thy blessed SACRIFICE be mine,
And sanctify this ALTAR to be thine.

George Herbert

Easter Wings

Lord, who createdst man in wealth and store,
Though foolishly he lost the same,
Decaying more and more,
Till he became
5   Most poore.

With thee
O let me rise
As larks, harmoniously,
And sing this day thy victories:
10 Then shall the fall further the flight in me.

My tender age in sorrow did beginne
And still with sicknesses and shame.
Thou didst so punish sinne,
That I became
15   Most thinne.

With thee
Let me combine,
And feel thy victorie:
For, if I imp my wing on thine,
20 Affliction shall advance the flight in me.

George Herbert

Man

My God, I heard this day
That none doth build a stately habitation,
But he that means to dwell therein.
What house more stately hath there been,
Or can be, than is Man? to whose creation
All things are in decay.
For Man is ev'ry thing,
And more: he is a tree, yet bears more fruit;
A beast, yet is, or should be more:
Reason and speech we only bring.
Parrots may thank us, if they are not mute,
They go upon the score.
Man is all symmetry,
Full of proportions, one limb to another,
And all to all the world besides:
Each part may call the furthest, brother;
For head with foot hath private amity,
And both with moons and tides.
Nothing hath got so far,
But man hath caught and kept it, as his prey.
His eyes dismount the highest star:
He is in little all the sphere.
Herbs gladly cure our flesh, because that they
Find their acquaintance there.
For us the winds do blow,
The earth doth rest, heav'n move, and fountains flow.
Nothing we see but means our good,

As our delight or as our treasure:
The whole is either our cupboard of food,
30   Or cabinet of pleasure.
The stars have us to bed;
Night draws the curtain, which the sun withdraws;
33   Music and light attend our head.
All things unto our flesh are kind
In their descent and being; to our mind
36   In their ascent and cause.
Each thing is full of duty:
Waters united are our navigation;
39   Distinguishèd, our habitation;
Below, our drink; above, our meat;
Both are our cleanliness. Hath one such beauty?
42   Then how are all things neat?
More servants wait on Man
Than he'll take notice of: in every path
45 He treads down that which doth befriend him
When sickness makes him pale and wan.
O mighty love! Man is one world, and hath
48   Another to attend him.
Since then, my God, thou hast
So brave a palace built, O dwell in it,
51   That it may dwell with thee at last!
Till then, afford us so much wit,
That, as the world serves us, we may serve thee,
54   And both thy servants be.

George Herbert

On My First Son

Farewell, thou child of my right hand, and joy;

My sin was too much hope of thee, lov'd boy.

3   Seven years tho' wert lent to me, and I thee pay,

Exacted by thy fate, on the just day.

O, could I lose all father now! For why

6   Will man lament the state he should envy?

To have so soon 'scap'd world's and flesh's rage,

And if no other misery, yet age?

9   Rest in soft peace, and, ask'd, say, "Here doth lie

Ben Jonson his best piece of poetry."

For whose sake henceforth all his vows be such,

12   As what he loves may never like too much.

Ben Jonson

Echo's Song for Narcissus

Slow, slow, fresh fount, keep time with my salt tears;

Yet slower, yet, O faintly, gentle springs!

List to the heavy part the music bears,

Woe weeps out her division, when she sings.

Droop herbs and flowers;

Fall grief in showers;

Our beauties are not ours.

O, I could still,

Like melting snow upon some craggy hill,

Drop, drop, drop, drop,

Since nature's pride is now a withered daffodil.

Ben Jonson

My Picture Left in Scotland

I now think Love is rather deaf than blind,
For else it could not be
That she,
Whom I adore so much, should so slight me
And cast my love behind.
I'm sure my language to her was as sweet,
And every close did meet
In sentence of as subtle feet,
As hath the youngest He
That sits in shadow of Apollo's tree.

O, but my conscious fears,
That fly my thoughts between,
Tell me that she hath seen
My hundred of gray hairs,
Told seven and forty years
Read so much waste, as she cannot embrace
My mountain belly and my rocky face;
And all these through her eyes have stopp'd her ears.

Ben Jonson

That Women Are But Men's Shadows

Follow a shadow, it still flies you;
Seem to fly it, it will pursue:
So court a mistress, she denies you;
Let her alone, she will court you.
Say, are not women truly then
Styled but the shadows of us men?
At morn and even shades are longest,
At noon they are or short or none;
So men at weakest, they are strongest,
But grant us perfect, they're not known.
Say, are not women truly then
Styled but the shadows of us men?

Ben Jonson

On a Drop of Dew

See how the orient dew,
Shed from the bosom of the morn
Into the blowing roses,
Yet careless of its mansion new,
For the clear region where 'twas born
Round in itself incloses:

And in its little globe's extent,
Frames as it can its native element.
How it the purple flow'r does slight,
Scarce touching where it lies,
But gazing back upon the skies,
Shines with a mournful light,

Like its own tear,
Because so long divided from the sphere.
Restless it rolls and unsecure,
Trembling lest it grow impure,
Till the warm sun pity its pain,
And to the skies exhale it back again.

So the soul, that drop, that ray
Of the clear fountain of eternal day,
Could it within the human flow'r be seen,
Remembering still its former height,
Shuns the sweet leaves and blossoms green,
And recollecting its own light,

Does, in its pure and circling thoughts, express
The greater heaven in an heaven less.
28   In how coy a figure wound,
        Every way it turns away:
So the world excluding round,
        Yet receiving in the day,

32   Dark beneath, but bright above,
        Here disdaining, there in love.
How loose and easy hence to go,
How girt and ready to ascend,
36   Moving but on a point below,
It all about does upwards bend.

Such did the manna's sacred dew distill,
White and entire, though congealed and chill,
40 Congealed on earth: but does, dissolving, run
Into the glories of th' almighty sun.

Andrew Marvell

Ode: Intimations of Immortality
from Recollections of Early Childhood

The child is father of the man;
And I could wish my days to be
Bound each to each by natural piety.

(Wordsworth, *My Heart Leaps Up*)

There was a time when meadow, grove, and stream,

The earth, and every common sight,

To me did seem

Apparelled in celestial light,

5 The glory and the freshness of a dream.

It is not now as it hath been of yore;—

Turn wheresoe'er I may,

By night or day.

The things which I have seen I now can see no more.

10 The Rainbow comes and goes,

And lovely is the Rose,

The Moon doth with delight

Look round her when the heavens are bare,

Waters on a starry night

15 Are beautiful and fair;

The sunshine is a glorious birth;

But yet I know, where'er I go,

That there hath past away a glory from the earth.

20   Now, while the birds thus sing a joyous song,

And while the young lambs bound

As to the tabor's sound,

To me alone there came a thought of grief:

A timely utterance gave that thought relief,

25   And I again am strong:

The cataracts blow their trumpets from the steep;

No more shall grief of mine the season wrong;

I hear the Echoes through the mountains throng,

The Winds come to me from the fields of sleep,

30   And all the earth is gay;

Land and sea

Give themselves up to jollity,

And with the heart of May

Doth every Beast keep holiday;—

35   Thou Child of Joy,

Shout round me, let me hear thy shouts, thou happy Shepherd-boy.

Ye blessèd creatures, I have heard the call

Ye to each other make; I see

The heavens laugh with you in your jubilee;

40   My heart is at your festival,

My head hath its coronal,

The fulness of your bliss, I feel—I feel it all.

170 | Variable

Oh evil day! if I were sullen

While Earth herself is adorning,

45 This sweet May-morning,

And the Children are culling

On every side,

In a thousand valleys far and wide,

Fresh flowers; while the sun shines warm,

50 And the Babe leaps up on his Mother's arm:—

I hear, I hear, with joy I hear!

—But there's a Tree, of many, one,

A single field which I have looked upon,

Both of them speak of something that is gone;

55 The Pansy at my feet

Doth the same tale repeat:

Whither is fled the visionary gleam?

Where is it now, the glory and the dream?

Our birth is but a sleep and a forgetting:

60 The Soul that rises with us, our life's Star,

Hath had elsewhere its setting,

And cometh from afar:

Not in entire forgetfulness,

And not in utter nakedness,

65 But trailing clouds of glory do we come

From God, who is our home:

Heaven lies about us in our infancy!

Shades of the prison-house begin to close

Upon the growing Boy,

70 But he beholds the light, and whence it flows,

He sees it in his joy;

The Youth, who daily farther from the east
Must travel, still is Nature's Priest,
And by the vision splendid
75   Is on his way attended;
At length the Man perceives it die away,
And fade into the light of common day.

Earth fills her lap with pleasures of her own;
Yearnings she hath in her own natural kind,
80   And, even with something of a Mother's mind,
And no unworthy aim,
The homely Nurse doth all she can
To make her Foster-child, her Inmate Man,
Forget the glories he hath known,
85   And that imperial palace whence he came.

Behold the Child among his new-born blisses,
A six years' Darling of a pigmy size!
See, where 'mid work of his own hand he lies,
Fretted by sallies of his mother's kisses,
90   With light upon him from his father's eyes!
See, at his feet, some little plan or chart,
Some fragment from his dream of human life,
Shaped by himself with newly-learn{e}d art
A wedding or a festival,
95   A mourning or a funeral;
And this hath now his heart,
And unto this he frames his song:

172 | Variable

Then will he fit his tongue

To dialogues of business, love, or strife;

But it will not be long

Ere this be thrown aside,

And with new joy and pride

The little Actor cons another part;

Filling from time to time his "humorous stage"

With all the Persons, down to palsied Age,

That Life brings with her in her equipage;

As if his whole vocation

Were endless imitation.

Thou, whose exterior semblance doth belie

Thy Soul's immensity;

Thou best Philosopher, who yet dost keep

Thy heritage, thou Eye among the blind,

That, deaf and silent, read'st the eternal deep,

Haunted for ever by the eternal mind,—

Mighty Prophet! Seer blest!

On whom those truths do rest,

Which we are toiling all our lives to find,

In darkness lost, the darkness of the grave;

Thou, over whom thy Immortality

Broods like the Day, a Master o'er a Slave,

A Presence which is not to be put by;

Thou little Child, yet glorious in the might

Of heaven-born freedom on thy being's height,

Why with such earnest pains dost thou provoke

The years to bring the inevitable yoke,

Thus blindly with thy blessedness at strife?

Full soon thy Soul shall have her earthly freight,
And custom lie upon thee with a weight,
Heavy as frost, and deep almost as life!

130 O joy! that in our embers
Is something that doth live,
That Nature yet remembers
What was so fugitive!
The thought of our past years in me doth breed
135 Perpetual benediction: not indeed
For that which is most worthy to be blest;
Delight and liberty, the simple creed
Of Childhood, whether busy or at rest,
With new-fledged hope still fluttering in his breast:—
140 Not for these I raise
The song of thanks and praise
But for those obstinate questionings
Of sense and outward things,
Fallings from us, vanishings;
145 Blank misgivings of a Creature
Moving about in worlds not realised,
High instincts before which our mortal Nature
Did tremble like a guilty thing surprised:
But for those first affections,
150 Those shadowy recollections,
Which, be they what they may
Are yet the fountain-light of all our day,
Are yet a master-light of all our seeing;

174 | Variable

Uphold us, cherish, and have power to make

155   Our noisy years seem moments in the being

Of the eternal Silence: truths that wake,

To perish never;

Which neither listlessness, nor mad endeavour,

Nor Man nor Boy,

160   Nor all that is at enmity with joy,

Can utterly abolish or destroy!

Hence in a season of calm weather

Though inland far we be,

Our Souls have sight of that immortal sea

165   Which brought us hither,

Can in a moment travel thither,

And see the Children sport upon the shore,

And hear the mighty waters rolling evermore.

Then sing, ye Birds, sing, sing a joyous song!

170   And let the young Lambs bound

As to the tabor's sound!

We in thought will join your throng,

Ye that pipe and ye that play,

Ye that through your hearts to-day

175   Feel the gladness of the May!

What though the radiance which was once so bright

Be now for ever taken from my sight,

Though nothing can bring back the hour

Of splendor in the grass, of glory in the flower;

180   We will grieve not, rather find

Strength in what remains behind;

In the primal sympathy

Which having been must ever be;

In the soothing thoughts that spring

185   Out of human suffering;

In the faith that looks through death,

In years that bring the philosophic mind.

And O, ye Fountains, Meadows, Hills, and Groves,

Forebode not any severing of our loves!

190   Yet in my heart of hearts I feel your might;

I only have relinquished one delight

To live beneath your more habitual sway.

I love the Brooks which down their channels fret,

Even more than when I tripped lightly as they;

195   The innocent brightness of a new-born Day

Is lovely yet;

The Clouds that gather round the setting sun

Do take a sober coloring from an eye

That hath kept watch o'er man's mortality;

200   Another race hath been, and other palms are won.

Thanks to the human heart by which we live,

Thanks to its tenderness, its joys, and fears,

To me the meanest flower that blows can give

Thoughts that do often lie too deep for tears.

William Wordsworth

176 | Variable

Kubla Khan;
Or, a vision in a dream. A Fragment.

In Xanadu did Kubla Khan
A stately pleasure-dome decree:
Where Alph, the sacred river, ran
Through caverns measureless to man
5   Down to a sunless sea.
So twice five miles of fertile ground
With walls and towers were girdled round;
And there were gardens bright with sinuous rills,
Where blossomed many an incense-bearing tree;
10 And here were forests ancient as the hills,
   Enfolding sunny spots of greenery.

But oh! that deep romantic chasm which slanted
Down the green hill athwart a cedarn cover!
15   A savage place! as holy and enchanted
As e'er beneath a waning moon was haunted
By woman wailing for her demon-lover!
And from this chasm, with ceaseless turmoil seething,
As if this earth in fast thick pants were breathing,
20   A mighty fountain momently was forced:
Amid whose swift half-intermitted burst
Huge fragments vaulted like rebounding hail,
Or chaffy grain beneath the thresher's flail:
And mid these dancing rocks at once and ever
25   It flung up momently the sacred river.
Five miles meandering with a mazy motion
Through wood and dale the sacred river ran,
Then reached the caverns measureless to man,

S. Coleridge | 177

And sank in tumult to a lifeless ocean;
30   And 'mid this tumult Kubla heard from far
Ancestral voices prophesying war!
The shadow of the dome of pleasure
Floated midway on the waves;
Where was heard the mingled measure
35   From the fountain and the caves.
It was a miracle of rare device,
A sunny pleasure-dome with caves of ice!

A damsel with a dulcimer
40   In a vision once I saw:
It was an Abyssinian maid
And on her dulcimer she played,
Singing of Mount Abora.
Could I revive within me
45   Her symphony and song,
To such a deep delight 'twould win me,
That with music loud and long,
I would build that dome in air,
That sunny dome! those caves of ice!
50   And all who heard should see them there,
And all should cry, Beware! Beware!
His flashing eyes, his floating hair!
Weave a circle round him thrice,
And close your eyes with holy dread
55   For he on honey-dew hath fed,
And drunk the milk of Paradise.

Samuel Taylor Coleridge

178 | *Variable*

Gerard Manley Hopkins
POEMS (1918)

Author's Preface

The poems in this book are written some in Running Rhythm, the common rhythm in English use, some in Sprung Rhythm, and some in a mixture of the two. And those in the common rhythm are some counterpointed, some not.

Common English rhythm, called Running Rhythm above, is measured by feet of either two or three syllables and (putting aside the imperfect feet at the beginning and end of lines and also some unusual measures, in which feet seem to be paired together and double or composite feet to arise) never more or less.

Every foot has one principal stress or accent, and this or the syllable it falls on may be called the Stress of the foot and the other part, the one or two unaccented syllables, the Slack. Feet (and the rhythms made out of them) in which the stress comes first are called Falling Feet and Falling Rhythms, feet and rhythm in which the slack comes first are called Rising Feet and Rhythms, and if the stress is between two slacks there will be Rocking Feet and Rhythms. These distinctions are real and true to nature; but for purposes of scanning it is a great convenience to follow the example of music and take the stress always first, as the accent or the chief account always comes first in a musical bar. If this is done there will be in common English verse only two possible feet—the so-called accentual Trochee and Dactyl, and correspondingly only two possible uniform rhythms, the so-called Trochaic and Dactylic. But they may be mixed and then what the Greeks called a Logaoedic Rhythm arises. These are the facts and according to these the scanning of ordinary regularly-written English verse is very simple indeed and to bring in other principles is here unnecessary. . . .

Sprung Rhythm, as used in this book, is measured by feet of from one to four syllables, regularly, and for particular effects any number of weak or slack syllables may be used. It has one stress, which falls on the only syllable, if there is only one, if there are more, then scanning as above, on the first, and so gives rise to four sorts of feet, a monosyllable and the so-called accentual Trochee, Dactyl, and the First Paeon. And there will be four corresponding natural rhythms; but nominally the feet are mixed and any one may follow any other. And hence Sprung Rhythm differs from Running Rhythm in having or being only one nominal rhythm, a mixed or 'logaoedic' one, instead of three, but on the other hand in having twice the flexibility of foot, so that any two stresses may either follow one another running or be divided by one, two, or three slack syllables. But strict Sprung Rhythm cannot be counterpointed. In Sprung Rhythm, as in logaoedic rhythm generally, the feet are assumed to be equally long or strong and their seeming inequality is made up by pause or stressing.

Remark also that it is natural in Sprung Rhythm for the lines to be rove over, that is for the scanning of each line immediately to take up that of the one before, so that if the first has one or more syllables at its end the other must have so many the less at its beginning; and in fact the scanning runs on without break from the beginning, say, of a stanza to the end and all the stanza is one long strain, though written in lines asunder.

Two licenses are natural to Sprung Rhythm. The one is rests, as in music; but of this an example is scarcely to be found in this book, unless in the *Echoes,* second line. The other is hangers or outrides, that is one, two, or three slack syllables added to a foot and not counting in the nominal scanning. They are so called because they seem to hang below the line or ride forward or backward from it in another dimension than the line itself, according to a principle needless to explain here. These outriding half feet or hangers are marked by a loop underneath them, and plenty of them will be found. The other marks are easily understood, namely accents, where the reader might be in doubt which syllable should have the stress; slurs, that is loops over syllables, to tie them together into the time of one; little loops at the end of a line to shew that the rhyme goes on to the first letter of the next line; what in music are called pauses [symbol], to shew that the syllable should be dwelt on; and twirls [symbol], to mark reversed or counterpointed rhythm.

Note on the nature and history of Sprung Rhythm—Sprung Rhythm is the most natural of things. For (1) it is the rhythm of common speech and of written prose, when rhythm is perceived in them. (2) It is the rhythm of all but the most monotonously regular music, so that in the words of choruses and refrains and in songs written closely to music it arises. (3) It is found in nursery rhymes, weather saws, and so on; because, however these may have been once made in running rhythm, the terminations having dropped off by the change of language, the stresses come together and so the rhythm is sprung. (4) It arises in common verse when reversed or counterpointed, for the same reason.

But nevertheless in spite of all this and though Greek and Latin lyric verse, which is well known, and the old English verse seen in *Pierce Ploughman* are in sprung rhythm, it has in fact ceased to be used since the Elizabethan age, Greene being the last writer who can be said to have recognized it. For perhaps there was not, down to our days, a single, even short, poem in English in which sprung rhythm is employed—not for single effects or in fixed places—but as the governing principle of the scansion. I say this because the contrary has been asserted: if it is otherwise the poem should be cited.

180 | *Variable*

Pied Beauty

Glory be to God for dappled things –
For skies of couple-color as a brinded cow;
For rose-moles all in stipple upon trout that swim;
Fresh-firecoal chestnut-falls; finches' wings;
Landscape plotted and pieced – fold, fallow, and plough;
And áll trádes, their gear and tackle and trim.

All things counter, original, spare, strange;
Whatever is fickle, freckled (who knows how?)
With swift, slow; sweet, sour; adazzle, dim;
He fathers-forth whose beauty is past change:
Praise him.

Gerard Manley Hopkins

Carrion Comfort

Not, I'll not, carrion comfort, Despair, not feast on thee;
Not untwist—slack they may be—these last strands of man
In me ór, most weary, cry I can no more. I can;
4   Can something, hope, wish day come, not choose not to be.
But ah, but O thou terrible, why wouldst thou rude on me
Thy wring-world right foot rock? lay a lionlimb against me? scan
With darksome devouring eyes my bruisèd bones? and fan,
8   O in turns of tempest, me heaped there; me frantic to avoid thee and flee?

Why? That my chaff might fly; my grain lie, sheer and clear.
Nay in all that toil, that coil, since (seems) I kissed the rod,
12   Hand rather, my heart lo! lapped strength, stole joy, would laugh, chéer.
Cheer whom though? the hero whose heaven-handling flung me, fóot tród
Me? or me that fought him? O which one? is it each one? That night, that year
Of now done darkness I wretch lay wrestling with (my God!) my God.

Gerard Manley Hopkins

182 | Variable

Spring and Fall

to a young child

Márgarét, áre you gríeving
Over Goldengrove unleaving?
Leáves like the things of man, you
4   With your fresh thoughts care for, can you?
Ah! ás the heart grows older
It will come to such sights colder
By and by, nor spare a sigh
8   Though worlds of wanwood leafmeal lie;
And yet you wíll weep and know why.
Now no matter, child, the name:
Sórrow's spríngs áre the same.
12   Nor mouth had, no nor mind, expressed
What heart heard of, ghost guessed:
It ís the blight man was born for,
It is Margaret you mourn for.

Gerard Manley Hopkins

The Windhover
To Christ our Lord

I caught this morning morning's minion, king-
    dom of daylight's dauphin, dapple-dawn-drawn Falcon, in his riding
    Of the rolling level underneath him steady air, and striding
4 High there, how he rung upon the rein of a wimpling wing
In his ecstasy! then off, off forth on swing,
    As a skate's heel sweeps smooth on a bow-bend: the hurl and gliding
    Rebuffed the big wind. My heart in hiding
8 Stirred for a bird, – the achieve of, the mastery of the thing!

Brute beauty and valour and act, oh, air, pride, plume, here
    Buckle! AND the fire that breaks from thee then, a billion
Times told lovelier, more dangerous, O my chevalier!

12   No wonder of it: shéer plód makes plough down sillion
Shine, and blue-bleak embers, ah my dear,
    Fall, gall themselves, and gash gold-vermilion.

Gerard Manley Hopkins

184 | Variable

A Moment

The clouds had made a crimson crown
Above the mountains high.
The stormy sun was going down
In a stormy sky.

Why did you let your eyes so rest on me,
And hold your breath between?
In all the ages this can never be
As if it had not been.

Mary Elizabeth Coleridge

Jealousy

'The myrtle bush grew shady
Down by the ford.'
3 'Is it even so?' said my lady.
'Even so!' said my lord.
'The leaves are set too thick together
6 For the point of a sword.

'The arras in your room hangs close,
9 No light between!
You wedded one of those that see unseen.'
'Is it even so?' said the King's Majesty.
12 'Even so!' said the Queen.

Mary Elizabeth Coleridge

Shiloh: A Requiem

(April, 1862)

Skimming lightly, wheeling still,

The swallows fly low

3   Over the field in clouded days,

The forest-field of Shiloh—

Over the field where April rain

6   Solaced the parched ones stretched in pain

Through the pause of night

That followed the Sunday fight

9   Around the church of Shiloh—

The church so lone, the log-built one,

That echoed to many a parting groan

12   And natural prayer

Of dying foemen mingled there—

Foemen at morn, but friends at eve—

15   Fame or country least their care:

(What like a bullet can undeceive!)

But now they lie low,

18   While over them the swallows skim,

And all is hushed at Shiloh.

Herman Melville

AND DEATH shall have no dominion.

Dead man naked they shall be one

With the man in the wind and the west moon;

When their bones are picked clean and the clean bones gone,

They shall have stars at elbow and foot;

Though they go mad they shall be sane,

Though they sink through the sea they shall rise again;

Though lovers be lost love shall not;

And death shall have no dominion.

And death shall have no dominion.

Under the windings of the sea

They lying long shall not die windily;

Twisting on racks when sinews give way,

Strapped to a wheel, yet they shall not break;

Faith in their hands shall snap in two,

And the unicorn evils run them through;

Split all ends up they shan't crack;

And death shall have no dominion.

And death shall have no dominion.

No more may gulls cry at their ears

Or waves break loud on the seashores;

Where blew a flower may a flower no more

Lift its head to the blows of the rain;

Though they be mad and dead as nails,

Heads of the characters hammer through daisies;

Break in the sun till the sun breaks down,

And death shall have no dominion.

Dylan Thomas

The Lockless Door

It went many years,
But at last came a knock,
And I thought of the door
With no lock to lock.

I blew out the light,
I tip-toed the floor,
And raised both hands
In prayer to the door.

But the knock came again
My window was wide;
I climbed on the sill
And descended outside.

Back over the sill
I bade a "Come in"
To whoever the knock
At the door may have been.

So at a knock
I emptied my cage
To hide in the world
And alter with age.

Robert Frost

Tree at my Window

Tree at my window, window tree,
My sash is lowered when night comes on;
But let there never be curtain drawn
Between you and me.

Vague dream-head lifted out of the ground,
And thing next most diffuse to cloud,
Not all your light tongues talking aloud
Could be profound.

But tree, I have seen you taken and tossed,
And if you have seen me when I slept,
You have seen me when I was taken and swept
And all but lost.

That day she put our heads together,
Fate had her imagination about her,
Your head so much concerned with outer,
Mine with inner, weather.

Robert Frost

Lord Fulke Greville, 193

John Donne, 194

George Herbert, 196

Ben Jonson, 198

Aphra Behn, 200

Andrew Marvell, 202

John Keats, 208

Percy Bysshe Shelley, 214

Mary Elizabeth Coleridge, 220

William Butler Yeats, 222

Edna St. Vincent Millay, 226

Robert Frost, 236

Muse with Lyre,
by Henri-Jean Guillaume Martin

VERSE ITERATIVE

A line-length reiterates indefinitely.

Eurydice Follows Orpheus to the Upper World

Eurydice Torn from Orpheus

Caelica 99

Down in the depth of mine iniquity,
That ugly center of infernal spirits;
Where each sin feels her own deformity,
In those peculiar torments she inherits,
Depriv'd of human graces, and divine,
Even there appears this saving God of mine.

And in this fatal mirror of transgression,
Shows man as fruit of his degeneration,
The error's ugly infinite impression,
Which bears the faithless down to desperation;
Depriv'd of human graces, and divine,
Even there appears this saving God of mine.

In power and truth, Almighty and eternal,
Which on the sin reflects strange desolation,
With glory scourging all the Sprites infernal,
And uncreated hell with unprivation;
Depriv'd of human graces, not divine,
Even there appears this saving God of mine.

For on this sp'ritual cross condemned lying,
To pains infernal by eternal doom,
I see my Saviour for the same sins dying,
And from that hell I fear'd, to free me, come;
Depriv'd of human graces, not divine,
Thus hath his death rais'd up this soul of mine.

Lord Brooke Fulke Greville

194 | *Iterative*

A Valediction Forbidding Mourning

As virtuous men pass mildly away,

And whisper to their souls to go,

Whilst some of their sad friends do say

4   The breath goes now, and some say, No:

So let us melt, and make no noise,

No tear-floods, nor sigh-tempests move;

'Twere profanation of our joys

8   To tell the laity our love.

Moving of th' earth brings harms and fears,

Men reckon what it did, and meant;

But trepidation of the spheres,

12   Though greater far, is innocent.

Dull sublunary lovers' love

(Whose soul is sense) cannot admit

Absence, because it doth remove

16   Those things which elemented it.

But we by a love so much refined,

That our selves know not what it is,

Inter-assured of the mind,

20 Care less, eyes, lips, and hands to miss.

Our two souls therefore, which are one,

Though I must go, endure not yet

A breach, but an expansion,

24 Like gold to airy thinness beat.

If they be two, they are two so

As stiff twin compasses are two;

Thy soul, the fixed foot, makes no show

28 To move, but doth, if the other do.

And though it in the center sit,

Yet when the other far doth roam,

It leans and hearkens after it,

32 And grows erect, as that comes home.

Such wilt thou be to me, who must,

Like th' other foot, obliquely run;

Thy firmness makes my circle just,

36 And makes me end where I begun.

John Donne

196 | *Iterative*

Church Monuments

While that my soul repairs to her devotion,

Here I intomb my flesh, that it betimes

3   May take acquaintance of this heap of dust;

To which the blast of death's incessant motion,

Fed with the exhalation of our crimes,

6   Drives all at last. Therefore I gladly trust

My body to this school, that it may learn

To spell his elements, and find his birth

9   Written in dusty heraldry and lines;

Which dissolution sure doth best discern,

Comparing dust with dust, and earth with earth.

12   These laugh at jet, and marble put for signs,

To sever the good fellowship of dust,

And spoil the meeting. What shall point out them,

15   When they shall bow, and kneel, and fall down flat

To kiss those heaps, which now they have in trust?

Dear flesh, while I do pray, learn here thy stem

18   And true descent: that when thou shalt grow fat,

And wanton in thy cravings, thou mayst know,

That flesh is but the glass, which holds the dust

21   That measures all our time; which also shall

Be crumbled into dust. Mark, here below,

How tame these ashes are, how free from lust,

24   That thou mayst fit thyself against thy fall.

George Herbert

Colossians 3:3
Our life is hid with Christ in God.

My words and thoughts do both express this notion,
That Life hath with the sun a double motion.
The first Is straight, and our diurnal friend;
The other Hid, and doth obliquely bend.
One life is wrapt In flesh, and tends to earth:
The other winds towards Him, whose happy birth
Taught me to live here so, That still one eye
Should aim and shoot at that which Is on high;
Quitting with daily labour all My pleasure,
To gain at harvest an eternal Treasure.

George Herbert

198 | *Iterative*

A Celebration of Charis:
His Excuse for Loving

Let it not your wonder move,

Less your laughter, that I love.

Though I now write fifty years,

4   I have had, and have, my peers;

Poets, though divine, are men,

Some have lov'd as old again.

And it is not always face,

8   Clothes, or fortune, gives the grace;

Or the feature, or the youth.

But the language and the truth,

With the ardour and the passion,

12   Gives the lover weight and fashion.

If you then will read the story,

First prepare you to be sorry

That you never knew till now

16   Either whom to love or how;

But be glad, as soon with me,

When you know that this is she

Of whose beauty it was sung;

20   She shall make the old man young,

Keep the middle age at stay,

And let nothing high decay,

Till she be the reason why

24   All the world for love may die.

Ben Jonson

Evening: Barents Sea

The trawl of unquiet mind drops astern
Great lucid streamers bar the sky ahead
3   (bifurcated banners at a tourney)
light alchemizes the brass on the bridge
into sallow gold
6   now the short northern
autumn day closes quickly
                                              the thin coast
9   (of grey Norway is it, or of Russia?)
distinguished only as a formal change
in the pattern of clouds on our port side
12   on the deck the strung lights illuminate no
movement but the sullen swill of water
in the washer, but the unnatural way
15   dead starfish and disregarded dabs swim
in the strict seas surging through the bilges
and out. A fishgut hangs like a hank of
18   hair from the iron grill in a pound board
brighter now that the sun, the fishfinder's
green bleep catches the skipper's intentness
21   and the trawl is down, is out, is catching!

Ben Jonson

Love Armed
Song from Abdelazar

Love in Fantastic Triumph sat,
Whilst Bleeding Hearts around him flowed,
For whom Fresh pains he did Create,
And strange Tyrannic power he showed;
From thy Bright Eyes he took his fire,
Which round about, in sport he hurled;
But 'twas from mine he took desire
Enough to undo the Amorous World.

From me he took his sighs and tears,
From thee his Pride and Cruelty;
From me his Languishments and Fears,
And every Killing Dart from thee;
Thus thou and I, the God have armed,
And set him up a Deity;
But my poor Heart alone is harmed,
Whilst thine the Victor is, and free.

Aphra Behn

A thousand Martyrs I have made,
All sacrific'd to my desire;
A thousand Beauties have betray'd,
That languish in resistless Fire.
The untam'd Heart to hand I brought,
And fixt the wild and wand'ring Thought.

I never vow'd nor sigh'd in vain
But both, tho' false, were well receiv'd.
The Fair are pleas'd to give us pain,
And what they wish is soon believ'd.
And tho' I talked of Wounds and Smart,
Loves Pleasures only toucht my Heart.

Alone the Glory and the Spoil
I always Laughing bore away;
The Triumphs, without Pain or Toil,
Without the Hell, the Heav'n of Joy.
And while I thus at random rove
Despise the Fools that whine for Love.

Aphra Behn

The Definition of Love

My love is of a birth as rare
As 'tis for object strange and high;
It was begotten by Despair
Upon Impossibility.

Magnanimous Despair alone
Could show me so divine a thing
Where feeble Hope could ne'er have flown,
But vainly flapp'd its tinsel wing.

And yet I quickly might arrive
Where my extended soul is fixt,
But Fate does iron wedges drive,
And always crowds itself betwixt.

For Fate with jealous eye does see
Two perfect loves, nor lets them close;
Their union would her ruin be,
And her tyrannic pow'r depose.

And therefore her decrees of steel
Us as the distant poles have plac'd,
20 (Though love's whole world on us doth wheel)
Not by themselves to be embrac'd;

Unless the giddy heaven fall,
And earth some new convulsion tear;
24 And, us to join, the world should all
Be cramp'd into a planisphere.

As lines, so loves oblique may well
Themselves in every angle greet;
28 But ours so truly parallel,
Though infinite, can never meet.

Therefore the love which us doth bind,
But Fate so enviously debars,
32 Is the conjunction of the mind,
And opposition of the stars.

Andrew Marvell

204 | *Iterative*

To His Coy Mistress

Had we but world enough and time,

This coyness, lady, were no crime.

We would sit down, and think which way

To walk, and pass our long love's day.

Thou by the Indian Ganges' side

Shouldst rubies find; I by the tide

Of Humber would complain. I would

Love you ten years before the flood,

And you should, if you please, refuse

Till the conversion of the Jews.

My vegetable love should grow

Vaster than empires and more slow;

An hundred years should go to praise

Thine eyes, and on thy forehead gaze;

Two hundred to adore each breast,

But thirty thousand to the rest;

An age at least to every part,

And the last age should show your heart.

For, lady, you deserve this state,

Nor would I love at lower rate.

But at my back I always hear

Time's wingèd chariot hurrying near;

And yonder all before us lie

Deserts of vast eternity.

Thy beauty shall no more be found;

Nor, in thy marble vault, shall sound

28 My echoing song; then worms shall try

That long-preserved virginity,

And your quaint honour turn to dust,

And into ashes all my lust;

32 The grave's a fine and private place,

But none, I think, do there embrace.

Now therefore, while the youthful hue

Sits on thy skin like morning dew,

36 And while thy willing soul transpires

At every pore with instant fires,

Now let us sport us while we may,

And now, like amorous birds of prey,

40 Rather at once our time devour

Than languish in his slow-chapped power.

Let us roll all our strength and all

Our sweetness up into one ball,

44 And tear our pleasures with rough strife

Through the iron gates of life:

Thus, though we cannot make our sun

Stand still, yet we will make him run.

Andrew Marvell

206 | *Iterative*

A Dialogue
Between the Soul and the Body

SOUL

O who shall, from this dungeon, raise

A soul enslav'd so many ways?

With bolts of bones, that fetter'd stands

In feet, and manacled in hands;

5 Here blinded with an eye, and there

Deaf with the drumming of an ear;

A soul hung up, as 'twere, in chains

Of nerves, and arteries, and veins;

Tortur'd, besides each other part,

10 In a vain head, and double heart.

BODY

O who shall me deliver whole

From bonds of this tyrannic soul?

Which, stretch'd upright, impales me so

That mine own precipice I go;

15 And warms and moves this needless frame,

(A fever could but do the same)

And, wanting where its spite to try,

Has made me live to let me die.

A body that could never rest,

20 Since this ill spirit it possest.

SOUL

What magic could me thus confine
Within another's grief to pine?
Where whatsoever it complain,
I feel, that cannot feel, the pain;
25 And all my care itself employs;
That to preserve which me destroys;
Constrain'd not only to endure
Diseases, but, what's worse, the cure;
And ready oft the port to gain,
30 Am shipwreck'd into health again.

BODY

But physic yet could never reach
The maladies thou me dost teach;
Whom first the cramp of hope does tear,
And then the palsy shakes of fear;
35 The pestilence of love does heat,
Or hatred's hidden ulcer eat;
Joy's cheerful madness does perplex,
Or sorrow's other madness vex;
Which knowledge forces me to know,
40 And memory will not forego.
What but a soul could have the wit
To build me up for sin so fit?
So architects do square and hew
Green trees that in the forest grew.

Andrew Marvell

Ode to a Nightingale

My heart aches, and a drowsy numbness pains
My sense, as though of hemlock I had drunk,
Or emptied some dull opiate to the drains
One minute past, and Lethe-wards had sunk:
'Tis not through envy of thy happy lot,
But being too happy in thine happiness,—
That thou, light-winged Dryad of the trees
In some melodious plot
Of beechen green, and shadows numberless,
Singest of summer in full-throated ease.

O, for a draught of vintage! that hath been
Cool'd a long age in the deep-delved earth,
Tasting of Flora and the country green,
Dance, and Provençal song, and sunburnt mirth!
O for a beaker full of the warm South,
Full of the true, the blushful Hippocrene,
With beaded bubbles winking at the brim,
And purple-stained mouth;
That I might drink, and leave the world unseen,
And with thee fade away into the forest dim
:

Fade far away, dissolve, and quite forget
What thou among the leaves hast never known,
The weariness, the fever, and the fret
Here, where men sit and hear each other groan;
25   Where palsy shakes a few, sad, last gray hairs,
Where youth grows pale, and spectre-thin, and dies;
Where but to think is to be full of sorrow
And leaden-eyed despairs,
Where Beauty cannot keep her lustrous eyes,
30   Or new Love pine at them beyond to-morrow.

Away! away! for I will fly to thee,
Not charioted by Bacchus and his pards,
But on the viewless wings of Poesy,
Though the dull brain perplexes and retards:
35   Already with thee! tender is the night,
And haply the Queen-Moon is on her throne,
Cluster'd around by all her starry Fays;
But here there is no light,
Save what from heaven is with the breezes blown
40   Through verdurous glooms and winding mossy ways.

210 | *Iterative*

I cannot see what flowers are at my feet,
Nor what soft incense hangs upon the boughs,
But, in embalmed darkness, guess each sweet
Wherewith the seasonable month endows
45 The grass, the thicket, and the fruit-tree wild;
White hawthorn, and the pastoral eglantine;
Fast fading violets cover'd up in leaves;
And mid-May's eldest child,
The coming musk-rose, full of dewy wine,
50 The murmurous haunt of flies on summer eves.

Darkling I listen; and, for many a time
I have been half in love with easeful Death,
Call'd him soft names in many a mused rhyme,
To take into the air my quiet breath;
55 Now more than ever seems it rich to die,
To cease upon the midnight with no pain,
While thou art pouring forth thy soul abroad
In such an ecstasy!
Still wouldst thou sing, and I have ears in vain—
60 To thy high requiem become a sod.

Thou wast not born for death, immortal Bird!

No hungry generations tread thee down;

65 The voice I hear this passing night was heard

In ancient days by emperor and clown:

Perhaps the self-same song that found a path

Through the sad heart of Ruth, when, sick for home,

She stood in tears amid the alien corn;

70 The same that oft-times hath

Charm'd magic casements, opening on the foam

Of perilous seas, in faery lands forlorn.

Forlorn! the very word is like a bell

To toll me back from thee to my sole self!

75 Adieu! the fancy cannot cheat so well

As she is fam'd to do, deceiving elf.

Adieu! adieu! thy plaintive anthem fades

Past the near meadows, over the still stream,

Up the hill-side; and now 'tis buried deep

80 In the next valley-glades:

Was it a vision, or a waking dream?

Fled is that music:—Do I wake or sleep?

John Keats

212 | *Iterative*

Ode on a Grecian Urn

Thou still unravish'd bride of quietness,

Thou foster-child of silence and slow time,

Sylvan historian, who canst thus express

A flowery tale more sweetly than our rhyme:

5   What leaf-fring'd legend haunts about thy shape

Of deities or mortals, or of both,

In Tempe or the dales of Arcady?

What men or gods are these? What maidens loth?

What mad pursuit? What struggle to escape?

10   What pipes and timbrels? What wild ecstasy?

Heard melodies are sweet, but those unheard

Are sweeter; therefore, ye soft pipes, play on;

Not to the sensual ear, but, more endear'd,

Pipe to the spirit ditties of no tone:

15   Fair youth, beneath the trees, thou canst not leave

Thy song, nor ever can those trees be bare;

Bold Lover, never, never canst thou kiss,

Though winning near the goal yet, do not grieve;

She cannot fade, though thou hast not thy bliss,

20   For ever wilt thou love, and she be fair!

Ah, happy, happy boughs! that cannot shed

Your leaves, nor ever bid the Spring adieu;

And, happy melodist, unwearied,

For ever piping songs for ever new;

25   More happy love! more happy, happy love!

For ever warm and still to be enjoy'd,

For ever panting, and for ever young;

All breathing human passion far above,

That leaves a heart high-sorrowful and cloy'd,

30   A burning forehead, and a parching tongue.

Who are these coming to the sacrifice?

To what green altar, O mysterious priest,

Lead'st thou that heifer lowing at the skies,

And all her silken flanks with garlands drest?

35   What little town by river or sea shore,

Or mountain-built with peaceful citadel,

Is emptied of this folk, this pious morn?

And, little town, thy streets for evermore

Will silent be; and not a soul to tell

40   Why thou art desolate, can e'er return.

O Attic shape! Fair attitude! with brede

Of marble men and maidens overwrought,

With forest branches and the trodden weed;

Thou, silent form, dost tease us out of thought

45   As doth eternity: Cold Pastoral!

When old age shall this generation waste,

Thou shalt remain, in midst of other woe

Than ours, a friend to man, to whom thou say'st,

"Beauty is truth, truth beauty,—that is all

50   Ye know on earth, and all ye need to know."

John Keats

214 | *Iterative*

Mont Blanc:
Lines Written in the Vale of Chamouni

I

The everlasting universe of things
Flows through the mind, and rolls its rapid waves,
Now dark—now glittering—now reflecting gloom—
4   Now lending splendor, where from secret springs
The source of human thought its tribute brings
Of waters—with a sound but half its own,
Such as a feeble brook will oft assume,
8   In the wild woods, among the mountains lone,
Where waterfalls around it leap for ever,
Where woods and winds contend, and a vast river
Over its rocks ceaselessly bursts and raves.

II

12   Thus thou, Ravine of Arve—dark, deep Ravine—
Thou many-color'd, many-voiced vale,
Over whose pines, and crags, and caverns sail
Fast cloud-shadows and sunbeams: awful scene,
16   Where Power in likeness of the Arve comes down
From the ice-gulfs that gird his secret throne,
Bursting through these dark mountains like the flame
Of lightning through the tempest;—thou dost lie,
20   Thy giant brood of pines around thee clinging,
Children of elder time, in whose devotion

The chainless winds still come and ever came
To drink their odours, and their mighty swinging
24   To hear—an old and solemn harmony;
Thine earthly rainbows stretch'd across the sweep
Of the aethereal waterfall, whose veil
Robes some unsculptur'd image; the strange sleep
28   Which when the voices of the desert fail
Wraps all in its own deep eternity;
Thy caverns echoing to the Arve's commotion,
A loud, lone sound no other sound can tame;
32   Thou art pervaded with that ceaseless motion,
Thou art the path of that unresting sound—
Dizzy Ravine! and when I gaze on thee
I seem as in a trance sublime and strange
36   To muse on my own separate fantasy,
My own, my human mind, which passively
Now renders and receives fast influencings,
Holding an unremitting interchange
40   With the clear universe of things around;
One legion of wild thoughts, whose wandering wings
Now float above thy darkness, and now rest
Where that or thou art no unbidden guest,
44   In the still cave of the witch Poesy,
Seeking among the shadows that pass by
Ghosts of all things that are, some shade of thee,
Some phantom, some faint image; till the breast
48   From which they fled recalls them, thou art there!

216 | *Iterative*

III

Some say that gleams of a remoter world
Visit the soul in sleep, that death is slumber,
And that its shapes the busy thoughts outnumber

52

Of those who wake and live.—I look on high;
Has some unknown omnipotence unfurl'd
The veil of life and death? or do I lie

56

In dream, and does the mightier world of sleep
Spread far around and inaccessibly
Its circles? For the very spirit fails,
Driven like a homeless cloud from steep to steep

60

That vanishes among the viewless gales!
Far, far above, piercing the infinite sky,
Mont Blanc appears—still, snowy, and serene;
Its subject mountains their unearthly forms

64

Pile around it, ice and rock; broad vales between
Of frozen floods, unfathomable deeps,
Blue as the overhanging heaven, that spread
And wind among the accumulated steeps;

68

A desert peopled by the storms alone,
Save when the eagle brings some hunter's bone,
And the wolf tracks her there—how hideously
Its shapes are heap'd around! rude, bare, and high,

72

Ghastly, and scarr'd, and riven.—Is this the scene
Where the old Earthquake-daemon taught her young
Ruin? Were these their toys? or did a sea
Of fire envelop once this silent snow?

76 None can reply—all seems eternal now.
The wilderness has a mysterious tongue
Which teaches awful doubt, or faith so mild,
So solemn, so serene, that man may be,
80 But for such faith, with Nature reconcil'd;
Thou hast a voice, great Mountain, to repeal
Large codes of fraud and woe; not understood
By all, but which the wise, and great, and good
84 Interpret, or make felt, or deeply feel.

IV

The fields, the lakes, the forests, and the streams,
Ocean, and all the living things that dwell
Within the daedal earth; lightning, and rain,
88 Earthquake, and fiery flood, and hurricane,
The torpor of the year when feeble dreams
Visit the hidden buds, or dreamless sleep
Holds every future leaf and flower; the bound
92 With which from that detested trance they leap;
The works and ways of man, their death and birth,
And that of him and all that his may be;
All things that move and breathe with toil and sound
96 Are born and die; revolve, subside, and swell.
Power dwells apart in its tranquillity,
Remote, serene, and inaccessible:

100

218 | *Iterative*

And this, the naked countenance of earth,

On which I gaze, even these primeval mountains

Teach the adverting mind. The glaciers creep

104 Like snakes that watch their prey, from their far fountains,

Slow rolling on; there, many a precipice

Frost and the Sun in scorn of mortal power

Have pil'd: dome, pyramid, and pinnacle,

108 A city of death, distinct with many a tower

And wall impregnable of beaming ice.

Yet not a city, but a flood of ruin

Is there, that from the boundaries of the sky

112 Rolls its perpetual stream; vast pines are strewing

Its destin'd path, or in the mangled soil

Branchless and shatter'd stand; the rocks, drawn down

From yon remotest waste, have overthrown

116 The limits of the dead and living world,

Never to be reclaim'd. The dwelling-place

Of insects, beasts, and birds, becomes its spoil;

Their food and their retreat for ever gone,

120 So much of life and joy is lost. The race

Of man flies far in dread; his work and dwelling

Vanish, like smoke before the tempest's stream,

And their place is not known. Below, vast caves

124 Shine in the rushing torrents' restless gleam,

Which from those secret chasms in tumult welling

Meet in the vale, and one majestic River,

The breath and blood of distant lands, for ever

128   Rolls its loud waters to the ocean-waves,

Breathes its swift vapours to the circling air.

V

Mont Blanc yet gleams on high:—the power is there,

The still and solemn power of many sights,

132   And many sounds, and much of life and death.

In the calm darkness of the moonless nights,

In the lone glare of day, the snows descend

Upon that Mountain; none beholds them there,

136   Nor when the flakes burn in the sinking sun,

Or the star-beams dart through them. Winds contend

Silently there, and heap the snow with breath

Rapid and strong, but silently! Its home

140   The voiceless lightning in these solitudes

Keeps innocently, and like vapour broods

Over the snow. The secret Strength of things

Which governs thought, and to the infinite dome

144   Of Heaven is as a law, inhabits thee!

And what were thou, and earth, and stars, and sea,

If to the human mind's imaginings

Silence and solitude were vacancy?

Percy Bysshe Shelley

The Other Side of a Mirror

I sat before my glass one day,
And conjured up a vision bare,
Unlike the aspects glad and gay,
That erst were found reflected there –
The vision of a woman, wild
With more than womanly despair.

Her hair stood back on either side
A face bereft of loveliness.
It had no envy now to hide
What once no man on earth could guess.
It formed the thorny aureole
Of hard unsanctified distress.

Her lips were open – not a sound
Came through the parted lines of red.
Whate'er it was, the hideous wound
In silence and in secret bled.
No sigh relieved her speechless woe,
She had no voice to speak her dread.

And in her lurid eyes there shone
The dying flame of life's desire,
21   Made mad because its hope was gone,
And kindled at the leaping fire
Of jealousy, and fierce revenge,
24   And strength that could not change nor tire.

Shade of a shadow in the glass,
O set the crystal surface free!
27   Pass – as the fairer visions pass –
Nor ever more return, to be
The ghost of a distracted hour,
30   That heard me whisper, "I am she!"

Mary Elizabeth Coleridge

Sailing to Byzantium

I

That is no country for old men. The young
In one another's arms, birds in the trees,
—Those dying generations—at their song,
4 The salmon-falls, the mackerel-crowded seas,
Fish, flesh, or fowl, commend all summer long
Whatever is begotten, born, and dies.
Caught in that sensual music all neglect
8 Monuments of unageing intellect.

II

An aged man is but a paltry thing,
A tattered coat upon a stick, unless
Soul clap its hands and sing, and louder sing
12 For every tatter in its mortal dress,
Nor is there singing school but studying
Monuments of its own magnificence;
And therefore I have sailed the seas and come
16 To the holy city of Byzantium.

III

O sages standing in God's holy fire

As in the gold mosaic of a wall,

Come from the holy fire, perne in a gyre,

20   And be the singing-masters of my soul.

Consume my heart away; sick with desire

And fastened to a dying animal

It knows not what it is; and gather me

24   Into the artifice of eternity.

IV

Once out of nature I shall never take

My bodily form from any natural thing,

But such a form as Grecian goldsmiths make

28   Of hammered gold and gold enamelling

To keep a drowsy Emperor awake;

Or set upon a golden bough to sing

To lords and ladies of Byzantium

32   Of what is past, or passing, or to come.

William Butler Yeats

The Second Coming

Turning and turning in the widening gyre
The falcon cannot hear the falconer;
Things fall apart; the centre cannot hold;
Mere anarchy is loosed upon the world,
The blood-dimmed tide is loosed, and everywhere
The ceremony of innocence is drowned;
The best lack all conviction, while the worst
Are full of passionate intensity.
Surely some revelation is at hand;
Surely the Second Coming is at hand.
The Second Coming! Hardly are those words out
When a vast image out of Spiritus Mundi
Troubles my sight: somewhere in sands of the desert
A shape with lion body and the head of a man,
A gaze blank and pitiless as the sun,
Is moving its slow thighs, while all about it
Reel shadows of the indignant desert birds.
The darkness drops again; but now I know
That twenty centuries of stony sleep
Were vexed to nightmare by a rocking cradle,
And what rough beast, its hour come round at last,
Slouches towards Bethlehem to be born?

William Butler Yeats

Do not go gentle into that good night,
Old age should burn and rave at close of day;
3   Rage, rage against the dying of the light.

Though wise men at their end know dark is right,
Because their words had forked no lightning they
6   Do not go gentle into that good night.

Good men, the last wave by, crying how bright
Their frail deeds might have danced in a green bay,
9   Rage, rage against the dying of the light.

Wild men who caught and sang the sun in flight,
And learn, too late, they grieved it on its way,
12   Do not go gentle into that good night.

Grave men, near death, who see with blinding sight
Blind eyes could blaze like meteors and be gay,
15   Rage, rage against the dying of the light.

And you, my father, there on the sad height,
Curse, bless, me now with your fierce tears, I pray.
18   Do not go gentle into that good night.
Rage, rage against the dying of the light.

Dylan Thomas

226 | *Iterative*

Renascence

All I could see from where I stood

Was three long mountains and a wood;

I turned and looked another way,

4   And saw three islands in a bay.

So with my eyes I traced the line

Of the horizon, thin and fine,

Straight around till I was come

8   Back to where I'd started from;

And all I saw from where I stood

Was three long mountains and a wood.

Over these things I could not see;

12   These were the things that bounded me;

And I could touch them with my hand,

Almost, I thought, from where I stand.

And all at once things seemed so small

16   My breath came short, and scarce at all.

But, sure, the sky is big, I said;

Miles and miles above my head;

So here upon my back I'll lie

20   And look my fill into the sky.

And so I looked, and, after all,

The sky was not so very tall.

The sky, I said, must somewhere stop,

24   And—sure enough!—I see the top!

The sky, I thought, is not so grand;

I 'most could touch it with my hand!

And reaching up my hand to try,

28   I screamed to feel it touch the sky.

I screamed, and—lo!—Infinity

Came down and settled over me;

Forced back my scream into my chest,

32   Bent back my arm upon my breast,

And, pressing of the Undefined

The definition on my mind,

Held up before my eyes a glass

36   Through which my shrinking sight did pass

Until it seemed I must behold

Immensity made manifold;

Whispered to me a word whose sound

40   Deafened the air for worlds around,

And brought unmuffled to my ears

The gossiping of friendly spheres,

The creaking of the tented sky,

44   The ticking of Eternity.

228 | *Iterative*

I saw and heard, and knew at last

The How and Why of all things, past,

And present, and forevermore.

48   The Universe, cleft to the core,

Lay open to my probing sense

That, sick'ning, I would fain pluck thence

But could not,—nay! But needs must suck

52   At the great wound, and could not pluck

My lips away till I had drawn

All venom out.—Ah, fearful pawn!

For my omniscience paid I toll

56   In infinite remorse of soul.

All sin was of my sinning, all

Atoning mine, and mine the gall

Of all regret. Mine was the weight

60   Of every brooded wrong, the hate

That stood behind each envious thrust,

Mine every greed, mine every lust.

And all the while for every grief,

64   Each suffering, I craved relief

With individual desire,—

Craved all in vain! And felt fierce fire

About a thousand people crawl;

68   Perished with each,—then mourned for all!

A man was starving in Capri;

He moved his eyes and looked at me;

I felt his gaze, I heard his moan,

72 And knew his hunger as my own.

I saw at sea a great fog bank

Between two ships that struck and sank;

A thousand screams the heavens smote;

76 And every scream tore through my throat.

No hurt I did not feel, no death

That was not mine; mine each last breath

That, crying, met an answering cry

80 From the compassion that was I.

All suffering mine, and mine its rod;

Mine, pity like the pity of God.

Ah, awful weight! Infinity

84 Pressed down upon the finite Me!

My anguished spirit, like a bird,

Beating against my lips I heard;

Yet lay the weight so close about

88 There was no room for it without.

And so beneath the weight lay I

And suffered death, but could not die.

230 | *Iterative*

Long had I lain thus, craving death,

92   When quietly the earth beneath

Gave way, and inch by inch, so great

At last had grown the crushing weight,

Into the earth I sank till I

96   Full six feet under ground did lie,

And sank no more,—there is no weight

Can follow here, however great.

From off my breast I felt it roll,

100   And as it went my tortured soul

Burst forth and fled in such a gust

That all about me swirled the dust.

Deep in the earth I rested now;

104   Cool is its hand upon the brow

And soft its breast beneath the head

Of one who is so gladly dead.

And all at once, and over all

108   The pitying rain began to fall;

I lay and heard each pattering hoof

Upon my lowly, thatched roof,

And seemed to love the sound far more

112   Than ever I had done before.

For rain it hath a friendly sound

To one who's six feet underground;

And scarce the friendly voice or face:

116   A grave is such a quiet place.

The rain, I said, is kind to come

And speak to me in my new home.

I would I were alive again

120   To kiss the fingers of the rain,

To drink into my eyes the shine

Of every slanting silver line,

To catch the freshened, fragrant breeze

124   From drenched and dripping apple-trees.

For soon the shower will be done,

And then the broad face of the sun

Will laugh above the rain-soaked earth

128   Until the world with answering mirth

Shakes joyously, and each round drop

Rolls, twinkling, from its grass-blade top.

How can I bear it; buried here,

132   While overhead the sky grows clear

And blue again after the storm?

O, multi-colored, multiform,

232 | *Iterative*

Beloved beauty over me,

136   That I shall never, never see

Again! Spring-silver, autumn-gold,

That I shall never more behold!

Sleeping your myriad magics through,

140   Close-sepulchred away from you!

O God, I cried, give me new birth,

And put me back upon the earth!

Upset each cloud's gigantic gourd

144   And let the heavy rain, down-poured

In one big torrent, set me free,

Washing my grave away from me!

I ceased; and through the breathless hush

148   That answered me, the far-off rush

Of herald wings came whispering

Like music down the vibrant string

Of my ascending prayer, and—crash!

152   Before the wild wind's whistling lash

The startled storm-clouds reared on high

And plunged in terror down the sky,

And the big rain in one black wave

156   Fell from the sky and struck my grave.

Millay | 233

I know not how such things can be;

I only know there came to me

A fragrance such as never clings

160   To aught save happy living things;

A sound as of some joyous elf

Singing sweet songs to please himself,

And, through and over everything,

164   A sense of glad awakening.

The grass, a-tiptoe at my ear,

Whispering to me I could hear;

I felt the rain's cool finger-tips

168   Brushed tenderly across my lips,

Laid gently on my sealed sight,

And all at once the heavy night

Fell from my eyes and I could see,—

172   A drenched and dripping apple-tree,

A last long line of silver rain,

A sky grown clear and blue again.

And as I looked a quickening gust

176   Of wind blew up to me and thrust

Into my face a miracle

Of orchard-breath, and with the smell,—

I know not how such things can be!—

180   I breathed my soul back into me.

234 | *Iterative*

Ah! Up then from the ground sprang I
And hailed the earth with such a cry
As is not heard save from a man
184 Who has been dead, and lives again.

About the trees my arms I wound;
Like one gone mad I hugged the ground;
I raised my quivering arms on high;
188 I laughed and laughed into the sky,
Till at my throat a strangling sob
Caught fiercely, and a great heart-throb
Sent instant tears into my eyes;
192 O God, I cried, no dark disguise
Can e'er hereafter hide from me
Thy radiant identity!

Thou canst not move across the grass
196 But my quick eyes will see Thee pass,
Nor speak, however silently,
But my hushed voice will answer Thee.
I know the path that tells Thy way
200 Through the cool eve of every day;
God, I can push the grass apart
And lay my finger on Thy heart!

The world stands out on either side

No wider than the heart is wide;

3 Above the world is stretched the sky,—

No higher than the soul is high.

The heart can push the sea and land

6 Farther away on either hand;

The soul can split the sky in two,

And let the face of God shine through.

9 But East and West will pinch the heart

That can not keep them pushed apart;

And he whose soul is flat—the sky

12 Will cave in on him by and by.

Edna St. Vincent Millay

236 | *Iterative*

For Once, Then, Something

Others taunt me with having knelt at well-curbs
Always wrong to the light, so never seeing
3   Deeper down in the well than where the water
Gives me back in a shining surface picture
Me myself in the summer heaven godlike
6   Looking out of a wreath of fern and cloud puffs.
Once, when trying with chin against a well-curb,
I discerned, as I thought, beyond the picture,
9   Through the picture, a something white, uncertain,
Something more of the depths—and then I lost it.
Water came to rebuke the too clear water.
12 One drop fell from a fern, and lo, a ripple
Shook whatever it was lay there at bottom,
Blurred it, blotted it out. What was that whiteness?
15 Truth? A pebble of quartz? For once, then, something.

Robert Frost

Acquainted with the Night

I have been one acquainted with the night.
I have walked out in rain—and back in rain.
3   I have outwalked the furthest city light.

I have looked down the saddest city lane.
I have passed by the watchman on his beat
6   And dropped my eyes, unwilling to explain.

I have stood still and stopped the sound of feet
When far away an interrupted cry
9   Came over houses from another street,

But not to call me back or say good-bye;
And further still at an unearthly height,
12   One luminary clock against the sky
Proclaimed the time was neither wrong nor right.
I have been one acquainted with the night.

Robert Frost

Emily Dickinson, 241

Edna St. Vincent Millay, 245

Wallace Stevens, 246

Hilda Doolittle (H.D.), 250

e.e. cummings, 257

Ezra Pound, 262

T.S. Eliot, 287

FREE VERSE

Irregular line, rhythm, rhyme, syntax.

La Muse, Picasso

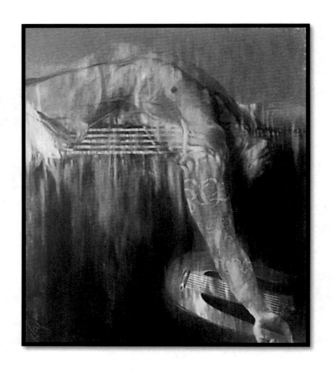

The Death of Orpheus
Antonio García Vega

Banish Air from Air—
Divide Light if you dare—
They'll meet

3

While Cubes in a Drop
Or Pellets of Shape

6

Fit—
Films cannot annul
Odors return whole

9

Force Flame
And with a Blonde push
Over your impotence

12

Flits Steam.

Emily Dickinson

242 | Free Verse

After great pain, a formal feeling comes—
The Nerves sit ceremonious, like Tombs—
The stiff Heart questions 'was it He, that bore,'
And 'Yesterday, or Centuries before'?

5 The Feet, mechanical, go round—
A Wooden way
Of Ground, or Air, or Ought—
Regardless grown,
A Quartz contentment, like a stone—

10 This is the Hour of Lead—
Remembered, if outlived,
As Freezing persons, recollect the Snow—
First - Chill - then Stupor - then the letting go—

Emily Dickinson

One need not be a Chamber—to be Haunted—
One need not be a House—
The Brain has Corridors—surpassing
Material Place—

Far safer, of a Midnight Meeting
External Ghost
Than its interior Confronting—
That Cooler Host.

Far safer, through an Abbey gallop,
The Stones a'chase—
Than Unarmed, one's a'self encounter—
In lonesome Place—

Ourself behind ourself, concealed—
Should startle most—
Assassin hid in our Apartment—
Be Horror's least.

The Body—borrows a Revolver—
He bolts the Door—
O'erlooking a superior spectre—
Or More—

Emily Dickinson

244 | *Dickinson*

In Winter in my Room
I came upon a Worm—
Pink, lank and warm—
But as he was a worm
And worms presume
Not quite with him at home—
Secured him by a string
To something neighboring
And went along.

A Trifle afterward
A thing occurred
I'd not believe it if I heard
But state with creeping blood—
A snake with mottles rare
Surveyed my chamber floor
In feature as the worm before
But ringed with power—

The very string with which
I tied him—too
When he was mean and new
That string was there—

I shrank—"How fair you are"!
Propitiation's claw—
"Afraid," he hissed
"Of me"?
"No cordiality"—
He fathomed me—
Then to a Rhythm Slim
Secreted in his Form
As Patterns swim
Projected him.

That time I flew
Both eyes his way
Lest he pursue
Nor ever ceased to run
Till in a distant Town
Towns on from mine
I set me down
This was a dream.

Emily Dickinson

Spring

To what purpose, April, do you return again?

Beauty is not enough.

3   You can no longer quiet me with the redness

Of little leaves opening stickily.

I know what I know.

6   The sun is hot on my neck as I observe

The spikes of the crocus.

The smell of the earth is good.

9   It is apparent that there is no death.

But what does that signify?

Not only under ground are the brains of men

12   Eaten by maggots.

Life in itself

Is nothing,

15   An empty cup, a flight of uncarpeted stairs.

It is not enough that yearly, down this hill,

April

18   Comes like an idiot, babbling and strewing flowers.

Edna St. Vincent Millay

246 | *Free Verse*

The Snow Man

One must have a mind of winter
To regard the frost and the boughs
Of the pine-trees crusted with snow;

And have been cold a long time
To behold the junipers shagged with ice,
The spruces rough in the distant glitter

Of the January sun; and not to think
Of any misery in the sound of the wind,
In the sound of a few leaves,

Which is the sound of the land
Full of the same wind
That is blowing in the same bare place

For the listener, who listens in the snow,
And, nothing himself, beholds
Nothing that is not there and the nothing that is.

Wallace Stevens

The Emperor of Ice-Cream

Call the roller of big cigars,

The muscular one, and bid him whip

In kitchen cups concupiscent curds.

4   Let the wenches dawdle in such dress

As they are used to wear, and let the boys

Bring flowers in last month's newspapers.

Let be be finale of seem.

8   The only emperor is the emperor of ice-cream.

Take from the dresser of deal,

Lacking the three glass knobs, that sheet

On which she embroidered fantails once

12   And spread it so as to cover her face.

If her horny feet protrude, they come

To show how cold she is, and dumb.

Let the lamp affix its beam.

16   The only emperor is the emperor of ice-cream.

Wallace Stevens

248 | *Free Verse*

Thirteen Ways of Looking at a Blackbird

I
Among twenty snowy mountains,
The only moving thing
Was the eye of the blackbird.

II
I was of three minds,
Like a tree
In which there are three blackbirds.

III
The blackbird whirled in the autumn winds.
It was a small part of the pantomime.

IV
A man and a woman
Are one.
A man and a woman and a blackbird
Are one.

V
I do not know which to prefer,
The beauty of inflections
Or the beauty of innuendoes,
The blackbird whistling
Or just after.

VI

Icicles filled the long window
With barbaric glass.
The shadow of the blackbird
Crossed it, to and fro.
The mood
Traced in the shadow
An indecipherable cause.

VII

O thin men of Haddam,
Why do you imagine golden birds?
Do you not see how the blackbird
Walks around the feet
Of the women about you?

VIII

I know noble accents
And lucid, inescapable rhythms;
But I know, too,
That the blackbird is involved
In what I know.

IX

When the blackbird flew out of sight,
It marked the edge
Of one of many circles.

X

At the sight of blackbirds
Flying in a green light,
Even the bawds of euphony
Would cry out sharply.

XI

He rode over Connecticut
In a glass coach.
Once, a fear pierced him,
In that he mistook
The shadow of his equipage
For blackbirds.

XII

The river is moving.
The blackbird must be flying.

XIII

It was evening all afternoon.
It was snowing
And it was going to snow.
The blackbird sat
In the cedar-limbs.

Wallace Stevens

250 | Free Verse

Sea Garden

I

You are clear
O rose, cut in rock,
hard as the descent of hail.

I could scrape the color
from the petals
like spilt dye from a rock.

If I could break you
I could break a tree.

If I could stir
I could break a tree—
I could break you.

II

O wind, rend open the heat,
cut apart the heat,
rend it to tatters.

Fruit cannot drop
through this thick air—
fruit cannot fall into heat
that presses up and blunts
the points of pears
and rounds the grapes.

Cut the heat—
plough through it,
turning it on either side
of your path.

H.D.

At Baia

I should have thought
in a dream you would have brought
some lovely, perilous thing,
orchids piled in a great sheath,
as who would say (in a dream)
I send you this,
who left the blue veins
of your throat unkissed.

Why was it that your hands
(that never took mine)
your hands that I could see
drift over the orchid heads
so carefully,
your hands, so fragile, sure to lift
so gently, the fragile flower stuff–
ah, ah, how was it
You never sent (in a dream)

the very form, the very scent,
not heavy, not sensuous,
but perilous—perilous—
of orchids, piled in a great sheath,
and folded underneath on a bright scroll
some word:

Flower sent to flower;
for white hands, the lesser white,
less lovely of flower leaf,

or

Lover to lover, no kiss,
no touch, but forever and ever this.

H.D.

252 | *Free Verse*

Eurydice*

I

So you have swept me back,
I who could have walked with the live souls
above the earth,
I who could have slept among the live
flowers
at last;

so for your arrogance
and your ruthlessness
I am swept back
where dead lichens drip
dead cinders upon moss of ash;

so for your arrogance
I am broken at last,
I who had lived unconscious,
who was almost forgot;

if you had let me wait
I had grown from listlessness
into peace,
if you had let me rest with the dead,
I had forgot you
and the past.

II

Here only flame upon flame
and black among the red sparks,
streaks of black and light
grown colorless;

why did you turn back,
that hell should be reinhabited
of myself thus
swept into nothingness?

why did you glance back?
why did you hesitate for that moment?
why did you bend your face
caught with the flame of the upper
earth,
above my face?

what was it that crossed my face
with the light from yours
and your glance?
what was it you saw in my face?
the light of your own face,
the fire of your own presence?

---

* See p. 310 for the story of Eurydice and Orpheus.

What had my face to offer
but reflex of the earth,
hyacinth color
caught from the raw fissure in the rock
where the light struck,
and the color of azure crocuses
and the bright surface of gold crocuses
and of the wind-flower,
swift in its veins as lightning
and as white.

III

Saffron from the fringe of the earth,
wild saffron that has bent
over the sharp edge of earth,
all the flowers that cut through the
earth,
all, all the flowers are lost;

everything is lost,
everything is crossed with black,
black upon black
and worse than black,
this colorless light.

IV

Fringe upon fringe
of blue crocuses,
crocuses, walled against blue of themselves,
blue of that upper earth,
blue of the depth upon depth of flowers,
lost;

flowers,
if I could have taken once my breath of
them,
enough of them,
more than earth,
even than of the upper earth,
had passed with me
beneath the earth;

if I could have caught up from the earth,
the whole of the flowers of the earth,
if once I could have breathed into myself
the very golden crocuses
and the red,
and the very golden hearts of the first
saffron,
the whole of the golden mass,
the whole of the great fragrance,
I could have dared the loss.

254 | Free Verse

What had my face to offer
but reflex of the earth,
hyacinth color
caught from the raw fissure in the rock
where the light struck,
and the color of azure crocuses
and the bright surface of gold crocuses
and of the wind-flower,
swift in its veins as lightning
and as white.

III

Saffron from the fringe of the earth,
wild saffron that has bent
over the sharp edge of earth,
all the flowers that cut through the
earth,
all, all the flowers are lost;

everything is lost,
everything is crossed with black,
black upon black
and worse than black,
this colorless light.

IV

Fringe upon fringe
of blue crocuses,
crocuses, walled against blue of themselves,
blue of that upper earth,
blue of the depth upon depth of flowers,
lost;

flowers,
if I could have taken once my breath of
them,
enough of them,
more than earth,
even than of the upper earth,
had passed with me
beneath the earth;

if I could have caught up from the earth,
the whole of the flowers of the earth,
if once I could have breathed into myself
the very golden crocuses
and the red,
and the very golden hearts of the first
saffron,
the whole of the golden mass,
the whole of the great fragrance,
I could have dared the loss.

V

So for your arrogance
and your ruthlessness
I have lost the earth
and the flowers of the earth,
and the live souls above the earth,
and you who passed across the light
and reached
ruthless;

you who have your own light,
who are to yourself a presence,
who need no presence;

yet for all your arrogance
and your glance,
I tell you this:

such loss is no loss,
such terror, such coils and strands and
pitfalls
of blackness,
such terror
is no loss;
hell is no worse than your earth
above the earth,

hell is no worse,
no, nor your flowers
nor your veins of light
nor your presence,
a loss;

my hell is no worse than yours
though you pass among the flowers and
speak
with the spirits above earth.

VI

Against the black
I have more fervor
than you in all the splendor of that place,
against the blackness
and the stark grey
I have more light;

and the flowers,
if I should tell you,
you would turn from your own fit paths
toward hell,
turn again and glance back
and I would sink into a place
even more terrible than this.

VII

At least I have the flowers of myself,
and my thoughts, no god
can take that;
I have the fervor of myself for a presence
and my own spirit for light;

and my spirit with its loss
knows this;
though small against the black,
small against the formless rocks,
hell must break before I am lost;

before I am lost,
hell must open like a red rose
for the dead to pass.

H.D.

the bigness of cannon

is skilful,

3   but i have seen

death's clever enormous voice

which hides in a fragility

6   of poppies. . . .

i say that sometimes

on these long talkative animals

9   are laid fists of huger silence.

I have seen all the silence

filled with vivid noiseless boys

12   at Roupy

i have seen

between barrages,

15   the night utter ripe unspeaking girls.

e.e. cummings

258 | *Free Verse*

since feeling is first
who pays any attention
3   to the syntax of things
will never wholly kiss you;

wholly to be a fool
6   while Spring is in the world

my blood approves,
and kisses are a better fate
9   than wisdom
lady i swear by all flowers. Don't cry
—the best gesture of my brain is less than
12   your eyelids' flutter which says

we are for each other; then
laugh, leaning back in my arms
15   for life's not a paragraph

And death i think is no parenthesis

e.e. cummings

in Just—
spring   when the world is mud-
luscious the little
lame balloonman

whistles   far   and wee

and eddieandbill come
running from marbles and
piracies and it's
spring

when the world is puddle-wonderful

the queer
old balloonman whistles
far   and   wee
and bettyandisbel come dancing

from hop-scotch and jump-rope and

it's
spring
and

            the

                goat-footed

balloonMan   whistles
far
and
wee

e.e. cummings

260 | *Free Verse*

into the strenuous briefness
Life:
handorgans and April
4   darkness,friends

i charge laughing.
Into the hair-thin tints
of yellow dawn,
8   into the women-colored twilight

i smilingly
glide. I
into the big vermilion departure
12   swim,sayingly;

(Do you think?)the
i do,world
is probably made
16   of roses & hello:

(of solongs and,ashes)

e.e. cummings

when god lets my body be

20   when god lets my body be

From each brave eye shall sprout a tree

fruit dangles therefrom

24

the purpled world will dance upon

Between my lips which did sing

28   a rose shall beget the spring

that maidens whom passions wastes

will lay between their little breasts

32   My strong fingers beneath the snow

Into strenuous birds shall go

my love walking in the grass

36

their wings will touch with their face

and all the while shall my heart be

40   With the bulge and nuzzle of the sea

e.e. cummings

262 | *Free Verse*

> *The apparition of these faces in the crowd:*
> *Petals, on a wet, black bough.*

"In a Station at the Metro"
by Ezra Pound (Gaudier-Brzeska, 1916)

Three years ago in Paris I got out of a "metro" train at La Concorde, and saw suddenly a beautiful face, and then another and another, and then a beautiful child's face, and then another beautiful woman, and I tried all that day to find words for what this had meant to me, and I could not find any words that seemed to me worthy, or as lovely as that sudden emotion. And that evening, as I went home along the Rue Raynouard, I was still trying and I found, suddenly, the expression. I do not mean that I found words, but there came an equation . . . not in speech, but in little splotches of color. It was just that—a "pattern," or hardly a pattern, if by "pattern" you mean something with a "repeat" in it. But it was a word, the beginning, for me, of a language in color. I do not mean that I was unfamiliar with the kindergarten stories about colors being like tones in music. I think that sort of thing is nonsense. If you try to make notes permanently correspond with particular colors, it is like tying narrow meanings to symbols.

That evening, in the Rue Raynouard, I realized quite vividly that if I were a painter, or if I had, often, that kind of emotion, of even if I had the energy to get paints and brushes and keep at it, I might found a new school of painting that would speak only by arrangements in color.

And so, when I came to read Kandinsky's chapter on the language of form and color, I found little that was new to me. I only felt that someone else understood what I understood, and had written it out very clearly. It seems quite natural to me that an artist should have just as much pleasure in an arrangement of planes or in a pattern of figures, as in painting portraits of fine ladies, or in portraying the Mother of God as the symbolists bid us.

When I find people ridiculing the new arts, or making fun of the clumsy odd terms that we use in trying to talk of them amongst ourselves; when they laugh at our talking about the "ice-block quality" in Picasso, I think it is only because they do not know what thought is like, and they are familiar only with argument and gibe and opinion. That is to say, they can only enjoy what they have been brought up to consider enjoyable, or what some essayist has talked about in mellifluous phrases. They think only "the shells of thought," as de Gourmont calls them; the thoughts that have been already thought out by others

Any mind that is worth calling a mind must have needs beyond the existing categories of language, just as a painter must have pigments or shades more numerous than the existing names of the colors.

Perhaps this is enough to explain the words in my "Vortex": *Every concept, every emotion, presents itself to the vivid consciousness in some primary form. It belongs to the art of this form.*

That is to say, my experience in Paris should have gone into paint. If instead of color I had perceived sound or planes in relation, I should have expressed it in music or in sculpture. Color was, in that instance, the "primary pigment"; I mean that it was the first adequate equation that came into consciousness. The Vorticist uses the "primary pigment." Vorticism is art before it has spread itself into flaccidity, into elaboration and secondary application.

264 | *Free Verse*

What I have said of one vorticist art can be transposed for another vorticist art. But let me go on then with my own branch of vorticism, about which I can probably speak with greater clarity. All poetic language is the language of exploration. Since the beginning of bad writing, writers have used images as ornaments. The point of Imagism is that it does not use images as ornaments. The image is itself the speech. The image is the word beyond formulated language.

I once saw a small child go to an electric light switch and say, "Mamma, can I open the light?" She was using the age-old language of exploration, the language of art. It was a sort of metaphor, but she was not using it as ornamentation.

One is tired of ornamentations, they are all a trick, and any sharp person can learn them.

The Japanese have had the sense of exploration. They have understood the beauty of this sort of knowing. A Chinaman said long ago that if a man can't say what he has to say in twelve lines he had better keep quiet. The Japanese have evolved the still shorter form of the hokku.

"The fallen blossom flies back to its branch:
A butterfly."

That is the substance of a very well-known hokku. Victor Plarr tells me that once, when he was walking over snow with a Japanese naval officer, they came to a place where a cat had crossed the path, and the officer said," Stop, I am making a poem." Which poem was, roughly, as follows:—

> "The footsteps of the cat upon the snow:
> (are like) plum-blossoms."

The words "are like" would not occur in the original, but I add them for clarity.

80   The "one image poem" is a form of super-position, that is to say, it is one idea set on top of another. I found it useful in getting out of the impasse in which I had been left by my metro emotion. I wrote a thirty-line poem, and destroyed it because it was what we call work "of second intensity." Six months later I made a poem half that length; a year later I
85   made the following hokku-like sentence:—

> "The apparition of these faces in the crowd:
> Petals, on a wet, black bough."

I dare say it is meaningless unless one has drifted into a certain
90   vein of thought. In a poem of this sort one is trying to record the precise instant when a thing outward and objective transforms itself, or darts into a thing inward and subjective.

Ezra Pound

266 | *Free Verse*

Hugh Selwyn Mauberley
(Life And Contacts)

Vocat aestus in umbram.[1]
Nemesianus *Eclogues* IV

E. P. ODE POUR L'ÉLECTION DE SON SÉPULCHRE [2]

For three years, out of key with his time,

He strove to resuscitate the dead art

Of poetry; to maintain "the sublime"

96   In the old sense. Wrong from the start—

No, hardly, but, seeing he had been born

In a half savage country, out of date;

Bent resolutely on wringing lilies from the acorn;

100   Capaneus[3]; trout for factitious bait:

Ἴδμεν γάρ τοι πάνθ', ὅσ' ἐνὶ Τροίη [4]

Caught in the unstopped ear;

Giving the rocks small lee-way

104   The chopped seas held him, therefore, that year.

---

[1] [*Come hither, fair Meroe.*] *The heat calls us to the shade.*

[2] Cf. "Ode of choice for his tomb," title of Ronsard's (*Odes*, IV.1). Italicized subtexts cited are all taken from John Jenkins Espey, *Ezra Pound's Mauberley: A Study in Composition* (Faber, 1955)—though often translated into English by me.

[3] Capaneus stood at the city wall during the war of the Seven against Thebes and shouted that Zeus himself could not stop him from invading it. Zeus struck Capaneus with a thunderbolt, and Evadne threw herself on her husband's funeral pyre. In Dante's Inferno, he continues violently to blaspheme Jove even as fire rains down on him supine upon burning sands. All such historical facts and context cited in these notes are taken from Wikipedia.org articles.

[4] *For we have seen all that in wide Troy the Argives and Trojans endured through the will of the gods, and we know all things that come to pass on the fruitful earth.* From *Odyssey* XII, first line of the Sirens' song, heard only by Odysseus.

Pound | *267*

His true Penelope was Flaubert,

He fished by obstinate isles;

Observed the elegance of Circe's hair[5]

108   Rather than the mottoes on sun-dials.

Unaffected by "the march of events",[6]

He passed from men's memory in *l'an trentiesme*

De son eage;[7] the case presents

112   No adjunct to the Muses' diadem.

II

The age demanded an image

Of its accelerated grimace,

Something for the modern stage,

116   Not, at any rate, an Attic grace;

Not, not certainly, the obscure reveries

Of the inward gaze;

Better mendacities

120   Than the classics in paraphrase!

The "age demanded" chiefly a mold in plaster,

Made with no loss of time,

A prose cinema, not, not assuredly, alabaster

124   Or the "sculpture" of rhyme.

[5] The goddess who turned Odysseus' men into swine; with Hermes' help he resisted her bewitchments and then lay with the god for a year on her island before departing for the underworld equipped with her counsels and magical provisions.

[6] *The march of events rules and overrules human action,* Treaty of Paris, President William McKinley.

[7] *In the thirtieth year of my age, when I had drunk down all my shames ....* François Villon, *Le Grand Testament.*

268 | *Free Verse*

III

The tea-rose, tea-gown, etc.[8]

Supplants the mousseline of Cos,[9]

The pianola "replaces"

128 Sappho's *barbitos.*[10]

Christ follows Dionysus,

Phallic and ambrosial

Made way for macerations;[11]

132 Caliban casts out Ariel.[12]

All things are a flowing,

Sage Heraclitus says;

But a tawdry cheapness

136 Shall reign throughout our days.

Even the Christian beauty

Defects—after Samothrace;[13]

We see *το καλόν* [14]

140 Decreed in the market place.

---

[8] The tea-rose is a mid-19th C. French hybrid, the first of modern garden roses. A tea-gown, characterized by unstructured lines and light fabrics, was popular in the mid-19th C. for informal entertaining at home—cf. Henry James' opening description of Rosanna Gaw in *The Ivory Tower: ... mistress as she might have been of the most expensive modern aids to the constitution of a "figure", lived, as they said of her, in wrappers and tea-gowns ...".*

[9] Greek island renowned in Roman times for its beautiful muslin.

[10] Ancient Greek lute or lyre. The 19th C. pianola, a self-playing piano fitted with pneumatics and punched sheet music, was also fitted with control levers so that the pianolist could sound as if he could play far more difficult music than he was able to.

[11] Literally, the steeping of crushed grapes in wine-making. In French, also mortifications of the flesh: ... *the pale eunuch exhausted by mortifications* [*macérations*] ..., from Flaubert's description of the high priest Schahabarim in "Salammbô".

[12] The one the beast-man, the other the aerial sprite, ruled over by Prospero's magic in Shakespeare's *The Tempest.*

[13] Greek island associated with the cults of Dionysius.

[14] The beautiful, noble, or good.

Faun's flesh is not to us,

Nor the saint's vision.

We have the press for wafer;

144   Franchise for circumcision.

All men, in law, are equals.

Free of Peisistratus,[15]

We choose a knave or an eunuch

148   To rule over us.

A bright Apollo,

τίν' ἄνδρα, τίν' ἤρωα, τινα θεόν,[16]

What god, man, or hero

152   Shall I place a tin wreath upon?

IV

These fought, in any case,

and some believing,

pro domo, in any case ...[17]

156   Some quick to arm,

some for adventure,

some from fear of weakness,

some from fear of censure,

160   some for love of slaughter, in imagination,

learning later ...[18]

---

[15] Populist Athenian tyrant who seized power but then secured prosperity, and fostered Attic unity with the cult of Dionysius.

[16] *What God, what hero, and yes, what man shall we loudly praise?* First line of Pindar's *Ode to Theron*, a tribute to the Sicilian victor of an Olympic chariot race.

[17] *For the home,* or household.

[18] Compare the tributes of Love to the dead Adonis as described in Bion of Smyrna: *One puts his arrows on the funeral bed, one his bow, one a feather from his win, one his quiver. This one unties Adonis's sandal, others carry water in a golden bowl; one washes the wounds, one, standing behind Adonis, fans him with his wings ...."* Tr. Philippe Legrand, *Bucoliques Grecs*, in Espey's *A Study in Composition* (n. 2 above).

270 | *Free Verse*

164   some in fear, learning love of slaughter;

         Died some *pro patria,*

         non dulce non et decor ...[19]

         walked eye-deep in hell

168   believing in old men's lies, then unbelieving

         came home, home to a lie,

         home to many deceits,

         home to old lies and new infamy;

172   usury age-old and age-thick

         and liars in public places.

         Daring as never before, wastage as never before.

         Young blood and high blood,

176   Fair cheeks, and fine bodies;

         fortitude as never before

180   frankness as never before,

         disillusions as never told in the old days,

         hysterias, trench confessions,

         laughter out of dead bellies.

[19] Cf. Horace, Odes: *It is a sweet thing and fitting to die for one's country.*

V

184   There died a myriad,

And of the best, among them,

For an old bitch gone in the teeth,

For a botched civilization.

188   Charm, smiling at the good mouth,

Quick eyes gone under earth's lid,

For two gross of broken statues,

For a few thousand battered books.

YEUX GLAUQUES [20]

192   Gladstone was still respected,

When John Ruskin produced

"Kings' Treasuries";[21] Swinburne

And Rossetti still abused.

196   Fetid Buchanan lifted up his voice

When that faun's head of hers

Became a pastime for

Painters and adulterers.[22]

---

[20] *Sea-green or glassy eyes. Cf. "Caerulei oculi" by Thophile Gautier in* Emaux et Camées: *A mysterious woman whose beauty troubled my senses stayed standing silent at the edge of the resounding waves. Her eyes, where the sky was reflected, with the vacant blue bespangled by their sparkling moisture mingled the glassy greens of the sea [teintes glauques]...." Cf. Flaubert's* L'Education Sentimentale: "*A pitiless energy rested in his glassy-green eyes [yeux glauques], colder than eyes made of glass."

[21] *I want to speak to you about the treasures hidden in books; and about the way we find them, and the way we lose them.... I say first we have despised literature. What do we, as a nation, care about books? In* Sesame and Lilies.

[22] Robert Buchanan wrote a critique of poet Dante Gabriel Rossetti, who painted nudes of his wife Elizabeth Siddal.

272 | *Free Verse*

200 The Burne-Jones cartons

Have preserved her eyes;

Still, at the Tate, they teach

Cophetua to rhapsodize;[23]

204 Thin like brook-water,

With a vacant gaze.

The English Rubaiyat was still-born

In those days.[24]

208 The thin, clear gaze, the same

Still darts out faun-like from the half-ruin'd face,

Questing and passive ....

"Ah, poor Jenny's case" ...[25]

212 Bewildered that a world

Shows no surprise

At her last *maquero's*[26]

Adulteries.

"SIENA MI FE', DISFECEMI MAREMMA" [27]

---

[23] Sir Edward Burne-Jones painted Elizabeth Siddal as a beggar-maid and himself as king in his painting *King Cophetua and the Beggar Maid,* hanging in the Tate Gallery in London

[24] *The Rubaiyat* of Omar Khayyam was a translation published in 1856 of 11ᵗʰ C. Persian poems promoted by Rosetti.

[25] Pound quotes from a poem "Jenny" by Rossetti about a prostitute, which Buchanan attacked.

[26] Procurer or pimp.

[27] Cf. Dante *Purgatorio:* [*Remember me, who am pious,*] *Siena made me, Maremma unmade me.* La Pia in Purgatorio V, who repented in the hour of her violent death at the hands of her husband in the Maremma, the south of Tuscany.

Pound | 273

216
Among the pickled fetuses and bottled bones,

Engaged in perfecting the catalogue,

I found the last scion of the

Senatorial families of Strasbourg, Monsieur Verog.

220
For two hours he talked of Gallifet;

Of Dowson; of the Rhymers' Club;

Told me how Johnson (Lionel) died

By falling from a high stool in a pub ...[28]

224
But showed no trace of alcohol

At the autopsy, privately performed—

Tissue preserved—the pure mind

Arose toward Newman as the whiskey warmed.[29]

228
Dowson found harlots cheaper than hotels;

Headlam for uplift; Image impartially imbued

With raptures for Bacchus, Terpsichore and the Church.[30]

So spoke the author of *The Dorian Mood,*[31]

232
M. Verog, out of step with the decade,

Detached from his contemporaries,

Neglected by the young,

Because of these reveries.

[28] Marquis de Galliffet, French general in the Franco-Prussian war. Ernest Dowson and Lionel Johnson were members of a poetry club that met at a Fleet St. London pub.

[29] Cardinal John Henry Newman, Protestant apologist who converted to Roman Catholicism, as did Dowson and Johnson.

[30] Stewart Headlam and Selwyn Image, clerics who were poets; the former was forced to resign his curacy because of an avowed interest in dance and drama. Terpsichore is the Greek muse of dance.

[31] *The Dorian Mood*, book published in 1896 by Victor Plarr, head librarian at the Royal College of Surgeons in London—presumably *Monsieur Verog*—and a friend of Dowson and Johnson.

274 | *Free Verse*

BRENNEBAUM

236 The sky-like limpid eyes,
 The circular infant's face,
 The stiffness from spats to collar
 Never relaxing into grace;

240 The heavy memories of Horeb, Sinai and the forty years,[32]
 Showed only when the daylight fell
 Level across the face
 Of Brennbaum "The Impeccable."

MR. NIXON

244 In the cream gilded cabin of his steam yacht
 Mr. Nixon advised me kindly, to advance with fewer
 Dangers of delay. "Consider
  "Carefully the reviewer.

248 "I was as poor as you are;
 "When I began I got, of course,
 "Advance on royalties, fifty at first," said Mr. Nixon,
 "Follow me, and take a column,
252 "Even if you have to work free.

 "Butter reviewers. From fifty to three hundred
 "I rose in eighteen months;
 "The hardest nut I had to crack
256 "Was Dr. Dundas.

---

[32] God spoke to Moses from the burning bush on Mount Horeb and gave him the ten commandments on Mount Sinai.

Pound | 275

"I never mentioned a man but with the view

"Of selling my own works.

"The tip's a good one, as for literature

260   "It gives no man a sinecure."

And no one knows, at sight a masterpiece.

And give up verse, my boy,

There's nothing in it."

*   *   *   *

264   Likewise a friend of Bloughram's once advised me:[33]

Don't kick against the pricks,

Accept opinion. The "Nineties" tried your game

And died, there's nothing in it.

X

268   Beneath the sagging roof

The stylist has taken shelter,

Unpaid, uncelebrated,

At last from the world's welter

272   Nature receives him,

With a placid and uneducated mistress

He exercises his talents

And the soil meets his distress.

---

[33] *You do despise me; your ideal of life Is not the bishop's: you would not be I.* Bishop Flougram from Robert Browning's *Bishop Blougram's Apology*, the bishop's dramatic monologue in defense of his pragmatism, addressed to a skeptical journalist.

276 | *Free Verse*

276   The haven from sophistications and contentions

Leaks through its thatch;

He offers succulent cooking;

The door has a creaking latch.

XI

280   "Conservatrix of Milésien" [34]

Habits of mind and feeling,

Possibly. But in Ealing

With the most bank-clerkly of Englishmen? [35]

284   No, "Milésian" is an exaggeration.

No instinct has survived in her

Older than those her grandmother

Told her would fit her station.

XII

288   "Daphne with her thighs in bark

Stretches toward me her leafy hands," — [36]

Subjectively. In the stuffed-satin drawing-room

I await The Lady Valentine's commands,

292   Knowing my coat has never been

Of precisely the fashion

To stimulate, in her,

A durable passion;

---

[34] Milesian tales of love and adventure is a genre prominent in ancient Greek and Roman literature, usually of a titillating nature. The name refers to Aristides of Miletus' ribald tales of adventurous sex set in luxurious Miletus, translated into Latin by Sisenna as *Milesiae fabulae*, which inspired Petronius and Ovid. The name also refers to mythical Gaels from Iberia who settle in Ireland after sailing the earth for centuries under their captain Milesius, in the medieval Irish Christian pseudo-history *Lebor Gabála Érenn*.

[35] An affluent London suburb at the time.

[36] By a wrathful curse of Cupid's against Apollo, the naiad Daphne became the object of the infatuated god's chase, who caught her; but Daphne invoked her father, a river god, who changed her into a laurel tree.

Poetry, her border of ideas,

296   Doubtful, somewhat, of the value

Of well-gowned approbation

Of literary effort,

But never of The Lady Valentine's vocation:

300   Poetry, her border of ideas,
The edge, uncertain, but a means of blending

With other strata

Where the lower and higher have ending;

304   A hook to catch the Lady Jane's attention,

A modulation toward the theatre,

Also, in the case of revolution,

A possible friend and comforter.

                *   *   *   *

308   Conduct, on the other hand, the soul

"Which the highest cultures have nourished"[37]

To Fleet St. where

Dr. Johnson flourished;

312   Beside this thoroughfare

The sale of half-hose has

Long since superseded the cultivation

Of Pierian roses.[38]

---

[37] Cf. Jules Laforgue, "Complainte des Pianos qu'on Entend dans les Quatiers Aisés": *Lead the soul that Letters have well nourished, The pianos, the pianos, in affluent neighborhoods! First evenings, without an overcoat, a chaste stroll, To the complaints of nerves misunderstood or broken..*

[38] The Pierian Spring was the sacred birthplace of the Muses: *But ever shall you lie dead, and there shall be no remembrance of you, not then, nor thereafter, for you have not any roses of Pieria; obscure shall you wander even in the house of Hades, flitting among the shadowy dead.* Sappho, "To one who loved not poetry".

278 | Free Verse

Envoi (1919)

316   Go, dumb-born book,

Tell her that sang me once that song of Lawes:
Hadst thou but song
As thou hast subjects known,

320   Then were there cause in thee that should condone
Even my faults that heavy upon me lie
And build her glories their longevity.

Tell her that sheds
324   Such treasure in the air,
Recking naught else but that her graces give
Life to the moment,
I would bid them live
328   As roses might, in magic amber laid,
Red overwrought with orange and all made
One substance and one color
Braving time.

332   Tell her that goes
With song upon her lips
But sings not out the song, nor knows
The maker of it, some other mouth,
336   May be as fair as hers,
Might, in new ages, gain her worshippers,
When our two dusts with Waller's shall be laid,[40]
Siftings on siftings in oblivion,
340   Till change hath broken down
All things save Beauty alone.

[40] Cf. Edmund Waller: *Go, lovely rose! Tell her that wastes her time and me, That now she knows, When I resemble her to thee, How sweet and fair she seems to be.*

Part II
1920

(MAUBERLEY)

Vacuos exercet aera morsus.[41]

I

Turned from the *eau-forte*
Par Jaquemart[42]
To the strait head
4   Of Messalina:[43]

"His True Penelope
Was Flaubert,"
And his tool
8   The engraver's.

Firmness,
Not the full smile,
His art, but an art
12   In profile;

Colorless
Pier Francesca,
Pisanello lacking the skill
16   To forge Achaia.[44]

---

[41] Written a year later, this sequel's sections parallel the original sequentially. The epigraph is from Ovid's *Metamorphoses*. *The hound presses hard, and matches its pace, seems to grip it, and does not grip it, and worries at the air with its empty snapping* (Tr. A.S. Kline, *ovid.lib.virginia.edu*). The preternatural dog Laelaps, destined by Zeus to catch everything it chased, was set by Cephalus on the Teumessian fox, sent by the gods to punish Theban children for the city's crime. Zeus resolved the endless chase by turning the two beasts into stones, cast into the sky as the constellations *Canis major* and *Canis minor*.

[42] Etching by Jules Jacquemart, known for detailed etching of idyllic landscape; *eau-forte* is the acid used in.

[43] Wife of Roman emperor Claudius, known for licentious conduct and court intrigue, ordered murdered by Claudius; commemorated in profile on ancient Roman coins.

[44] Renaissance painter Piero della Francesca and medallion-maker Antonio di Puccio Pisano, known for serene humanism in their works. Achaia was known for ancient Greek medallion work of superior quality.

280 | *Free Verse*

II

Qu'est ce qu'ils savent de l'amour, et qu'est ce qu'ils peuvent comprendre?
S'ils ne comprennent pas la poésie, s'ils ne sentent pas la musique, qu'est ce
qu'ils peuvent comprendre de cette passion en comparaison avec laquelle la
20   *rose est grossière et le parfum des violettes un tonnerre?* —CAID ALI [45]

       For three years, diabolus in the scale,[46]

       He drank ambrosia,

       All passes, ANANGKE[48] prevails,

24   Came end, at last, to that Arcadia.

       He had moved amid her phantasmagoria,[47]

       Amid her galaxies,

       NUKTIS 'AGALMA

       .   .   .   .

28   Drifted ... drifted precipitate

       Asking time to be rid of ...

       Of his bewilderment; to designate

       His new found orchid. ...

---

[45] *What do they know of love, and what can they understand? If they do not understand poetry, if they do not hear music, what can they understand about this passion in comparison with which the rose is coarse and the scent of violets clamorous.* Le Caïd was a buffoonish comic opera set in Algiers.

[46] The *diabolus in music* refers to the most discordant musical interval, the augmented fourth—banned from Church music—halfway between the two most commonly used pure intervals, associated with the Trinity.

[47] *Of course I moved among miracles. It was all phantasmagoric ...* Lambert Strether in Henry James' novel *The Ambassadors.*

[48] *ANANGKE* means *Necessity* and NUKTIS 'AGALMA *Night's glory,* which Greek bucolic poet Bion of Smyrna uses to apostrophize Venus as the evening or vesper star: *Hesperus, golden light of loving Aphrodite, dear Hesperus, blue Night's glory* [nuktos agalma]. In Bion's poem *The Wings,* Eros says his birth was *under the reign of necessity.* Hesiod says Eros was born primordially of Chaos and blessed the union of Gaia and Uranus to give birth to the cosmos. But in later tales Eros is made a child of illicit sexual unions by Aphrodite, and is one of the *Erotes* or winged love gods. Similarly, Hesiod says Aphrodite was born of the white foam when Cronus' threw his father Uranus' severed genitals into the sea; appearing out of the foam, she floated on a scallop shell to the island of Cypress. However, in Homer, she is the child of Zeus and nymph Dione, and the licentious wife of Hephaestus, and the mother of Cupid by Ares, and the mother of Aeneas by King Anchises of Dardania, crippled by Zeus' thunderbolt for bedding a goddess.

Pound | 281

32   Unable in the supervening blankness

        To sift TO AGATHON[49] from the chaff

        Until he found his sieve ...

        Ultimately, his seismograph:

36   —Given that is his "fundamental passion,"

        This urge to convey the relation

        Of eye-lid and cheek-bone

        By verbal manifestations;

40   To present the series

        Of curious heads in medallion—

        He had passed, inconscient, full gaze,

        The wide-banded irides

44   And Botticellian sprays implied

        In their diastasis;[50]

        Which anæsthesis, noted a year late,

        And weighed, revealed his great affect,

48   (Orchid), mandate

        Of Eros, a retrospect.[51]

            .   .   .

        Mouths biting empty air,

        The still stone dogs,

52   Caught in metamorphosis, were

        Left him as epilogues.[52]

[49] *The good, brave, noble,* in ancient Greek.

[50] In Sandro Botticelli's painting *Birth of Venus,* Venus arises out of ocean spray—*aphros* means foam, whence *Aphrodite.* Diastasis is the distance between the eyes, governed in classical painting by ideal proportions.

[51] ὄρχις/ὄρχεις (m.) in Greek means testicle(s) or ovary/ovaries as well as orchid (f.). Similarly, *iris* refers to the eye as well as to the flower.

[52] See note on the Latin epigraph, which did not appear in all publications of the poem.

282 | *Free Verse*

"THE AGE DEMANDED"
VIDE POEM II

56 For this agility chance found
 Him of all men, unfit
 As the red-beaked steeds of
 The Cytherian for a chain bit.[53]

60 The glow of porcelain
 Brought no reforming sense
 Ṭo his perception
 Of the social inconsequence.

64 Thus, if her color
 Came against his gaze,
 Tempered as if
 It were through a perfect glaze

68 He made no immediate application
 Of this to relation of the state
 To the individual, the month was more temperate
 Because this beauty had been.

 . . . . .

72 The coral isle, the lion-colored sand
 Burst in upon the porcelain revery:
 Impetuous troubling
 Of *his imagery.*

 . . . . .

---

[53] Aphrodite's chariot was pulled by white doves (the beaks and feet of which are in fact red).

Pound | 283

76   Mildness, amid the neo-Nietzschean clatter,[54]

His sense of graduations,

Quite out of place amid

Resistance to current exacerbations,

80   Invitation, mere invitation to perceptivity

Gradually led him to the isolation

Which these presents place

Under a more tolerant, perhaps, examination.

84   By constant elimination

The manifest universe

Yielded an armor

Against utter consternation,

88   A Minoan undulation,[55]

Seen, we admit, amid ambrosial circumstances

Strengthened him against

The discouraging doctrine of chances,

92   And his desire for survival,

Faint in the most strenuous moods,

Became an Olympian *apathein*[56]

In the presence of selected perceptions.

---

[54] Nietzsche's writings came late to England, but provoked strongly divided partisan reactions in the press.

[55] "Minoan" is archeological coinage for an artistically sophisticated Bronze Age civilization, urban and seafaring, unearthed in the 19th C.; the term is based on the myth of King Minos of Crete, son of Zeus and Europa, who punitively exacted from Athens every nine years a sacrificial tribute of seven boys and seven girls, sent into the labyrinth created by Daedalus, to be devoured by the Minotaur, born of a bull and Minos' wife. The Minotaur was slain by Theseus with the help of Minos' daughter Ariadne, herself betrayed by him. After a death by treachery, Minos became a judge in Hades, with Aeacus and Rhadamanthus. Rhadamanthus judged the souls of Asians, and Aeacus judged Europeans, and Minos decided their fate.

[56] A modern neologism: an infinitive from Greek noun *apátheia*—impassibility, insensibility, freedom from emotion—derived from adjective *apathés*—not having suffered, without experience of, unaffected by—formed from privative ἀ- and the noun *páthos*—any effect in a thing, including an affection or passion.

284 | *Free Verse*

96   A pale gold, in the aforesaid pattern,

The unexpected palms

Destroying, certainly, the artist's urge,

Left him delighted with the imaginary

100   Audition of the phantasmal sea-surge,

Incapable of the least utterance or composition,

Emendation, conservation of the "better tradition,"

Refinement of medium, elimination of superfluities,

104   August attraction or concentration.

Nothing, in brief, but maudlin confession,

Irresponse to human aggression,

Amid the precipitation, down-float

108   Of insubstantial manna,[57]

Lifting the faint *susurrus*

Of his subjective *hosannah.*[58]

Ultimate affronts to

112   Human redundancies;

Non-esteem of self-styled "his betters"

Leading, as he well knew,

To his final

116   Exclusion from the world of letters.

---

[57] Manna is the bread-like flakes sent from heaven to the Hebrews by God for their daily bread during their forty years of wandering in the desert; in Christianity it is a figurative type of the eucharist, the bread-like wafer of holy communion.

[58] *Susurrus* is Latin for a whisper or murmur; certain prayers of the Mass are said by the priest *secreto*, or in a low voice. *Hosannah,* like *alleluia,* is a Hebraism of praise in the liturgy of the Church.

Pound | 285

IV

Scattered Moluccas[59]

Not knowing, day to day,

The first day's end, in the next noon;

120   The placid water

Unbroken by the Simoon;[60]

Thick foliage

Placid beneath warm suns,

124   Tawn fore-shores

Washed in the cobalt of oblivions;

Or through dawn-mist

The grey and rose

128   Of the juridical

Flamingoes;

A consciousness disjunct,

Being but this overblotted

132   Series

Of intermittences;

Coracle[61] of Pacific voyages,

The unforecasted beach;

136   Then on an oar

Read this:

"I was

And I no more exist;

140   "Here drifted

An hedonist."

---

[59] An archipelago in the east of Indonesia, the "Spice Islands" famous for nutmeg, clove, mace, which are exclusively found there, and for palm-lined beaches and coral reefs.

[60] A hot, dry, dust-laden wind blowing in the desert, especially in the Sahara and Middle East.

[61] A small, rounded, lightweight boat.

286 | *Free Verse*

MEDALLION

144
Luini in porcelain! [62]

The grand piano

Utters a profane

Protest with her clear soprano.

148
The sleek head emerges

From the gold-yellow frock

As Anadyomene in the opening

Pages of Reinach. [63]

152
Honey-red, closing the face-oval,

A basket-work of braids which seem as if they were

Spun in King Minos' hall

From metal, or intractable amber;

156
The face-oval beneath the glaze,

Bright in its suave bounding-line, as,

Beneath half-watt rays,

The eyes turn topaz.

Ezra Pound [64]

[62] Bernardino Luini was a painter in DaVinci's circle known for graceful female figures with elongated eyes.

[63] The print in Salomon's Reinach's *Apollo* is of Venus Anadyomene—Greek for *rising from the sea*—an iconic presentation of Venus born as a woman from the sea off Paphos. A motif of the goddess wringing out her hair is often repeated in antiquity, and in ancient painting by Apelles of Kos on a scallop shell, symbol of the female vulva.

[64] Cf. Pound's *Canto LXXIV,* apostrophizing *Venus Hesphoros,* the morning star, from his Pisan prison cell:

> *Time is not, Time is the evil, beloved*
> *Beloved the hours βροδοδἄκτυλος **   rosy-fingered
> > *as against the half-light of the window*
> > *with the sea beyond making horizon*
> > *le contre-jour * the line of the cameo*   focal view in art of silhouetting back-light
> > *profile "to carve Achaia"**   Cf. "to forge Achaia" above
> > > *a dream passing over the face in the half-light*
> > > *Venere, Cytherea "aut Rhodon"* Others will praise bright Rhodes or Mytilene,* Horace
> > > *vento ligure, veni*   Wind of Liguria, come
> > *"Beauty is difficult" sd */Mr. Beardsley*   sea-drowned

The Love Song of J. Alfred Prufrock

S'io credesse che mia risposta fosse
A persona che mai tornasse al mondo,
Questa fiamma staria senza piu scosse.
Ma percioche giammai di questo fondo
Non torno vivo alcun, s'i'odo il vero,
Senza tema d'infamia ti rispondo.[1]

Let us go then, you and I,
When the evening is spread out against the sky
Like a patient etherized upon a table;
Let us go, through certain half-deserted streets,
5 The muttering retreats
Of restless nights in one-night cheap hotels
And sawdust restaurants with oyster-shells:
Streets that follow like a tedious argument
Of insidious intent
10 To lead you to an overwhelming question ...
Oh, do not ask, "What is it?"
Let us go and make our visit.

---

[1] Did I think that my reply were to someone ever to return to earth, the flickering of this tongue of flame would cease forever; but as no one has ever returned alive from this ditch—if what I hear is true—I answer you without fear of infamy. Guido da Montefeltro is speaking to Dante in the eighth circle of hell, Malebolge (Evil Ditches), where fraud without intended malice is punished. Inferno, in Divina Commedia, Dante Alighieri.

288 | *Free Verse*

In the room the women come and go
Talking of Michelangelo.

15   The yellow fog that rubs its back upon the window-panes,
The yellow smoke that rubs its muzzle on the window-panes,
Licked its tongue into the corners of the evening,
Lingered upon the pools that stand in drains,
Let fall upon its back the soot that falls from chimneys,

20   Slipped by the terrace, made a sudden leap,
And seeing that it was a soft October night,
Curled once about the house, and fell asleep.

And indeed there will be time
For the yellow smoke that slides along the street,

25   Rubbing its back upon the window-panes;
There will be time, there will be time
To prepare a face to meet the faces that you meet;
There will be time to murder and create,
And time for all the works and days of hands

30   That lift and drop a question on your plate;
Time for you and time for me,
And time yet for a hundred indecisions,
And for a hundred visions and revisions,
Before the taking of a toast and tea.

35   In the room the women come and go
Talking of Michelangelo.

Eliot | 289

And indeed there will be time

To wonder, "Do I dare?" and, "Do I dare?"

Time to turn back and descend the stair,

40   With a bald spot in the middle of my hair—

(They will say: "How his hair is growing thin!")

My morning coat, my collar mounting firmly to the chin,

My necktie rich and modest, but asserted by a simple pin—

(They will say: "But how his arms and legs are thin!")

45   Do I dare

Disturb the universe?

In a minute there is time

For decisions and revisions which a minute will reverse.

For I have known them all already, known them all:

50   Have known the evenings, mornings, afternoons,

I have measured out my life with coffee spoons;

I know the voices dying with a dying fall

Beneath the music from a farther room.

          So how should I presume?

55   And I have known the eyes already, known them all—

The eyes that fix you in a formulated phrase,

And when I am formulated, sprawling on a pin,

When I am pinned and wriggling on the wall,

Then how should I begin

60   To spit out all the butt-ends of my days and ways?

              And how should I presume?

290 | *Free Verse*

And I have known the arms already, known them all—

Arms that are braceleted and white and bare

(But in the lamplight, downed with light brown hair!)

65 Is it perfume from a dress

That makes me so digress?

Arms that lie along a table, or wrap about a shawl.

   And should I then presume?

   And how should I begin?

70 Shall I say, I have gone at dusk through narrow streets

And watched the smoke that rises from the pipes

Of lonely men in shirt-sleeves, leaning out of windows? ...

I should have been a pair of ragged claws

Scuttling across the floors of silent seas.

75 And the afternoon, the evening, sleeps so peacefully!

Smoothed by long fingers,

Asleep ... tired ... or it malingers,

Stretched on the floor, here beside you and me.

Should I, after tea and cakes and ices,

80 Have the strength to force the moment to its crisis?

But though I have wept and fasted, wept and prayed,

Though I have seen my head (grown slightly bald) brought in upon
a platter,

I am no prophet—and here's no great matter;

85 I have seen the moment of my greatness flicker,

And I have seen the eternal Footman hold my coat, and snicker,

And in short, I was afraid.

Eliot | *291*

And would it have been worth it, after all,

After the cups, the marmalade, the tea,

90   Among the porcelain, among some talk of you and me,

Would it have been worth while,

To have bitten off the matter with a smile,

To have squeezed the universe into a ball

To roll it towards some overwhelming question,

95   To say: "I am Lazarus, come from the dead,

Come back to tell you all, I shall tell you all"—

If one, settling a pillow by her head

      Should say: "That is not what I meant at all;

      That is not it, at all."

100   And would it have been worth it, after all,

Would it have been worth while,

After the sunsets and the dooryards and the sprinkled streets,

After the novels, after the teacups, after the skirts that trail along the floor—

105   And this, and so much more?—

It is impossible to say just what I mean!

But as if a magic lantern threw the nerves in patterns on a screen:

Would it have been worth while

If one, settling a pillow or throwing off a shawl,

110   And turning toward the window, should say:

      "That is not it at all,

      That is not what I meant, at all."

292 | *Free Verse*

No! I am not Prince Hamlet, nor was meant to be;
Am an attendant lord, one that will do
115   To swell a progress, start a scene or two,
Advise the prince; no doubt, an easy tool,
Deferential, glad to be of use,
Politic, cautious, and meticulous;
Full of high sentence, but a bit obtuse;
120   At times, indeed, almost ridiculous—
Almost, at times, the Fool.
I grow old ... I grow old ...
I shall wear the bottoms of my trousers rolled.
Shall I part my hair behind?   Do I dare to eat a peach?
125   I shall wear white flannel trousers, and walk upon the beach.
I have heard the mermaids singing, each to each.

I do not think that they will sing to me.

I have seen them riding seaward on the waves
Combing the white hair of the waves blown back
130   When the wind blows the water white and black.
We have lingered in the chambers of the sea
By sea-girls wreathed with seaweed red and brown
Till human voices wake us, and we drown.

T.S. Eliot

THE WASTE LAND

*Nam Sibyllam quidem Cumis ego ipse oculis meis vidi in ampulla pendere,
et cum illae pueri dicerent:
"Σίβνλλα τί θέλεις; respondebat illa: άπο θανεῖν θέλω."*[5]

T.S. ELIOT

For Ezra Pound, *Il Miglior Fabbro*

I. The Burial of the Dead

April is the cruellest month, breeding

135   Lilacs out of the dead land, mixing

Memory and desire, stirring

Dull roots with spring rain.

138   Winter kept us warm, covering

Earth in forgetful snow, feeding

A little life with dried tubers.

141   Summer surprised us, coming over the Starnbergersee

With a shower of rain; we stopped in the colonnade,

And went on in sunlight, into the Hofgarten,

144   And drank coffee, and talked for an hour.

Bin gar keine Russin, stamm' aus Litauen, echt deutsch.[6]

And when we were children, staying at the arch-duke's,

---

[5] *I saw with my own eyes the Sibyl at Cumae hanging in a cage, and when the boys said to her: 'Sibyl, what do you want?' she answered: 'I want to die.'* This epigraph is from the comical Satyricon, a first century Latin work by Gaius Petronius about the adventures of an ex-gladiator: The Sibyl of Cumae was a prophetess in service to Apollo and a great beauty. Apollo wished to take her as his lover and offered her anything she desired. She asked to live for as many years as there were grains in a handful of dust. Apollo granted her wish, but still she refused to become his lover. In time, the Sibyl came to regret her boon as she grew old but did not die. She lived for hundreds of years, each year becoming smaller and frailer, Apollo having given her long life but not eternal youth. When the ostentatious Trimalchio speaks of her at his feast, she is but a tourist attraction, tiny, ancient, confined, and longing to die. *wasteland.windingway.org/epigraph*

[6] *I am not Russian; I come from Lithuania, a real German.*

294 | Free Verse

147 My cousin's, he took me out on a sled,

And I was frightened. He said, Marie,

Marie, hold on tight. And down we went.

150 In the mountains, there you feel free.

I read, much of the night, and go south in the winter.

What are the roots that clutch, what branches grow

153 Out of this stony rubbish? Son of man,[7]

You cannot say, or guess, for you know only

A heap of broken images, where the sun beats,

156 And the dead tree gives no shelter, the cricket no relief,[8]

And the dry stone no sound of water. Only

There is shadow under this red rock,[9]

159 (Come in under the shadow of this red rock),

And I will show you something different from either

Your shadow at morning striding behind you

162 Or your shadow at evening rising to meet you;

I will show you fear in a handful of dust.

---

[7] The title God gives Ezekiel at the start of his apocalyptic visions: *Son of man, stand up on your feet and I will speak to you. As he spoke, the Spirit came into me and raised me to my feet, and I heard him speaking to me. He said: "Son of man ... the people to whom I am sending you are obstinate and stubborn. Say to them, 'This is what the Sovereign Lord says.' And whether they listen or fail to listen—for they are a rebellious people—they will now that a prophet has been among them.* Ezekiel 2:1ff; see also Ch. 37 for the valley of dry bones. English Standard Version, biblehub.com/esv/ezekiel/2.htm

[8] *Remember also your Creator in the days of your youth, before the evil days come and the years draw near of which you will say, "I have no pleasure in them"; before the sun and the light and the moon and the stars are darkened and the clouds return after the rain, in the day when ... they are afraid also of what is high, and terrors are in the way; the almond tree blossoms, the grasshopper drags itself along, a and desire fails, because man is going to his eternal home, and the mourners go about the streets—... the dust returns to the earth as it was, and the spirit returns to God who gave it. Vanity of vanities, says the Preacher; all is vanity.* English Standard Version, 12:1ff, biblehub.com/esv/ecclesiastes/12.htm.

[9] *Behold, a king will reign in righteousness, and princes will rule in justice. Each will be like a hiding place from the wind, a shelter from the storm, like streams of water in a dry place, like the shade of a great rock in a weary land.* Isaiah 32:1ff. English Standard Version, biblehub.com/esv/isaiah/32.htm.

Eliot | 295

165   *Frisch weht der Wind*

             Der Heimat zu

             Mein Irisch Kind,

             Wo weilest du?[10]

        "You gave me hyacinths first a year ago;

168   "They called me the hyacinth girl."

        —Yet when we came back, late, from the Hyacinth garden,

        Your arms full, and your hair wet, I could not

171   Speak, and my eyes failed, I was neither

        Living nor dead, and I knew nothing,

        Looking into the heart of light, the silence.

174   *Oed' und leer das Meer.*[11]

        Madame Sosostris, famous clairvoyant,

177   Had a bad cold, nevertheless

        Is known to be the wisest woman in Europe,

        With a wicked pack of cards. Here, said she,

180   Is your card, the drowned Phoenician Sailor,

        (Those are pearls that were his eyes. Look!)

183   Here is Belladonna, the Lady of the Rocks,

        The lady of situations.

        Here is the man with three staves, and here the Wheel,

186   And here is the one-eyed merchant,[12] and this card,

---

[10] *Fresh blows the wind for home, my Irish child; where are you lingering?* Wagner, **Tristan und Isolde**, I,.5-8. A sailor sings sadly about the girl he left behind in his travels.

[11] *Wide and desolate is the sea.* Wagner, **Tristan und Isolde**, III.24. Tristan is sailing to England from Ireland to carry Isolde as a bride for his uncle, King Marke. Aboard the ship a young sailor sings a song about an Irish girl left behind. Isolde construes the sailor's song to be a mocking reference to herself, and hate wells up in her. In an outburst, she wishes that the seas would rise up and sink the ship, killing all.

[12] The one-eyed merchant and the Lady of the Rocks are not traditional Tarot cards. *Belladonna* means *beautiful woman* in Italian: cf. DaVinci's painting, *Madonna of the Rocks.* Belladonna is a drug or poison made from nightshade plants.

296 | *Free Verse*

Which is blank, is something he carries on his back,

Which I am forbidden to see. I do not find

189 The Hanged Man.[13] Fear death by water.

I see crowds of people, walking round in a ring.

Thank you. If you see dear Mrs. Equitone,

192 Tell her I bring the horoscope myself:

One must be so careful these days.

Unreal City,[14]

195 Under the brown fog of a winter dawn,

A crowd flowed over London Bridge, so many,

I had not thought death had undone so many.[15]

198 Sighs, short and infrequent, were exhaled,

And each man fixed his eyes before his feet.

---

[13] Three of the Tarot cards are traditional: the man with three staves, the Wheel of fortune, and The Hanged Man (hanged upside-down by one ankle from a T, an execution for traitors in Italy). In his notes, Eliot cites the Hanged God of Sir J.G. Fraser's *Golden Bough* (1922): "In the holy grove at Upsala ... human victims dedicated to Odin were regularly put to death by hanging or by a combination of hanging and stabbing, the man being strung up to a tree or a gallows and then wounded with a spear. Hence Odin was called the Lord of the Gallows or the God of the Hanged, and he is represented sitting under a gallows tree. Indeed he is said to have been sacrificed to himself: ... *I know that I hung on the windy tree For nine whole nights, Wounded with the spear, dedicated to Odin, Myself to myself.* www.bartleby.com/196/pages/page354.html

[14] For his "Unreal City" Eliot cites Baudelaire's "The Seven Old Men, To Victor Hugo": *Teeming, swarming city, city full of dreams, Where specters in broad day accost the passer-by!* Tr. W. Aggeler (1954), fleursdumal.org/poem/221.

[15] Dante, **Divine Comedy, Inferno III** (24ff): *Here sighs, with lamentations and loud moans, resounded through the air pierced by no star, that e'en I wept at entering. Various tongues, horrible languages, outcries of woe, accents of anger, voices deep and hoarse, with hands together smote that swell'd the sounds, made up a tumult, that forever whirls round through that air with solid darkness stain'd, like to the sand that in the whirlwind flies. I then, with horror yet encompast, cried: 'O master! what is this I hear? what race are these, who seem so overcome with woe?' He thus to me: 'This miserable fate suffer the wretched souls of those, who lived without or praise or blame, with that ill band of angels mix'd, who nor rebellious proved, Nor yet were true to God, but for themselves were only. From his bounds Heaven drove them forth not to impair his lustre; nor the depth of Hell receives them, lest the accursed tribe should glory thence with exultation vain.... These of death no hope may entertain: and their blind life so meanly passes, that all other lots they envy. Fame of them the world hath none, nor suffers; Mercy and Justice scorn them both. Speak not of them, but look, and pass them by.' And I, who straightway look'd, beheld a flag, which whirling ran around so rapidly, that it no pause obtain'd: and following came such a long train of spirits, I should ne'er Have thought that death so many had despoil'd.* (Harvard Classics: P.F. Collier & Son, 1909-14) bartleby.com/br/02001.html

Eliot | 297

201 Flowed up the hill and down King William Street,

To where Saint Mary Woolnoth kept the hours

With a dead sound on the final stroke of nine.

204 There I saw one I knew, and stopped him, crying: "Stetson!

"You who were with me in the ships at Mylae!

"That corpse you planted last year in your garden,

207 "Has it begun to sprout? Will it bloom this year?

"Or has the sudden frost disturbed its bed?

"Oh keep the Dog far hence, that's friend to men,

210 "Or with his nails he'll dig it up again![16]

"You! *hypocrite lecteur!—mon semblable,—mon frère!*"[17]

II. A Game of Chess

213 The Chair she sat in, like a burnished throne,

Glowed on the marble, where the glass

Held up by standards wrought with fruited vines

216 From which a golden Cupidon peeped out

(Another hid his eyes behind his wing)

Doubled the flames of sevenbranched candelabra

219 Reflecting light upon the table as

The glitter of her jewels rose to meet it,

From satin cases poured in rich profusion;

222 In vials of ivory and colored glass

Unstoppered, lurked her strange synthetic perfumes,

Unguent, powdered, or liquid—troubled, confused

---

[16] *Call for the robin-redbreast, and the wren, Since o'er shady groves they hover, And with leaves and flowers do cover The friendless bodies of unburied men. Call unto his funeral dole The ant, the field-mouse and the mole, To raise him hillocks that shall keep him warm, And (when gay tombs are robb'd) sustain no harm; But keep the wolf far thence, that's foe to men, For with his nails he'll dig them up again.* From "The White Devil," by John Webster, [Funeral Dirge for Marcello], English Literature (MacMillan Co., 1904), luminarium.org/sevenlit/webster/dirge.htm

[17] *You! Hypocrite reader! my like, my brother!* Baudelaire, **Fleurs du Mal** (Preface).

298 | Free Verse

225 And drowned the sense in odours; stirred by the air

That freshened from the window, these ascended

In fattening the prolonged candle-flames,

228 Flung their smoke into the laquearia,

Stirring the pattern on the coffered ceiling.

Huge sea-wood fed with copper

231 Burned green and orange, framed by the colored stone,

In which sad light a carvéd dolphin swam.

Above the antique mantel was displayed

234 As though a window gave upon the sylvan scene

The change of Philomel, by the barbarous king

So rudely forced; yet there the nightingale

237 Filled all the desert with inviolable voice

And still she cried, and still the world pursues,

"Jug Jug" to dirty ears.

240 And other withered stumps of time

Were told upon the walls; staring forms

Leaned out, leaning, hushing the room enclosed.

243 Footsteps shuffled on the stair.

Under the firelight, under the brush, her hair

Spread out in fiery points

246 Glowed into words, then would be savagely still.

"My nerves are bad tonight. Yes, bad. Stay with me.

"Speak to me. Why do you never speak. Speak.

249 "What are you thinking of? What thinking? What?

"I never know what you are thinking. Think."

I think we are in rats' alley

252 Where the dead men lost their bones.

"What is that noise?"

255	The wind under the door.
	"What is that noise now? What is the wind doing?"
	Nothing again nothing.
258	"Do
	"You know nothing? Do you see nothing? Do you remember
	"Nothing?"
261	I remember
	Those are pearls that were his eyes.
	"Are you alive, or not? Is there nothing in your head?"
264	But

O O O O that Shakespeherian Rag—

It's so elegant

267 So intelligent

"What shall I do now? What shall I do?"

"I shall rush out as I am, and walk the street

270 "With my hair down, so. What shall we do tomorrow?

"What shall we ever do?"

The hot water at ten.

273 And if it rains, a closed car at four.

And we shall play a game of chess,

Pressing lidless eyes and waiting for a knock upon the door.

276 When Lil's husband got demobbed, I said—

I didn't mince my words, I said to her myself,

HURRY UP PLEASE ITS TIME

279 Now Albert's coming back, make yourself a bit smart.

He'll want to know what you done with that money he gave you

To get yourself some teeth. He did, I was there.

282 You have them all out, Lil, and get a nice set,

He said, I swear, I can't bear to look at you.

300 | *Free Verse*

And no more can't I, I said, and think of poor Albert,

285 He's been in the army four years, he wants a good time,

And if you don't give it him, there's others will, I said.

Oh is there, she said. Something o' that, I said.

288 Then I'll know who to thank, she said, and give me a straight look.

HURRY UP PLEASE ITS TIME

If you don't like it you can get on with it, I said.

291 Others can pick and choose if you can't.

But if Albert makes off, it won't be for lack of telling.

You ought to be ashamed, I said, to look so antique.

294 (And her only thirty-one.)

I can't help it, she said, pulling a long face,

It's them pills I took, to bring it off, she said.

297 (She's had five already, and nearly died of young George.)

The chemist said it would be all right, but I've never been the same.

You are a proper fool, I said.

300 Well, if Albert won't leave you alone, there it is, I said,

What you get married for if you don't want children?

HURRY UP PLEASE ITS TIME

303 Well, that Sunday Albert was home, they had a hot gammon,

And they asked me in to dinner, to get the beauty of it hot—

HURRY UP PLEASE ITS TIME

306 HURRY UP PLEASE ITS TIME

Goonight Bill. Goonight Lou. Goonight May. Goonight.

Ta ta. Goonight. Goonight.

309 Good night, ladies, good night, sweet ladies, good night, good night.

III. The Fire Sermon

The river's tent is broken: the last fingers of leaf
Clutch and sink into the wet bank. The wind
Crosses the brown land, unheard. The nymphs are departed.
Sweet Thames, run softly, till I end my song.
The river bears no empty bottles, sandwich papers,
Silk handkerchiefs, cardboard boxes, cigarette ends
Or other testimony of summer nights. The nymphs are departed.
And their friends, the loitering heirs of city directors;
Departed, have left no addresses.
By the waters of Leman I sat down and wept . . .
Sweet Thames, run softly till I end my song,
Sweet Thames, run softly, for I speak not loud or long.
But at my back in a cold blast I hear
The rattle of the bones, and chuckle spread from ear to ear.

A rat crept softly through the vegetation
Dragging its slimy belly on the bank
While I was fishing in the dull canal
On a winter evening round behind the gashouse
Musing upon the king my brother's wreck
And on the king my father's death before him.

White bodies naked on the low damp ground
And bones cast in a little low dry garret,
Rattled by the rat's foot only, year to year.
But at my back from time to time I hear
The sound of horns and motors, which shall bring
Sweeney to Mrs. Porter in the spring.

302 | Free Verse

336 O the moon shone bright on Mrs. Porter

And on her daughter

They wash their feet in soda water

339 *Et O ces voix d'enfants, chantant dans la coupole!*[18]

Twit twit twit

Jug jug jug jug jug jug

342 So rudely forc'd.

Tereu[19]

Unreal City

345 Under the brown fog of a winter noon

Mr. Eugenides, the Smyrna merchant

Unshaven, with a pocket full of currants

348 C.i.f. London: documents at sight,

Asked me in demotic French

To luncheon at the Cannon Street Hotel

351 Followed by a weekend at the Metropole.

At the violet hour, when the eyes and back

Turn upward from the desk, when the human engine waits

354 Like a taxi throbbing waiting,

I Tiresias, though blind, throbbing between two lives,

Old man with wrinkled female breasts, can see

357 At the violet hour, the evening hour that strives

Homeward, and brings the sailor home from sea,

---

[18] *And O those children's voices singing in the dome!* Verlaine, *Parsifal*, a poem about a knight who resists all lust and desire so that he can drink from the Holy Grail.

[19] Tereus forced himself upon his wife's sister, Philomela, then cut her tongue out. Later he gave her to King Lynceus and told his wife her sister was dead. Philomela wove letters in a tapestry depicting Tereus's crime and sent it secretly to her sister Procne. When Procne recognized her sister and knew the crimes of Tereus, she in revenge killed her son by Tereus, Itys, and served his flesh in a meal at his father's table, and then fled with her sister. Tereus pursued the sisters to kill them, but all three were changed by the Olympian gods into birds: Tereus into a hoopoe, an onomatopoeic name from the male's loud mating song; Procne into a swallow, whose song is mournful; and Philomela, a nightingale—although the female nightingale has no song. *en.wikipedia.org/wiki/Tereus*

Eliot | 303

The typist home at teatime, clears her breakfast, lights

360   Her stove, and lays out food in tins.

Out of the window perilously spread

Her drying combinations touched by the sun's last rays,

363   On the divan are piled (at night her bed)

Stockings, slippers, camisoles, and stays.

I Tiresias, old man with wrinkled dugs

366   Perceived the scene, and foretold the rest—

I too awaited the expected guest.

He, the young man carbuncular, arrives,

369   A small house agent's clerk, with one bold stare,

One of the low on whom assurance sits

As a silk hat on a Bradford millionaire.

372   The time is now propitious, as he guesses,

The meal is ended, she is bored and tired,

Endeavours to engage her in caresses

375   Which still are unreproved, if undesired.

Flushed and decided, he assaults at once;

Exploring hands encounter no defence;

378   His vanity requires no response,

And makes a welcome of indifference.

(And I Tiresias have foresuffered all

381   Enacted on this same divan or bed;

I who have sat by Thebes below the wall

And walked among the lowest of the dead.)[20]

---

[20] Eliot quotes Ovid's **Metamorphoses:** *Jove, flush with wine, relaxed, jested with Juno, Your pleasure in love, said he, is greater than any husband's." She denied it, and it was decided to ask wise Tiresias' judgment, as he knew both sides of lovemaking. For he once struck with a staff two huge serpents mating in a green wood and, a thing wonderous to tell, was changed into a woman; he passed seven years in that shape. In the eighth year he saw the same serpents again and said: "Since in striking you there's power to*

304 | *Free Verse*

384 Bestows one final patronising kiss,

And gropes his way, finding the stairs unlit . . .

She turns and looks a moment in the glass,

387 Hardly aware of her departed lover;

Her brain allows one half-formed thought to pass:

"Well now that's done: and I'm glad it's over."

390 When lovely woman stoops to folly and

Paces about her room again, alone,

She smoothes her hair with automatic hand,

393 And puts a record on the gramophone.

"This music crept by me upon the waters"

And along the Strand, up Queen Victoria Street.

396 O City city, I can sometimes hear

Beside a public bar in Lower Thames Street,

The pleasant whining of a mandoline

399 And a clatter and a chatter from within

Where fishmen lounge at noon: where the walls

Of Magnus Martyr hold

402 Inexplicable splendor of Ionian white and gold.

  The river sweats

  Oil and tar

405 The barges drift

  With the turning tide

  Red sails

408 Wide

  To leeward, swing on the heavy spar.

---

change contraries to one another, I shall strike you again. He struck the serpents and was restored to his former shape, as he had been born. As chosen arbiter of the dispute in jest, he confirmed the words of Jove. But Saturnia took it hard and saying that judges are ever blind made him blind forever. Now no god may undo what another has done, but for the light he lost, the all powerful father granted him to know the future and lightened her punishment with this honor.

                        The barges wash

411   Drifting logs

                        Down Greenwich reach

                        Past the Isle of Dogs.

414   Weialala leia

                                    Wallala leialala

        Elizabeth and Leicester[21]

417   Beating oars

                        The stern was formed

                        A gilded shell

420   Red and gold

        The brisk swell

                        Rippled both shores

423   Southwest wind

                        Carried down stream

                        The peal of bells

426   White towers

        Weialala leia

                        Wallala leialala

429   "Trams and dusty trees.

        Highbury bore me. Richmond and Kew

        Undid me. By Richmond I raised my knees

432   Supine on the floor of a narrow canoe."

        "My feet are at Moorgate, and my heart

        Under my feet. After the event

435   He wept. He promised a 'new start.'

        I made no comment. What should I resent?"

---

[21] *In the afternoon we were in a barge, watching the games on the river. (The Queen) was alone with Lord Robert and myself on the poop, when they began to talk nonsense, and went so far that Lord Robert at last said, as I was on the spot there was no reason why they should not be married if the Queen pleased.* Letter of De Quadra to Philip of Spain, V. Froud, Elizabeth, Vol 1, Ch. iv (Eliot's note).

306 | *Free Verse*

"On Margate Sands.

438   I can connect

Nothing with nothing.

The broken fingernails of dirty hands.

441   My people humble people who expect

Nothing."
                  la la

444   To Carthage then I came[22]

Burning burning burning burning[23]

O Lord Thou pluckest me out

447   O Lord Thou pluckest

burning

IV. Death by Water

Phlebas the Phoenician, a fortnight dead,

450   Forgot the cry of gulls, and the deep sea swell

And the profit and loss.

---

[22] Eliot cites Augustine's Confessions: ...to Carthage then I came, where a cauldron of unholy loves sang all about mine ears and O Lord Thou pluckest me out.

[23] The Fire Sermon: ... *Then The Blessed One, having dwelt in Uruvela as long as he wished, proceeded on his wanderings in the direction of Gaya Head, accompanied by a great congregation of priests, a thousand in number, who had all of them been monks with matted hair. And there in Gaya, on Gaya Head, The Blessed One dwelt, together with the thousand priests. And there The Blessed One addressed the priests: All things, O priests, are on fire. And what, O priests, are all these things which are on fire? The eye, O priests, is on fire; forms are on fire; eye-consciousness is on fire; impressions received by the eye are on fire; and whatever sensation, pleasant, unpleasant, or indifferent, originates in dependence on impressions received by the eye, that also is on fire. And with what are these on fire? With the fire of passions, say I, with the fire of hatred, with the fire of infatuation, with birth, old age, death, sorrow, lamentation, misery, grief, and despair are they on fire.... The ear is on fire; sounds are on fire; ...the nose is on fire; odors are on fire; ...the tongue is on fire; tastes are on fire; ...the body is on fire; ideas are on fire; ...mind-consciousness is on fire; impressions received by the mind are on fire; and whatever sensation, pleasant, unpleasant, or indifferent, originates in dependence on impressions received by the mind, that also is on fire. And with what are these on fire? With the fire of passion, say I, with the fire of hatred, with the fire of lamentation; with birth, old age, death, sorrow, lamentation, misery, grief, and despair are they on fire.* Tr. H.C. Warren, in *Buddhism in Translation, wasteland.windingway.org/308/burning-burning-burning-burning*

Eliot | *307*

A current under sea

453 Picked his bones in whispers. As he rose and fell

He passed the stages of his age and youth

Entering the whirlpool.

456 Gentile or Jew

O you who turn the wheel and look to windward,

Consider Phlebas, who was once handsome and tall as you.

V. What the Thunder Said

459 After the torchlight red on sweaty faces

After the frosty silence in the gardens

After the agony in stony places

462 The shouting and the crying

Prison and palace and reverberation

Of thunder of spring over distant mountains

465 He who was living is now dead

We who were living are now dying

With a little patience

468 Here is no water but only rock

Rock and no water and the sandy road

The road winding above among the mountains

471 Which are mountains of rock without water

If there were water we should stop and drink

Amongst the rock one cannot stop or think

474 Sweat is dry and feet are in the sand

If there were only water amongst the rock

Dead mountain mouth of carious teeth that cannot spit

477 Here one can neither stand nor lie nor sit

There is not even silence in the mountains

But dry sterile thunder without rain

308 | Free Verse

480   There is not even solitude in the mountains

But red sullen faces sneer and snarl

From doors of mudcracked houses

483   If there were water

And no rock

If there were rock

486   And also water

And water

A spring

489   A pool among the rock

If there were the sound of water only

Not the cicada

492   And dry grass singing

But sound of water over a rock

Where the hermit-thrush sings in the pine trees

495   Drip drop drip drop drop drop drop

But there is no water

Who is the third who walks always beside you?

498   When I count, there are only you and I together

But when I look ahead up the white road

There is always another one walking beside you

501   Gliding wrapt in a brown mantle, hooded

I do not know whether a man or a woman

—But who is that on the other side of you?[24]

504   What is that sound high in the air

Murmur of maternal lamentation

Who are those hooded hordes swarming

507   Over endless plains, stumbling in cracked earth

---

[24] Eliot cites Acts, when two disciples on the road to Emmaus after the crucifixion talking of his death meet the newly risen Jesus without recognizing him.

Eliot | 309

Ringed by the flat horizon only

What is the city over the mountains

510   Cracks and reforms and bursts in the violet air

Falling towers

Jerusalem Athens Alexandria

513   Vienna London

Unreal

A woman drew her long black hair out tight

516   And fiddled whisper music on those strings

And bats with baby faces in the violet light

Whistled, and beat their wings

519   And crawled head downward down a blackened wall

And upside down in air were towers

Tolling reminiscent bells, that kept the hours

522   And voices singing out of empty cisterns and exhausted wells.

In this decayed hole among the mountains

In the faint moonlight, the grass is singing

525   Over the tumbled graves, about the chapel

There is the empty chapel, only the wind's home.

It has no windows, and the door swings,

528   Dry bones can harm no one.

Only a cock stood on the rooftree

Co co rico co co rico

531   In a flash of lightning. Then a damp gust

Bringing rain

Ganga was sunken, and the limp leaves

534   Waited for rain, while the black clouds

Gathered far distant, over Himavant.

310 | *Free Verse*

537 The jungle crouched, humped in silence.

Then spoke the thunder[25]

DA

540 *Datta*: what have we given?

My friend, blood shaking my heart

The awful daring of a moment's surrender

543 Which an age of prudence can never retract

By this, and this only, we have existed

Which is not to be found in our obituaries

546 Or in memories draped by the beneficent spider

Or under seals broken by the lean solicitor

In our empty rooms

549 DA

Dayadhvam: I have heard the key

Turn in the door once and turn once only

552 We think of the key, each in his prison

Thinking of the key, each confirms a prison

Only at nightfall, aethereal rumours

555 Revive for a moment a broken Coriolanus

DA

Damyata: The boat responded

558 Gaily, to the hand expert with sail and oar

---

[25] Cf. **Brihadaranyaka Upanishad** 5.2:1-3: *Three classes of Prajapati's sons lived a life of continence with their father Prajapati (Creator): the gods, men and Asuras. The gods on the completion of their term said, 'Please instruct us.' He told them the syllable 'Da': 'Have you understood?' (They) said, 'We have. You tell us: Control yourselves.' (He) said, 'Yes, you have understood.' —Then the men said to him, 'Please instruct us'. He told them the same syllable 'Da': 'Have you understood?' (They) said, 'We have. You tell us: Give.' (He) said, 'Yes, you have understood.' —Then the Asuras said to him, 'Please instruct us.' He told them the same syllable 'Da': 'Have you understood?' (They) said, 'We have. You tell us: Have compassion.' (He) said, 'Yes, you have understood.' That very thing is repeated by the heavenly voice, the cloud, as 'Da,' 'Da,' 'Da' 'Control yourselves,' 'Give,' and 'Have compassion.' Therefore one should learn these three: self control, charity and compassion.* Courtesy of *wasteland.windngway.org.*

Eliot | 311

The sea was calm, your heart would have responded

Gaily, when invited, beating obedient

561 To controlling hands

I sat upon the shore

Fishing, with the arid plain behind me

564 Shall I at least set my lands in order?[26]

London Bridge is falling down falling down falling down

Poi s'ascose nel foco che gli affina[27]

567 *Quando fiam uti chelidon*[28]—O swallow swallow

Le Prince d'Aquitaine à la tour abolie[29]

These fragments I have shored against my ruins

570 Why then Ile fit you. Hieronymo's mad againe.[30]

Datta. Dayadhvam. Damyata.
    Shantih   shantih   shantih[31]

---

[26] Isaiah 38:1. *Thus saith the Lord: Set thine house in order: for thou shalt die, and not live.* Eliot also cites the tale about the Fisher King, immortal guardian of the Holy Grail who, crippled by a magical wound for which his lands are desolate and infertile, spends his days fishing on a lake near his castle, until the knight Percival comes in search of the Holy Grail and heals the King, restoring fertility to the land and becoming keeper of the Grail.

[27] *"I pray you by that power conducting you to the summit of the staircase, recall then my pain." Then he hid himself in the fire that refines him.* Dante, *Purgatorio* XXVI. This final verse refers to Arnaut Daniel in the circle that punishes lust. In the next canto, Virgil must coax the terrified Dante to pass through this fire—as all souls must—to reach Beatrice.

[28] *When shall I become like the swallow.* "Pervigilium Veneris," a Latin poem of late antiquity written on the eve of the festival of Venus. It begins, *Let the one love tomorrow who has never loved, and let the one who has loved love* tomorrow, and it ends with the nightingale's song: *She sings; we are silent; when will my springtime come?* en.wikipedia.org/wiki/Pervigilium_Veneris

[29] From "El Desdichado," Gérard de Nerval: *I am the man of gloom,—the widower,—the unconsoled, The Prince of Aquitania, his tower in ruins: My only star is dead, and my constellated lute Bears the Black Sun of Melancholia. [...] I have dreamed in the grotto where the siren swims... And twice I have crossed Acheron victorious: modulating on the lyre of Orpheus Now the sighs of the saint, now the cry of the fairy.* (Tr. Rainey). link.springer.com/chapter/10.1057/9781137482846_52

[30] Thomas Kyd, *The Spanish Tragedy.* Hieronymo's son, Horatio, is murdered by a rival, driving Hieronymo mad as he plots revenge. *Ile fit you* (I'll oblige you) is from a scene where Hieronymo persuades the murderers to perform in a play for the king (IV.2).

[31] Peace, prayed at the end of an Upanishad. Eliot cites Philippians 4:7: The peace of God that passeth all understanding shall keep your hearts and minds through Christ Jesus.

ORPHEUS

Orpheus was the son of the Muse Calliope, patron of epic poetry,
and Apollo, god of poetry, who gave him his first lyre.
So beautiful was his singing that even animals, trees, and rocks
danced about him as he played.
He saved the Argonauts from the music of the Sirens by playing his own.

He married Eurydice, soon killed by a snakebite.
So overcome was Orpheus with grief that he sought his beloved in the land of the dead.
With his music he charmed the ferryman Charon
and the dog Cerberus who guarded the River Styx.
Then with the grief of his music he so moved Hades, King of the underworld,
that the god gave him leave take Eurydice back to the world of life and light,
if but leaving they look not back.

As Orpheus led his beloved up from the land of death,
seeing the Sun anew at the opening to the land of the living,
he turned back to share his delight with Eurydice,
and she vanished from his sight.

In the end, because Orpheus worshipped Apollo to the neglect of Dionysius,
the rival god drove Maenads to tear Orpheus to pieces in a Bacchic orgy.
His head, still singing, floated on his lyre to Lesbos,
where the Orphic oracle was established.

The Muses gathered up his limbs and buried them.
They placed his lyre in the heavens as a constellation.

In time the Orphic Oracle so surpassed Apollo's Delphic Oracle in renown
that Apollo bid the Orphic Oracle cease,
and it did.

The Head of Orpheus on his Lyre
by Gustav Moreau

INDEX: POEMS BY POET

BEHN
- One day the Amorous Lisander, *The Disappointment*—Ballad pp. 111-17.
- Love in Fantastic Triumph sat, *Love Armed*—Iterative p. 200.
- A thousand Martyrs I have made—Iterative p. 201.

BROWNING
- If thou must love me, let it be for nought, *Sonnets from the Portuguese* **14**—Sonnet p. 82.
- How do I love thee? Let me count the ways, *Sonnets from the Portuguese* **34**—Sonnet p. 83.
- What was he doing, the great god Pan, *A Musical Instrument*—Ballad pp. 122-23.

COLERIDGE, MARY ELIZABETH
- The myrtle bush grew shady, **Jealousy**—Variable, p. 185.
- The clouds had made a crimson crown, *A Moment*—Variable, p. 184.
- I sat before my glass one day, *The Other Side of a Mirror*—Iterative, p. 220.

COLERIDGE, SAMUEL
- In Xanadu did Kubla Khan, *Kubla Khan; Or, a vision in a dream*—Variable pp. 176-77.

cummings
- the bigness of cannon—Free p. 257.
- since feeling is first—Free p. 258.
- in Just—Free p. 259.
- into the strenuous briefness—Free, p. 260.
- when god lets my body be—Free, p. 261.

DICKENSON
- There's a certain Slant of light—Ballad p. 124.
- There is a solitude of space—Ballad p. 125.
- I died for beauty, but was scarce—Ballad p. 126.
- This World is not Conclusion—Ballad. p. 127.
- Banish Air from Air—Free p. 241.
- After great pain, a formal feeling comes—Free p. 242.
- One need not be a Chamber—to be Haunted—Free p. 243.
- In Winter in my Room—Free p. 244.

DONNE
- I am a little world made cunningly, *Holy Sonnet V*—Sonnet p. 60.
- Oh, to vex me, contraries meet in one, *Holy Sonnet XIX*—Sonnet p. 61.
- For God's sake hold your tongue, and let me love, *The Canonization*—Ballad pp. 106-7.
- Go and catch a falling star, *Song*—Ballad p. 108.
- Let man's soul be a sphere, and then, in this, *Good Friday, 1613.*—Variable p. 150.
- 'Tis the year's midnight, and it is the day's, *A Nocturnal Upon St. Lucy's Day*—Variable pp. 152-53.
- Busy old fool, unruly Sun, *The Sun Rising*—Variable p. 154.
- Let me pour forth, *A Valediction: Of Weeping*—Variable p. 155.
- As virtuous men pass mildly away, *A Valediction Forbidding Mourning*—Iterative pp. 194-95.

DOOLITTLE
- You are clear, *Sea Garden*—Free p. 250.
- I should have thought, *At Baia*—p. 251.
- So you have swept me back, **Eurydice**—pp. 252-54.

ELIOT
- Let us go then, you and I, *The Love Song of J. Alfred Prufrock*—Free pp. 287-92
- April is the cruellest month, breeding, *The Waste Land*—Free pp. 293-311.

FROST
- I found a dimpled spider, fat and white, *Design*—Sonnet p. 88.
- Love at the lips was touch, *To Earthward*—Ballad p. 144.
- Before man came to blow it right, *The Aim Was Song*—Ballad p. 145.
- It went many years, *The Lockless Door*—Variable p. 188.
- Tree at my window, window tree, *Tree at my Window*—Variable p. 189.
- Others taunt me with having knelt at well-curbs, *For Once, Then, Something*—Iterative p. 236.
- I have been one acquainted with the night, *Acquainted with the Night*—Iterative p. 237.

INDEX: POEMS BY POET

GREVILLE
- In night when colors all to black are cast, *Caelica 100*–Sonnet p. 58.
- The nurse-life wheat within his green husk growing, *Caelica 29*–Sonnet p. 59.
- Down in the depth of mine iniquity, *Caelica 99*–Iterative p. 193.

HERBERT
- Prayer the Church's banquet, angels' age, *Prayer* **(I)**–Sonnet p. 62.
- Wounded I sing, tormented I indite, *Joseph's Coat*–Sonnet p. 63.
- I struck the board, and cried, "No more, *The Collar*–Variable pp. 156–57.
- A broken ALTAR, Lord, thy servant rears, *The Altar*–Variable p. 158
- Lord, who createdst man in wealth and store, *Easter Wings*–Variable p. 159.
- My God, I heard this day, *Man*–Variable pp. 160–61.
- While that my soul repairs to her devotion, *Church Monuments*–Iterative p. 196.
- My words and thoughts do both expresse this notion, *Our life is hid with Christ in God*–Iterative p. 197.

HOPKINS
- As kingfishers catch fire, dragonflies draw flame–Sonnet p. 84.
- Thou art indeed just, Lord, if I contend–Sonnet p. 85.
- I wake and feel the fell of dark, not day.–Sonnet p. 86.
- The world is charged with the grandeur of God, *God's Grandeur*–Sonnet p. 87.
- Glory be to God for dappled things, *Pied Beauty*–Variable p. 180.
- Not, I'll not, carrion comfort, Despair, not feast on thee, *Carrion Comfort*–Variable p. 181.
- Márgarét, áre you gríeving, *Spring and Fall*–Variable p. 182.
- I caught this morning morning's minion, king, *The Windhover*–Variable p. 183.

JONSON
- Farewell, thou child of my right hand, and joy, *On My First Son*–Variable p. 162.
- Slow, slow, fresh fount, keep time with my salt tears, *Echo's Song for Narcissus*–Variable p. 163.
- I now think Love is rather deaf than blind, *My Picture Left in Scotland*–Variable p. 164.
- Follow a shadow, it still flies you, *That Women Are But Men's Shadows*–Variable p. 165.
- Let it not your wonder move, *A Celebration of Charis: His Excuse for Loving*–Iterative p. 198.
- The trawl of unquiet mind drops astern, *Evening: Barents Sea*–Iterative p. 199.

KEATS
- To Sleep, O soft embalmer of the still midnight, *To Sleep*–Sonnet p. 78.
- O what can ail thee, knight-at-arms, *La Belle Dame sans Merci: A Ballad*–Ballad pp. 118–19.
- My heart aches, and a drowsy numbness pains, *Ode to a Nightingale*–Iterative pp. 208–09.
- Thou still unravish'd bride of quietness, *Ode on a Grecian Urn*–Iterative pp. 212–13.

MARVELL
- See how the orient dew, *On a Drop of Dew*–Variable pp. 166–67.
- My love is of a birth as rare, *The Definition of Love*–Iterative pp. 202–03.
- Had we but world enough and time, *To His Coy Mistress*–Iterative pp. 204–05.
- O who shall, from this dungeon, raise, *A Dialogue Between the Soul and the Body*–Iterative pp. 206–07.

MELVILLE
- Skimming lightly, wheeling still, *Shiloh: A Requiem*–Variable p. 186.

MILLAY
- I, being born a woman and distressed–Sonnet p. 89.
- I think I should have loved you presently–Sonnet p. 90.
- Loving you less than life, a little less–Sonnet p. 91.
- Into the golden vessel of great song–Sonnet p. 92.
- When I too long have looked upon your face–Sonnet p. 93.
- Euclid alone has looked on Beauty bare–Sonnet p. 94.
- Still will I harvest beauty where it grows–Sonnet p. 95.
- All I could see from where I stood, *Renascence*–Iterative pp. 226–35.
- To what purpose, April, do you return again? *Spring*–Free, p. 245.

MILTON
- How soon hath Time, the subtle thief of youth, *Sonnets* **7**–Sonnet p. 76.
- When I consider how my light is spent, *Sonnets* 17–Sonnet p. 77.

INDEX: POEMS BY POET

POUND
- The apparition of these faces in the crowd, *"In A Station at the Metro"*—Free pp. 262–65.
- For three years out of key with his time, **Hugh Selwyn Mauberley**—Free pp. 266–86.

SHAKESPEARE
- When I do count the clock that tells the time, *Sonnets* 1—Meter p. 4.
- Shall I compare thee to a summer's day? *Sonnets* 18—Meter p. 5.
- From fairest creatures we desire increase, *Sonnets* 1—Sonnet p. 44.
- Weary with toil, I haste me to my bed, *Sonnets* 27—Sonnet p. 45.
- When, in disgrace with fortune and men's eyes, *Sonnets* 29—Sonnet p. 46.
- Was it the proud full sail of his great verse, *Sonnets* 86—Sonnet p. 47.
- What is your substance, whereof are you made, *Sonnets* 51—Sonnet p. 48.
- When my love swears that she is made of truth, *Sonnets* 138—Sonnet p. 49.
- That time of year thou mayst in me behold, *Sonnets* 73—Sonnet p. 50.
- Not mine own fears, nor the prophetic soul, *Sonnets* 107—Sonnet p. 51.
- They that have pow'r to hurt, and will do none, *Sonnets* 94—Sonnet p. 52.
- 'Tis better to be vile than vile esteemed, *Sonnets* 121—Sonnet p. 53.
- How like a winter hath my absence been, *Sonnets* 97—Sonnet p. 54.
- Let me not to the marriage of true minds, *Sonnets* 116—Sonnet p. 55.
- Th' expense of spirit in a waste of shame, *Sonnets* 129—Sonnet p. 56.
- So are you to my thoughts as food to life, *Sonnets* 75—Sonnet p. 57.

SHELLEY
- I met a traveller from an antique land, *Ozymandias*—Sonnet p. 79.
- The everlasting universe of things, *Mont Blanc*—Iterative pp. 214–19.

SIDNEY
- Loving in truth, and fain in verse my love to show—Sonnet p. 38.
- Come, Sleep! O Sleep, the certain knot of peace—Sonnet p. 39.
- Thou blind man's mark, thou fool's self-chosen snare—Sonnet p. 40.
- Leave me, O Love, which reachest but to dust—Sonnet p. 41.

SPENSER
- Like as a huntsman after weary chase—Sonnet p. 42.
- My love is like to ice, and I to fire—Sonnet p. 43.
- Calm was the day, and through the trembling air, *Prothalamion*—Ballad p. 99.

STEVENS
- The Snow Man—Free p. 246.
- The Emperor of Ice Cream—Free p. 247.
- Thirteen Ways of Looking at a Blackbird—Free p. 248.

THOMAS
- And death shall have no dominion—Variable p. 187.
- Do not go gentle into that good night—Iterative p. 225.

WILDE
- Tread lightly, she is near, *Requiescat*—Ballad p. 128.
- He did not wear his scarlet coat, *The Ballad of Reading Gaol*—Ballad p. 129–41.

WORDSWORTH
- The world is too much with us; late and soon—Sonnet p. 80.
- Surprised by joy—impatient as the Wind—Sonnet p. 81.
- I wandered lonely as a cloud—Ballad p. 120.
- There is a change—and I am poor, *A Complaint*—Ballad. p. 121.
- There was a time when meadow, grove, and stream, *Ode: Immortality*—Variable p. 168–75.

INDEX: POEMS BY POET

WROTH

Sonnets From Pamphilia to Amphilanthus
- When night's black mantle could most darkness prove, *Sonnet I*–Sonnet p. 64.
- Dear eyes, how well, indeed, you do adorn, *Sonnet II*–Sonnet p. 64.
- Yet is there hope. Then love but play thy part, *Sonnet III*–Sonnet p. 64.
- Venus unto the Gods a suit did move, *Sonnet IV*–Sonnet p. 64.
- Can pleasing sight, misfortune ever bring? *Sonnet V*–Sonnet p. 65.
- O strive not still to heap disdain on me, *Sonnet VI*–Sonnet p. 65.
- Love leave to urge, thou know'st thou hast the hand, *Sonnet VII*–Sonnet p. 65.
- Led by the power of grief, to wailings brought, *Sonnet VIII*–Sonnet p. 65.
- Be you all pleased? Your pleasures grieve not me, *Sonnet IX*–Sonnet p. 66.
- The weary traveller who tired sought, *Sonnet X*–Sonnet p. 66.
- You endless torments that my rest oppress, *Sonnet XI*–Sonnet p. 66.
- Cloyed with the torments of a tedious night, *Sonnet XII*–Sonnet p. 66.
- Dear, famish not what you yourself gave food, *Sonnet XIII*–Sonnet p. 67.
- Am I thus conquered? Have I lost the powers? *Sonnet XIV*–Sonnet p. 67.
- Love like a juggler, comes to play his prize, *Sonnet XV*–Sonnet p. 67.
- My pain, still smothered in my grieved breast, *Sonnet XVI*–Sonnet p. 67.
- Poor Love in chains, and fetters, like a thief, *Sonnet XVII*–Sonnet p. 68.
- Which should I better like of, day, or night, *Sonnet XVIII*–Sonnet p. 68.
- Come darkest night, becoming sorrow best, *Sonnet XIX*–Sonnet p. 68.
- The Sun which glads the earth at his bright sight, *Sonnet XX*–Sonnet p. 68.
- When I last saw thee, I did not thee see, *Sonnet XXI*–Sonnet p. 69.
- Cupid would needs make me a lover be, *Sonnet XXII*–Sonnet p. 69.
- When every one to pleasing pastime hies, *Sonnet XXIII*–Sonnet p. 69.
- Once did I hear an aged father say, *Sonnet XXIV*–Sonnet p. 69.
- Poor eyes be blind, the light behold no more, *Sonnet XXV*–Sonnet p. 70.
- Most blessed Night, the happy time for love, *Sonnet XXVI*–Sonnet p. 70.
- Fie treacherous Hope, why do you still rebel? *Sonnet XXVII*–Sonnet p. 70.
- Grief, killing grief, have not my torments been, *Sonnet XXVIII*–Sonnet p. 70.
- Fly hence, O joy, no longer here abide, *Sonnet XXIX*–Sonnet p. 71.
- You blessed shades, which give me silent rest, *Sonnet XXX*–Sonnet p. 71.
- After long trouble in a tedious way, *Sonnet XXXI*–Sonnet p. 71.
- How fast thou fliest, O Time, on love's swift wings, *Sonnet XXXII*–Sonnet p. 71.
- How many eyes hast thou, poor Love, to guard, *Sonnet XXXIII*–Sonnet p. 72.
- Take heed mine eyes, how you your looks do cast, *Sonnet XXXIV*–Sonnet p. 72.
- My heart is lost, what can I now expect, *Sonnet XXXV*–Sonnet p. 72.
- Juno, still jealous of her husband Jove, *Sonnet XXXVI*–Sonnet p. 72.
- Night, welcome art thou to my mind distressed, *Sonnet XXXVII*–Sonnet p. 73.
- What pleasure can a banished creature have, *Sonnet XXXVIII*–Sonnet p. 73.
- If I were given to mirth 'twould be more cross, *Sonnet XXXIX*–Sonnet p. 73.
- It is not love which you poor fools do deem, *Sonnet XL*–Sonnet p. 73.
- Late in the forest I did Cupid see, *Sonnet XLI*–Sonnet p. 74.
- If ever love had force in human breast, *Sonnet XLII*–Sonnet p. 74.
- O dearest eyes the lights, and guides of love, *Sonnet XLIII*–Sonnet p. 74.
- How fast thou hastest (O Spring) with swiftest speed, *Sonnet XLIV*–Sonnet p. 74.
- Good now be still, and do not me torment, *Sonnet XL*–Sonnet p. 75.
- Love, thou hast all, for now thou hast me made, *Sonnet XL*–Sonnet p. 75.
- O stay mine eyes, shed not these fruitless tears, *Sonnet XL*–Sonnet p. 75.
- How like a fire doth love increase in me, *Sonnet XL*–Sonnet p. 75.
- Love peruse me, seeke, and finde, **Song**, *The Countesse of Montgomery's Urania*–Ballad p. 110.

WYATT
- Whoso list to hunt, I know where is an hind–Sonnet p. 35.
- My galley chargèd with forgetfulness–Sonnet p. 36.
- The longë love that in my thought doth harbour–Sonnet p. 37.
- They flee from me that sometime did me seek–Variable p. 149.

YEATS
- My mother dandled me and sang, **Song from** *The Player Queen*–Ballad p. 142.
- I met the Bishop on the road, *Crazy Jane Talks with the Bishop*–Ballad p. 143.
- That is no country for old men. The young, *Sailing to Byzantium*–Iterative pp. 222-23.
- Turning and turning in the widening gyre, *The Second Coming*–Iterative p. 224.